ICONS OF ARCHITECTURE

THE 20th CENTURY

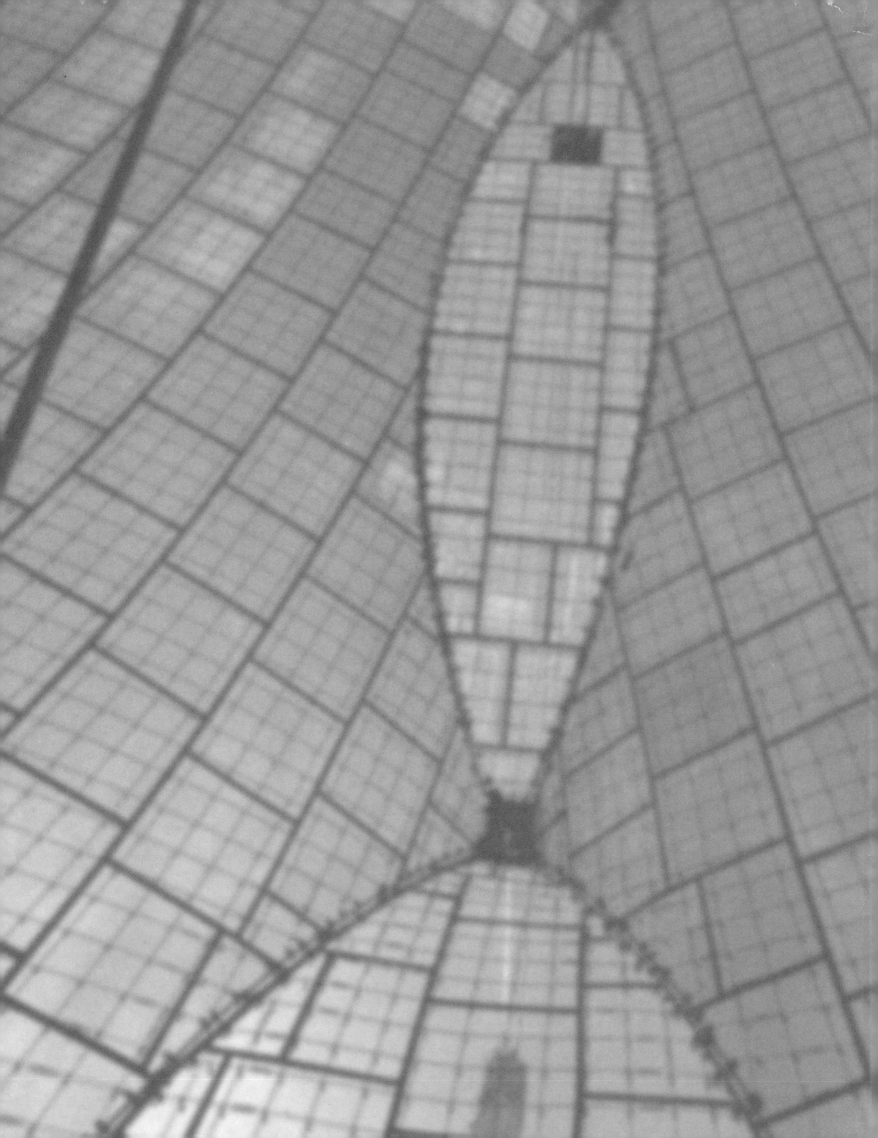

ICONS OF
ARCHITECTURE
THE 20th CENTURY

Edited by Sabine Thiel-Siling

With contributions by:

Wolfgang Bachmann, Christian Brensing, John Garton, Andrea Gleiniger, Dale A. Gyure, Ruth Hanisch, Mechthild Heuser, Hans Ibelings, Markus Jager, Teppo Jokinen, Wilhelm Klauser, Steffen Krämer, Reyer Kras, Vittorio Magnago Lampugnani, Bruno Maurer, Clare Melhuish, Kevin D. Murphy, Peter Murray, Elizabeth Prelinger, Charles L. Rosenblum, James S. Russell, Angeli Sachs, Manfred Sack, Sabine Schneider, Ulrich Maximilian Schumann, Pia Simmendinger, Wolfgang Sonne, Marie-Theres Stauffer, Wolfgang Jean Stock, Christian W. Thomsen, Wolfgang Voigt, Christine Waiblinger-Jens, Katharina Walterspiel, Claudine Weber-Hof, Carroll William Westfall, Richard Guy Wilson, and Victoria M. Young

Prestel

Munich · London · New York

Contents

1900

1950

1930

1940

1960

Contents

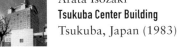

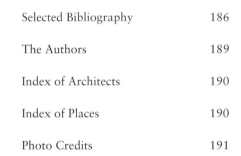
2000

1990

Of all the classical forms of art, architecture is the one most immediately bound up with our daily lives. Specific building types have been developed throughout the ages to accommodate all of our activities and needs: houses, day-care centers, schools, factories, offices, commercial buildings, churches, hospitals, museums, theaters, sports halls, stations, airports, and many others. Very often we are not aware of them as architecture, but take them for granted and use them as the necessary adjuncts of life. Certain structures nevertheless attract greater attention; they stir the emotions, are admired, loved, and accepted; or, conversely, they are rejected. It is at this juncture that architecture becomes a socially relevant topic, and one begins to speak of quality and aesthetics, functionalism, construction, and innovation.

In the light of the conditions prevailing at the end of the nineteenth century, which were brought about by the Industrial Revolution, the twentieth century has witnessed more rapid developments and advances in all fields of technology — including architecture and building technology — than ever before in the history of humankind. Now, on the threshold of the twenty-first century, taking a look back at the important buildings created in the past 100 years in our cultural sphere becomes an exciting and illuminating task.

This volume presents a review of this kind, in which we consider the highlights of twentieth-century architecture. Each of the buildings included here is spectacular in its own way: in the context of its times and its surroundings, by virtue of its structural achievements, its innovative use of materials, or its formal language, or perhaps because it represents the very first example of a new building type. Some of these buildings have become veritable places of pilgrimage for architectural enthusiasts, or have acquired a symbolic status as emblems of the cities or the nations in which they stand. Others that were once considered revolutionary and were acclaimed by the critics of their times have more or less been forgotten today. Naturally, the opposite is also true: many buildings that were misunderstood and condemned in their day now serve as models for later generations of architects, and are regarded as icons of twentieth-century architecture.

An unparalleled stylistic pluralism manifests itself in the buildings included here from the final decades of the twentieth century, so that the question as to what will prove of lasting value remains open.

The criteria for the selection of buildings and architects for this book were their significance in terms of architectural history, and their popularity, originality, or symbolic value. There are probably just as many celebrations of familiar works as there are surprises; as many well-loved examples as controversial ones. In any event, the selection is interesting and stimulating both for architectural enthusiasts and for those who would like to share in this enthusiasm.

I wish to extend a warm thanks to Professor Winfried Nerdinger, Director of the Architectural Museum of the University of Technology in Munich, for the valuable contribution he made in drawing up the initial list of projects. Thanks are also due to John Zukowsky, Curator of Architecture at the Art Institute of Chicago, and to Peter Murray, a member of the Royal Academy Architecture Committee in London, for broadening our perspective from an American and British point of view, respectively. Important impulses also came from Professor Vittorio Magnago Lampugnani and his team at the Department of Urban History at the Eidgenössische Technische Hochschule (ETH) in Zurich. With their Italian charm, Swiss precision, and European outlook, they made a major contribution to this book, for which we are greatly indebted.

I would also like to thank all of the authors, who not only wrote their contributions with a spontaneous sense of enthusiasm and a great deal of dedication, but who also supported this project in many other ways. In this context, special thanks are due to Wolfgang Jean Stock. Finally, I wish to express my gratitude to all the architects who supported this book's underlying concept and who placed illustrative material of exceptional quality at our disposal.

If this volume succeeds in arousing interest or indeed enthusiasm for architecture, in sharpening our awareness, and perhaps promoting a sense of responsibility for the built environment, one of its major aims will have been achieved. First and foremost, though, this should be a book to indulge and delight in. We wish our readers pleasure in the variety of the architecture they will find here, which we owe to the inventiveness and courage of the great master builders of the twentieth century.

Sabine Thiel-Siling
Prestel-Verlag

Antoni Gaudí

Sagrada Familia | BARCELONA, BEGUN 1884

Antoni Gaudí worked on the design of the Sagrada Familia (Holy Family) church in Barcelona from the age of 31 until his death 43 years later. From 1914 on he gave up all other commissions to concentrate on it, yet the most famous building in Barcelona remains incomplete, open to the sky.

Much admired by Salvador Dalí, and immensely popular with the people of Barcelona, the Sagrada Familia has been regarded by many critics as a curious novelty. The church was funded by private donations which gradually dried up as work progressed. The commission came to Gaudí on the resignation of the original architect, Francisco del Villar, and after the foundations had been laid. Gaudí supervised the completion of the crypt as originally conceived, but proceeded to develop a dramatically new interpretation of the Gothic in the church that haltingly rose above it, inspired by influences including the Catalan cultural and architectural heritage, and the contemporary writings of John Ruskin and E.-E. Viollet-le-Duc.

The famous Portal of the Nativity, which has been condemned by many critics for its vulgarity, drips with naturalistic sculpture, much of it cast from life — in total contrast to del Villar's Gothic revivalism. But, like the subsequent designs for the towers of the church, the south and west facades, the cloister, and the columns and vaults of the upper church, none of which were executed in Gaudí's lifetime, it represents a significant stage in the development of what he described as "Mediterranean Gothic."

Underlying the severe geometric aesthetic of the internal elevation of the eastern portal, the almost Moorish tapered form of the four spires with their suggestively Cubist finials, and the tense muscularity of the southern portal, is a strict structural agenda. This achieved its most sophisticated expression in the designs for the internal structure of columns and vaulting, developed through elaborate three-dimensional models. The complex system of tilted "tree-columns" and vaulting based on hyperboloid and hyperbolic paraboloid forms would have allowed the whole to be self-supporting, eliminating the need for flying buttresses, and, although conceived as a stone structure, it would most logically have been realized in reinforced concrete using modern methods.

Gaudí completely disregarded conventional architectural protocol in freely moving from one idea to another during the extended design process of the church, and happily combined a commitment to structural functionalism with an exuberant decorative display of craftsmanship in the modeling of the stonework and the wild polychromy of colored tile. The result was a unique architecture which had a particular resonance in the context of Barcelona's industrial expansion and Catalan nationalism. This gave Gaudí's work a significant populist dimension, but it is the generalized acceptance of architectural pluralism and Expressionism in the last 20 years which has opened the way to critical reevaluation of his work in relation to the history of modern architecture.   C. M.

ANTONI GAUDÍ

1852   Antoni Gaudí is born on June 25 in Reus, southwest of Barcelona, Spain

1878–82   After an apprenticeship as a blacksmith, Gaudí graduates in architecture from the Escola Superior d'Arquitectura in Barcelona; he subsequently becomes involved with the Catalan nationalist group, the Centre Excursionista; starts the Vicens House

1882   First commission from Count Eusebi Güell, a wealthy Barcelona textile manufacturer

1884   Work begins on the Sagrada Familia in Barcelona

1889–94   The Palacio Güell is completed; the Colonia Güell and Parc Güell follow, but are never finished; convent school of Santa Teresa de Jesus in Barcelona

1905–10   Casa Battló and the famous Casa Milá, Barcelona; Casa Fernandez–Andres, an office building for a textile merchant in León, Spain; in the last years of his life Gaudí establishes his workshop at the Sagrada Familia; takes up residence there in a single room

1926   Gaudí is killed on June 10 in a collision with a tram, and buried in the crypt of the Sagrada Familia

1

2

1 | Interior with view to sky
2 | Detail of figures around
     main portal
3 | Cross-section
4 | Plan
5 | Overall view

3

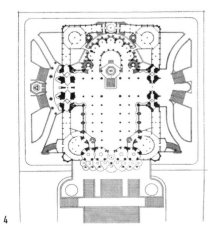

4

5

Hendrik Petrus Berlage

Stock Exchange | AMSTERDAM 1886; 1896-1903

1

HENDRIK PETRUS BERLAGE

1856	Born on February 21 in Amsterdam, the Netherlands
1875-78	Studies architecture at the Eidgenössisches Polytechnikum in Zurich, Switzerland
1881-89	After a Grand Tour finishing in Italy, he starts work in Theodor Sanders' architectural office in Amsterdam
1886	In his capacity as Sanders' associate, he submits a competition design for the Amsterdam Stock Exchange
1893-95	Villa Heymans, Groningen, the Netherlands
1896	Having set up his own office, Berlage receives the definitive commission for the Stock Exchange which was completed in 1903; in the same period, Berlage realizes another prominent Amsterdam building, the headquarters of the Dutch Diamond Workers' Union (ANDB)
1900-	During the first two decades of the new century, he works on his best known urban design scheme, the "Plan Zuid," a substantial southerly extension of Amsterdam that is eventually implemented in the 1920s and '30s
1914-20s	For the Kröller-Müller family, Berlage designs an office in London — Holland House (1914) — and a hunting lodge in Otterlo, the Netherlands (1915); in the 1920s he realizes the Mercatorplein Development in Amsterdam, the Usquert Town Hall, and the Christian Science Church in The Hague, the Netherlands
1934	Dies on August 12 in The Hague
1935	The Haags Gemeentemuseum, also in The Hague, is completed posthumously

Today known as the Beurs van Berlage (Berlage's Exchange), the Amsterdam Stock Exchange is regarded as the precursor of Dutch modern architecture. It consists of one large and two smaller halls plus the chamber of commerce, a post office, and a cafeteria, and functioned as an exchange for some 80 years. Today, however, the spaces where grain and stocks were once traded host concerts, while the large commodity exchange hall is used for exhibitions, events, and conferences.

The development of the Exchange design perfectly illustrates the still prevalent view that modern architecture began around the turn of the century with the renunciation of revivalism. Berlage's first design was a typical nineteenth-century variation on seventeenth-century Dutch architecture. But the robust design seems to have left the nineteenth century far behind — few stylistic allusions are perceptible, and the construction, rather than remaining hidden, is "honestly" exposed to view, such as the steel framework of the glazed roofs above the exchange halls. In this, the Exchange anticipated both functionalism and traditionalism, which were to raise these two aspects of building to dogma in the 1920s and '30s.

Compared with other buildings constructed in the Netherlands around 1900, the Exchange is remarkably plain — a logical consequence, according to Berlage, of the turbulent times in which he lived. He claimed that each great stylistic period of the past, from Gothic to Baroque, had coincided with a clearly organized society. Since such organization was, in his view, lacking, he thought it wise to postpone any decision about an appropriate architectural style until society stabilized. In the meantime, he argued, architects should content themselves with what he called "impressionistic architecture": an architecture in which the emphasis was placed on the broad outlines of planes and contours rather than on stylistic details. However austere the building appears as a result, its strict design is relieved by several splendid decorative features, such as Lambertus Zijl's sculptures, a vast frieze, and decoratively articulated keystones, all of which grace the facade.

Berlage based his design on thirteenth- and fourteenth-century Italian palazzi, such as Florence's Palazzo Vecchio and Volterra's Palazzo dei Priori, characterized by hermetic facades and massive towers. For him, this building type represented the quasi-democratic society of the Italian city-states, and as such, it was an appropriate metaphor for the kind of society the social democrat Berlage felt sure would come to be. The fact that he chose to render the Stock Exchange as a democratic symbol can be interpreted as a veiled criticism of liberal capitalism. For those for whom this criticism might have been too subtle, Berlage embellished the interior with an unmistakably anti-capitalist message in the form of three tile depictions by Jan Toorop, representing the feudal Past, the capitalist Present, and a beatific Future, that is, the hope for times in which the worker would no longer exploited.   H.I.

1 | View from road
2 | Exchange hall; now a concert hall
3 | Great hall; now exhibition space
4 | Cross-section
5 | Plan

2

3

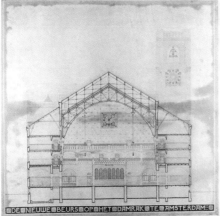

4

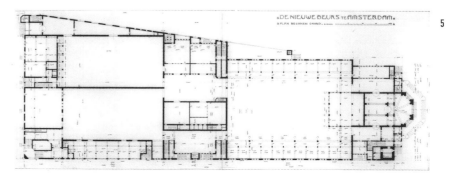

5

Charles Rennie Mackintosh

Glasgow School of Art | GLASGOW 1896-1899; 1907-1909

1

Charles Rennie Mackintosh's biography reveals that most of his major architectural achievements and design schemes were created parallel to his work on the Glasgow School of Art. Very few were subsequently realized. The art school is, therefore, not only his masterpiece; it also marks the most productive phase of his career. At the turn of the century, Mackintosh's fame extended far beyond Scotland, and he was closely linked with the Viennese Secession upon which he exerted a lasting influence. Today, the Glasgow School of Art is acclaimed as one of the outstanding works of architecture of early twentieth-century modernism. It is hardly conceivable, therefore, that — partly for personal, partly for economic reasons, but not least because his architecture met with little interest in his own country — Mackintosh was unable to secure a proper foothold as an architect in London and died completely impoverished in that city almost two decades after the completion of his finest building.

In 1896, a limited competition was held for the design of a new building to replace the existing Glasgow School of Art, which had become too small for its purpose. The competition

was won by the influential Glasgow architects Honeyman and Keppie, in whose office Mackintosh was employed. For financial reasons, it was not possible to erect the building in a single stage. In the first phase of building from 1897–99, roughly two-thirds of the development was completed: the central section and the east wing. The west wing was realized in a second phase of building from 1907–09, after Mackintosh had revised the plans. The studios were accommodated along the north-facing main front of the school in Renfrew Street and formed part of the first phase of development. This stone facade is, therefore, dominated by large divided studio windows. Positioned slightly off-center and in itself asymmetrical in character, the main entrance reveals a formal correspondence with the east face of the shorter east wing and creates a fascinating formal tension. Situated above the entrance is the principal's room, and behind this is the school museum. Sparing use is made of ornamentation, which is to be found only above the main portal, in the iron railings, the balcony balustrades, and the projecting bars installed at the bottom of the windows for cleaning purposes. Built at a later date, the west facade and the return south face reveal a clear tautening of the forms and might almost remind one of a cathedral tower. The most striking feature of this section of the building are the tall oriel windows to the two-story library. They form an essential part of the predominantly vertical articulation of the facade. The library itself is one of the finest and most important internal spaces designed by Mackintosh. It reveals a development from a style of lightly curving linear ornamentation to a stricter, primarily rectilinear structure of vertical and horizontal lines. In the second phase of construction, an attic story and a linking corridor between the two parts of the school were also added.

For Charles Rennie Mackintosh, being open to influences never meant the mere adoption or imitation of details. Nevertheless, in works like the Glasgow School of Art, he turned to earlier sources for inspiration — to the English Gothic style, to traditional Scottish houses and castles, and to the Arts and Crafts movement. Architectural theory and visual memory flowed into his independent architectural language in which growth and development led to variation. At the same time, the quality of variation embodied unity and function in a simple, yet grand, traditional, and extremely modern form.   A.S.

CHARLES RENNIE MACKINTOSH

1868	Born on June 7 in Glasgow, Scotland
1884	Commences training as an architect in the office of John Hutchinson; evening classes at the Glasgow School of Art
1889-	Assistant in the architectural practice of Honeyman and Keppie, Glasgow; partner from 1904-13
1890	Wins the Alexander Thomson Travel Scholarship
1891	Study trip to Italy
1893-95	*Glasgow Herald* offices
1894	Exhibition with Herbert MacNair and the Macdonald sisters, later known as the "Glasgow Four"; marries Margaret Macdonald in 1900 and works with her on most projects
1896	Participates in the competition for the Glasgow School of Art, which is won in 1897 by the architects Honeyman and Keppie; first stage of construction: 1896-99; second stage of construction: 1907-09
1896-	Design and fitting out of the Cranston Tearooms in Glasgow: Buchanan Street Tearooms (1896), Argyle Street Tearooms (1897-98, 1906), Ingram Street Tearooms (1900, 1907, 1909, 1910-11), Willow Tearooms (1903-04, 1917)
1900	Together with the "Glasgow Four," designs the Scottish exhibition space at the 8th exhibition of the Viennese Secession
1900-01	Windyhill House, Kilmacolm, Renfrewshire, Scotland
1901	Special prize in the competition for a "House of an Art Lover" organized by a journal for interior design
1902	Interior designs for the International Exhibition of Modern Decorative Art in Turin, Italy
1902-03	Hill House, Helensburgh, Dunbartonshire, Scotland; music salon for Fritz Wärndorfer, Vienna
1903-06	Scotland Street School, Glasgow
1915	Moves to London
1916-	Commissions for textile designs
1916-19	Interior design and redesign of the facade for a house at 78 Derngate, Northampton, England
1923	Moves to Port-Vendres, France, where he devotes much of his time to painting; international exhibitions of his watercolors
1927	Returns to London
1928	Dies on December 10 in London

1 | View of main front
2 | Main entrance in Renfrew Street
3 | West face
4 | View of library
5 | Elevation: drawing of main facade

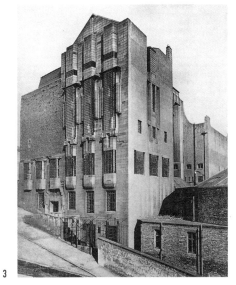

3

4

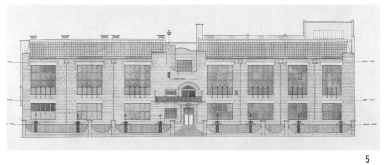

5

Daniel H. Burnham

Fuller Building (Flatiron) | NEW YORK CITY 1901–1903

1

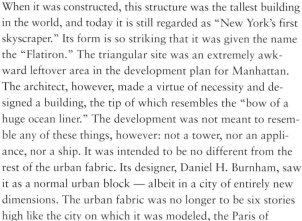

DANIEL H. BURNHAM

1846	Born on September 4 in Henderson, New York
1868–73	Training with William Le Baron Jenney and other Chicago architects
1873–91	Partnership with John Wellborn Root; Burnham and Root, Architects, Chicago
1881–82	Montauk Building, Chicago
1885–88	The Rookery, Chicago
1889–92	Monadnock Building, Chicago
1890–92	Masonic Temple, Chicago; Women's Temple, Chicago
1893	Overall planning of the World Columbian Exposition, Chicago
1894	Reliance Building, Chicago
1898–	Union Station, Pittsburgh, Pennsylvania, completed in 1902
1901–03	Fuller Building (Flatiron), New York City
1902	City plan for Washington, D.C., in collaboration with the architect Charles Follen McKim, the landscape architect Frederick Law Olmsted Jr., and the sculptor Augustus Saint Gaudens
1903	City plan for Cleveland, Ohio; Heyworth Building, Chicago
1903–07	Union Station, Washington, D.C.
1905	City plan for San Francisco; plans for Manila and Baguio, Philippines
1909	City plan for Chicago (with Edward H. Bennett)
1912	Dies on June 1 in Heidelberg, Germany

When it was constructed, this structure was the tallest building in the world, and today it is still regarded as "New York's first skyscraper." Its form is so striking that it was given the name the "Flatiron." The triangular site was an extremely awkward leftover area in the development plan for Manhattan. The architect, however, made a virtue of necessity and designed a building, the tip of which resembles the "bow of a huge ocean liner." The development was not meant to resemble any of these things, however: not a tower, nor an appliance, nor a ship. It was intended to be no different from the rest of the urban fabric. Its designer, Daniel H. Burnham, saw it as a normal urban block — albeit in a city of entirely new dimensions. The urban fabric was no longer to be six stories high like the city on which it was modeled, the Paris of Georges-Eugène Haussmann. It was to be increased to 21 stories; and it was to allow a maximum development of the site area. With this model in mind, Burnham wished to give the American metropolis of capitalist provenance, soaring disparately upwards, a new, unified, and definitive form. It was to outstrip the cultural model of Europe in much the same way as the American continent exceeded Europe in size.

Burnham, though, was not entirely certain whether his successors would follow his example. The same facade design extending around all three sides of the building and the crowning cornice strip which ties the structure together visually meant that what was intended as an egalitarian unit within the urban fabric might equally well be seen as a distinct and individual block. The elaborate ornamentation scarcely corresponds to that of the common Parisian town house of the Second Empire. It has more in common with the public buildings of the time, which were influenced by the rich style of the French Renaissance. Furthermore, the bay windows are so restrained that they actually accentuate the building's triangular form rather than counteract it.

Burnham hastened the development of steel-frame construction with stone and glass cladding and was well acquainted with market mechanisms. The greater individuality in the cityscape to which this led, however, was not, in Burnham's eyes, an unavoidable fate; it represented a challenge. At the World Columbian Exposition in Chicago in 1893, he had helped to make the classicistic beaux-arts concept of a unified urban space a generally admired ideal. He also played a leading role in the "City Beautiful" movement. The reworking of the scheme for the capital, Washington, D.C., in 1902, became a model for harmonious, artistic urban planning. Burnham's crowning achievement in this respect, however, was the plan he drew up in 1909 for Chicago, in which he proposed a city of gigantic uniform blocks in the mold of the Fuller Building.

"Don't make little plans. They lack the power to move men's hearts," was later to become Burnham's much-cited credo. Only large-scale ideal forms impress themselves on the mind and can thus be realized in the course of time, he argued. The Fuller Building, soaring into the New York sky, represents an autonomous fragment of a grand plan of this kind. With its promise of metropolitan beauty, it represents an enduring challenge that will retain its validity beyond the twentieth century.
                                                                        W. S.

1 | Detail of mezzanine story
2 | View from rear
3 | Plan
4 | View from south

2

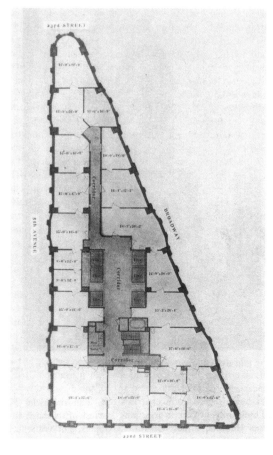

3

4

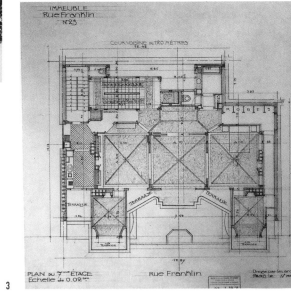

1 | Street face
2 | Elevation and section
3 | Eighth-floor plan
4 | Set-back upper floors
5 | Floral decoration to facade

1

2

3

Apartment Building, rue Franklin | PARIS 1903-1904

4

Two tenets of Auguste Perret's conception of architecture are in evidence in this building: that ornament and structural support are intimately connected, and that any architect who could express himself through a building's construction was a poet.

Since the nineteenth century, French architects had been attempting to develop fresh aesthetic approaches to the building materials and techniques of the modern age, rather than recycling existing stylistic elements more appropriate to traditional architectural technology. The apartment block on the rue Franklin at Passy, in the fashionable sixteenth arrondissement of Paris, was Perret's answer to the challenge of how best to employ reinforced concrete, and at the same time to express a break with the past.

In the rue Franklin apartment block, Perret demonstrated that architects building in reinforced concrete could profitably look to historic precedent without mimicking forms from earlier phases in the history of architecture. Here, Perret used a network of horizontal and vertical bands on the facade to express the underlying concrete frame, inviting comparison with trabeated classical masonry architecture. His design maximized glazed openings while minimizing the structurally-supporting material, a progressive aspect that is also visible in the plan. Perret designed a shallow U-shaped recess at the center of the front facade, which functions as an exterior light well, eliminating the need for a traditional space-consuming interior courtyard. This gave Perret more freedom to develop the interior, as is apparent in the first floor, or studio space, significant because it is arranged on an open plan. In this regard Perret anticipated the development of the modernist "free plan," so notable in the work of Le Corbusier. Perret also set back the upper stories of the facade to create roof terraces, features that likewise reappeared in Le Corbusier's work.

On the facade of the building, Perret establishes a dialogue between the modern concrete framing elements and the

glazed tile panels between them that are enlivened with floral motifs. The latter suggest that the building, although constructed of the same material as the factories and warehouses of the new industrial cities, is nonetheless connected with the natural world. These ceramic panels are not decorative elements affixed to the structure; instead, they are integral to it. There is no way to disassociate the flowers and leaves from the wall that they help to form. In this treatment we can perceive Perret's intention, similar to that of theorist E.-E. Viollet-le-Duc and Art Nouveau designers, to meld structure and ornament.

The proper relationship between these two aspects of architecture had also been the subject of debate in France and elsewhere in Europe since the nineteenth century, when industrialization made machine-produced objects inexpensive and ubiquitous. Perret's other ambition as an architect, to respond poetically to questions of construction rather than pure aesthetics, is achieved in the rue Franklin apartment block in that he does not mask the concrete structure, but uses the material to generate a modern yet historically relevant idiom.　　　　　K.D.M.

AUGUSTE PERRET

1874	Born on February 12 near Ixelles, Belgium
1881	Moves to Paris; studies at the Ecole Alsacienne
1891	Enters the Ecole des Beaux-Arts, Paris, where he studies with architect Julien Guadet; chooses not to receive a diploma because it would have prevented him from working as a building contractor
1903-04	Construction of the apartment block on rue Franklin, Paris, by Perret Frères, constructeurs en béton armé; the firm continues to build in reinforced concrete for 25 years
1905	Garage Marboeuf, 51 rue de Ponthieu, Paris
1911-13	Théatre des Champs-Elysées, Paris
1922-24	Church of Notre Dame at Le Raincy, France; widely published, it illustrates Perret's ability to adapt medieval (especially Gothic) precedent to modern concrete construction; intended as a monument to the soldiers who died in the Battle of the Ourcq (World War I)
1930-32	Apartment building at 51-55, rue Raynouard, Paris
1934-35	Mobilier National, Paris
1936	Musée des Travaux Publics, completed posthumously
1940	Architectural registration required by law; Perret named president of the Ordre des Architectes; following World War II, Perret is elected to the Institut de France
1949-56	Plan for the reconstruction of the French city of Le Havre destroyed during World War II; design for the church of St. Joseph (1952)
1954	Dies on February 28 in Paris

5

Otto Wagner

Postal Savings Bank | VIENNA 1903–1906; 1910–1912

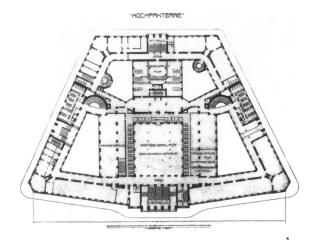

1

OTTO WAGNER

1841	Born on July 13 in Penzing near Vienna
1857–63	Studies architecture at the Polytechnic Institute in Vienna, at the Academy of Visual Arts in Vienna, and at the Academy for Building in Berlin
1870–73	Synagogue for the orthodox Jewish community in Budapest, Hungary
1879	Festive marque in Vienna for the procession staged by Hans Markat to mark the silver wedding anniversary of Emperor Franz Joseph and Empress Elisabeth
1882–84	Imperial and Royal Private Austrian States Bank, Vienna
1892–93	Participates in a competition to draw up an overall urban regulation plan for Vienna
1894	Appointed the head of a special class for architecture at the Academy of Visual Arts in Vienna; awarded the title Chief Public Building Officer
1894–	Construction of the Viennese suburban railway line, completed in 1900
1896	Publishes the first edition of *Moderne Architektur*; further editions appear in 1898, 1902,

	and, with a new title, *Die Baukunst unserer Zeit*, in 1913
1898–99	Housing blocks Köstlergasse 1, Köstlergasse 3, and Linke Wienzeile 40, Vienna; Wagner is both architect and developer
1899	Member of the Viennese Secession
1902–04	St. Leopold's Church in the psychiatric hospital, Baumgartnerhöhe, Vienna
1903–06	First stage of construction of the Postal Savings Bank, Vienna
1908	Lupus Sanatorium on the site of the Wilhelminenspital, Vienna
1910–12	Second stage of construction of the Postal Savings Bank, Vienna
1911	Publication of Wagner's main work on urban planning, *Die Grosstadt: Eine Studie über diese von Otto Wagner*
1918	Dies on April 11 in Vienna of deficiency disease caused by the war

If he could have had his way, Otto Wagner would have assumed sole responsibility for the planning of the entire area at the northeastern end of the Ringstrasse in Vienna, including the adjoining Stuben district, and would have impressed his own stamp upon the site. Despite his ambitious plans, he realized only one building: the Postal Savings Bank, and what began as something of an experiment ultimately turned out to be a major architectural accomplishment.

The set-back position of the building on the Ringstrasse meant that, although it formed part of a larger prestigious development, it was separated from it by an open public space. At first sight, the building's facades seem restrained and planar, but on closer examination they reveal themselves to be full of ornamentation. The thin marble skin over the brick structure makes no attempt to simulate monumental ashlar masonry. On the contrary, the lead-covered iron bolts and aluminum caps reveal the separation of core and skin. To achieve this degree of truth in materials, however, Wagner resorted to a lie: the slabs are not actually fixed by the pins, but are bedded in a conventional layer of mortar. In the middle section of the main facade, the bolts are increased in number to form a pattern over the entire surface. Wagner himself was open to other interpretations of this gesture. The decoration could be understood as an image of the "prosperity of the population" brought about by the virtue of thrift, the architect wrote in his report on the competition scheme. In his 1911 book about the metropolis, *Die Grosstadt: Eine Studie über diese von Otto Wagner*, Wagner also described the calm surfaces of the Postal Savings Bank as an expression of regularity and order.

Perhaps the most famous part of the building is the main banking hall. Situated in the center of this complex, it has a curved, frosted glass ceiling beneath a protective glazed roof and forms the translucent heart of the scheme. Externally, the building reveals a clear canonical division into three sections: a plinth story, the upper floors, and an attic story. Internally, the hall evokes the feeling of a basilica-like space, and represents the most immediate materialization of the doctrine Wagner formulated in 1896, according to which: "all modern forms must comply with the new material(s), the new requirements of our age.... They must represent our own better, democratic, self-assured, ideal being...." In light of this, the hieratic stelae that house the warm-air outlets in the main hall may be seen not only as a guarantee of modern comfort, but as an expression of this idea, as well. The careful choice of materials and forms, which alternate between display and pragmatism, can also be found in Wagner's interior design and furnishings for the Postal Savings Bank, the largest program of finishings the architect ever realized.   R.H.

1 | Plan of raised first-floor level
2 | Savings bank hall
3 | Main hall
4 | Part of the main facade
5 | Spiral staircase

4

2

3

5

1

2

1 | Hall
2 | Design perspective
3 | Hall
4 | Dining room
5 | East face after reconstruction in 1995

3

4

5

The Purkersdorf Sanatorium is without doubt one of Josef Hoffmann's most important architectural works. Yet the building conforms to only a limited extent with what one associates with this co-founder of the Viennese Werkstätten and later director of the School of Arts and Crafts in Vienna — the stronghold of "Viennese style" — who was to become the main target of designer Adolf Loos' venomous attacks.

The sanatorium, a convalescent home for members of Viennese society, was built on the edge of the Vienna Woods for Viktor Zuckerkandl. The active role the client himself played in the design is apparent from a number of differences between the work as executed and the preliminary design drawings that still exist. Above all, Zuckerkandl's idea of introducing a flat roof instead of the pitched roof foreseen by Hoffmann represented a drastic change to the design. This modification was undertaken for economic reasons and to create space for additional sickrooms. The resulting form is a seemingly simple composition of cubic volumes punctuated unobtrusively by windows. The articulation of the internal spaces had a great influence on the overall appearance of the facades. At first glance, their ascetic decoration, with narrow ornamental bands around the windows and to the central tract, seems somewhat frugal for Hoffmann; but it serves to integrate the square and rectangular window openings into the different volumes of the building. The willful proportions of the exterior are reflected in the sequences of spaces inside the sanatorium, which were fitted out in a restrained manner by the Viennese Werkstätten. The simplicity and brightness of the design were essential hygienic conditions for a sanatorium; at the same time, they also symbolized these conditions.

Hoffmann's origins in the school of Otto Wagner are more clearly evident in the sanatorium than in his later buildings. Wagner's rationalism is rendered by Hoffmann in a much more impressionistic manner, however; the pathos is toned down in favor of finer proportions and sets of relationships within the overall composition. In contrast to Wagner, whose often painstaking use of ornament served to elucidate the actual structure of his buildings, Hoffmann accommodates structural elements within his aesthetic concept, as can be seen in the downstand beams in the dining room of the Purkersdorf Sanatorium. The simplicity of form and the clarity of proportions achieved in this building represent an intermediate phase in Hoffmann's development. In his next major scheme, the Palais Stoclet in Brussels, his attention was focused less on simple proportions than on rich cadences in the coloration and combinations of materials. The sanatorium, therefore, is proof of the fact that this much maligned stylist also made a contribution to the unornamented tradition of the Modern Movement. Certainly that is how Hoffmann must have viewed the situation; otherwise he would hardly have said, when questioned about Le Corbusier's Pavillon d'Esprit Nouveau, that he had designed something similar himself 25 years earlier.   R.H.

JOSEF HOFFMANN

1870	Born on December 15 in Pirnitz, Moravia
1887	Attends the Imperial and Royal State Technical School in Brno, Moravia, with Adolf Loos
1892–95	Studies architecture at the Academy of Visual Arts in Vienna under Carl von Hasenauer and from 1894 under Otto Wagner
1897	Plays a major role in founding the Viennese Secession; designs an extensive series of exhibitions for this organization of artists
1899–	Teaches at the School for Arts and Crafts in Vienna (today, the College of Applied Arts)
1900–02	Ensemble of houses for Kolo Moser, Carl Moll, Hugo Henneberg, and Friedrich Viktor Spitzer erected on the Hohe Warte in Vienna
1903	Together with industrialists Fritz Wärndorfer and Kolo Moser, founds the Viennese Werkstätte; designs numerous arts and crafts objects for the Viennese Werkstätte and other specialized organizations until the former ceases production
1904	Sanatorium in Purkersdorf near Vienna
1905	Beer-Hoffmann House, Vienna
1905–11	Palais Stoclet, Brussels, Belgium
1908	Architectural planning for Kunstschau Vienna and design of the entrance structure
1913–15	Skywa-Primavesi House, Vienna
1914	Austrian Pavilion at the Werkbund Exhibition in Cologne, Germany
1923–25	Housing development for the "Klosehof" district of Vienna; Winarsky Hof housing scheme
1924–25	Sonja Knips House, Vienna; Austrian Pavilion at the International Exhibition of Arts and Crafts in Paris
1932	Terrace houses in the Viennese Werkbund estate (overall planning: Josef Frank)
1934	Austrian Pavilion for the biennial exhibition in Venice
1956	Dies on May 7 in Vienna

Eliel Saarinen

Main Station | HELSINKI 1904-1919

"We call for a style of iron and common sense!" the architects Sigurd Frosterus and Gustaf Strengell wrote in 1904 in a polemic against Eliel Saarinen's prizewinning competition scheme for the main station in Helsinki. The pamphlet led to a public debate about romanticism and rationalism in Finland and also had an influence on the formal language of the future station building.

At the turn of the century, Saarinen and his colleagues Herman Gesellius and Armas Lindgren were three of the leading representatives of the national-romantic movement in Finland. Like the National Museum building not far away, Saarinen's first design for the station contained a number of national-romantic motifs: heavy roof forms and squared rubble walls, small window openings and turrets of various forms. After the prize-giving ceremony, Saarinen went on a European tour to study the latest developments in station architecture. These new influences, together with the domestic criticism of his national-romantic formal language, had an effect on the development of the project, which went on until 1909. In the final design solution, emphasis was placed on the rational elements of the building. The turrets and figures of bears contained in earlier drawings vanished. In the final version, the "rational monumentality" of the building was accentuated: by the large semicircular window opening in the central hall, the huge statues on both sides of

the main entrance, the boldly articulated outer walls in red granite, and the massive, 50-meter-high tower.

According to the competition brief, the architect was originally commissioned to design only the external architecture of the station. Saarinen succeeded, however, in obtaining the commission for the internal design as well. The spatial program contained in the brief foresaw a central hall with ticket counters, an imperial waiting room, waiting halls with buffet facilities for second- and third-class passengers, a covered platform area (the covering was not executed, however), and a building for the railway administration. With high, vaulted, carefully articulated structural elements in reinforced concrete, with a functional organization and an expressive use of materials in combination with simple details, Saarinen created a building with clear lines that became a model of railway architecture and gave the city center of Helsinki a monumental focal point.

The outer structure of the new station was almost complete in 1914 when World War I broke out. This and the civil war in Finland in 1918 halted further work internally. It was only in February 1919 that the station could be taken into operation. Its festive inauguration took place on March 5, 1919. With the new Finnish constitution, the imperial waiting room had lost its original function, but it served the same purpose for the president of the young nation.   T.J.

ELIEL SAARINEN

1873	Born on August 20 in Rantasalmi, East Finland
1893-97	Studies architecture at the Polytechnic Institute (now the University of Technology) and painting at the University of Helsinki, Finland
1896	On December 10, together with Herman Gesellius (1874-1916) and Armas Lindgren (1874-1929), founds a joint architectural practice; their early works are expressions of Finnish national romanticism, which was influenced by Art Nouveau
1898	Gesellius, Lindgren, and Saarinen win the competition for the design of the Finnish Pavilion at the 1900 World Exposition in Paris and achieve international fame
1902-03	The three architects build their joint studio and residence in Hvitträsk near Helsinki, a *gesamtkunstwerk* in national-romantic style
1904	Saarinen wins the competition for Helsinki Main Station, completed in 1919; travels to England and Germany

1905	The joint office is dissolved; Gesellius continues to work with Saarinen until 1907
1910-15	Town planning for Munkkiniemi-Haaga near Helsinki
1912	Second prize in the competition for Canberra, the new capital of Australia
1918	Plan for greater Helsinki (not realized)
1922	Second prize in the Chicago Tribune Tower competition
1923	Moves to the U.S.
1925-	Architect for the Cranbrook Academy of Art in Bloomfield Hills, Michigan, founded by George and Ellen Scripps Booth
1937-	Collaboration with his son, Eero Saarinen (1910-61)
1948	Director of the Graduate Department of Architecture and City Planning at the Cranbrook Academy of Art
1950	Dies on July 1 in Bloomfield Hills, and is interred in the Hvitträsk forest

1

2

3

1 | Drawing of waiting room, 1910
2 | Main entrance
3 | Detail of entrance portal
4 | Overall view

4

Joseph Maria Olbrich

Hochzeitsturm and Exhibition Building | MATHILDENHÖHE, DARMSTADT (GERMANY) 1905-1908

Only when Joseph Maria Olbrich died at the age of 40, did it become clear to what great extent he had helped mold the image of the architect in society. He was indeed so popular that it is difficult to describe his art or his high aesthetic ideals as elitist. Frank Lloyd Wright was welcomed in Europe in 1910 as the "American Olbrich"; and Erich Mendelsohn wrote in 1919: "Incapable of creating anything itself after Olbrich's death, the leaderless profession again takes refuge behind the easy solutions of past systems."

Olbrich created the bulk of his oeuvre on the Mathildenhöhe in Darmstadt, Germany, where he headed the Grand Duchy of Hesse's colony of artists starting in 1899. With few exceptions, he built the colony to his own designs. To commemorate the marriage of the Grand Duke, the Hochzeitsturm (Wedding Tower) was also realized here as an observation point and as a landmark that was visible for miles around. The five crowning arches may be seen as a symbol of the fingers of a hand or as a reference to medieval city gates. The way the windows are distributed about the tower also

anticipates the free form of Cubist composition. The combination of bold formal design with the asymmetrical stressing of vertical and horizontal elements occasionally leads to Olbrich's inclusion under the broad heading of "Expressionism." In the year in which the Einstein Tower was commissioned, Erich Mendelsohn, the architect of that icon of Expressionism, described the Hochzeitsturm as having been a shining example for him.

Attached to the base of the tower is an extensive exhibition building of a much different character. The combination of geometric elements has parallels particularly in the work of Peter Behrens. Like Behrens, Olbrich found his way via this rationalist approach to a system of classical proportions. What is more, using this method of composition, he discovered that it was possible to integrate traditional elements into his work without difficulty.

What may seem like a return to classicism is in fact a logical development in Olbrich's oeuvre. Certain features of Biedermeier and Neoclassicism were present in his earlier work. In the way they structure the volumes of his buildings and lend them formal clarity, these elements come to assume an increasingly important role in Olbrich's architecture. He does not copy historical classicist buildings, but reconstructs the conditions that led to their creation, and relates them to the formal experience and functional needs of his time. The outcome is a classical quality that Olbrich rediscovered and employed in a strictly rational fashion.

Mendelsohn himself euphorically recognized this renewal of tradition: "Olbrich's strength forces all capable minds of his time to liberate the inner laws of architecture from centuries of incrustation and to formulate them anew."   U.M.S.

JOSEPH MARIA OLBRICH

1867	Born on November 22 in Troppau, Silesia
1882-86	Studies at the building department of the State Technical School in Vienna under Camillo Sitte
1890	Studies under Carl von Hasenauer at the Academy of Visual Arts in Vienna
1893	Wins the Rome Scholarship of the Academy in Vienna and travels in Italy and North Africa until May 1894
1894-98	Project leader in Otto Wagner's architectural office for Viennese suburban railway buildings
1897	Together with Josef Hoffmann, Kolo Moser, Gustav Klimt, and others, he founds the society of artists known as the Vienna Secession, whose headquarters building he erects by 1898
1899	Moves from Vienna to Darmstadt, Germany, to found and direct an artists' colony on the Mathildenhöhe at the request of Grand Duke Ernst-Ludwig of Hesse
1899-	Ernst-Ludwig House built as a studio on the Mathildenhöhe to Olbrich's designs, as well as

	residences for members and patrons of the artists' colony; the exhibition "A Document of German Art" held on the Mathildenhöhe (1901)
1903	Founding member of the Federation of German Architects (BDA)
1904	Second exhibition of the colony of artists on the Mathildenhöhe
1905-	Plans the Hochzeitsturm and exhibition building, Mathildenhöhe
1906-09	Builds the Tietz Department Store in Düsseldorf, Germany
1907	Moves part of his office to Düsseldorf, in the hopes of attaining the directorship of the School of Arts and Crafts; fails to do so; founding member of the German Werkbund; constructs the House of Upper Hesse and the exhibition building with the Hochzeitsturm, both completed in 1908 for the Hessian State Exhibition on the Mathildenhöhe
1908	Dies of leukemia on August 8 in Düsseldorf

2

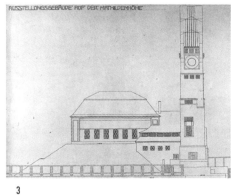

3

4

1 | Exhibition building
2 | Hochzeitsturm and exhibition building
3 | Elevational drawing
4 | Oblique view of ensemble

1 | Assembly hall
2 | Detail of courtyard face
3 | Corner detail
4 | Cover of international AEG journal,
   no. 6, Dec. 1913
5 | Cross-section

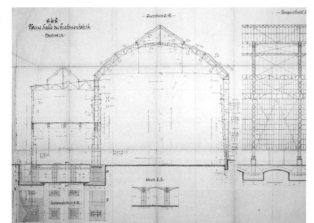

5

"A motor should look like a birthday present." With this motto, Peter Behrens was appointed artistic adviser to the AEG, Germany's General Electric Company, in 1907. Under his leadership, the unspectacular assembly hall of an electrical concern was transformed into a temple of labor and a cathedral of light. Flooded with sunlight by day, the hall shines at night in the light of its electric lamps. The AEG factory is regarded as Behrens' finest work and the incunabula of modern industrial architecture. At the point where the hall has to assert itself in the urban environment, it becomes part of an advertising concept aimed at a recognition of corporate identity.

It is hardly surprising, therefore, that Behrens used the company logo he himself had designed — the hexagonal AEG honeycomb — not only for the actual products, but for the architecture itself. One finds it both on the back of a tea kettle and on the temple front of the monumental main hall of the factory, where it decorates the pediment in place of ornamental figures.

Around the turn of the century, few architects were prepared to recognize technical innovation as an artistic challenge. The structure of a building remained a means to an end and had no influence on the outer form. All of this changed with Behrens' appointment. The "former painter" approached the assigment of a "factory" building with fewer prejudices than his colleagues who had been schooled in styles of architecture. Instead of concealing the different load-bearing systems of the two-bay hall behind bulwarks of stone, he exposed them to view in the long faces of the factory. The steel skeleton frame penetrates the glass skin, articulating and enclosing the building like a bracing corset. Sloping glass membranes take the place of massive vertical walls. The aesthetic of the finished hall is based on the fascination of the carcass structure. Nevertheless, Behrens was not content with the lattice beam construction that was common in those days. He transformed the seemingly fragile internal trussed girders, through which daylight floods, into closed box sections externally. Along the street face, they lend the skeleton frame a tectonic expressiveness and three-dimensional force that one finds in the colonnaded architecture of classical temples. Behrens built with iron, but thought in

stone. The horizontal beam that links the 14 steel columns at the top does indeed recall a frieze with metopes.

The pictorial quality of the structure is not so pronounced on the courtyard face. Its high degree of abstraction anticipates the modern steel and glass architecture of Mies van der Rohe, who worked on the Turbine Factory as a young architectural assistant in Behrens' office at that time.

"To build a factory in the form of a temple is to lie and disfigure the landscape," Mies himself remarked, referring to the imposing gable end of the main hall with its receding corner piers — a facade that was inspired by Egyptian models. In the 1920s, these were regarded as an offense against structural honesty, but they have guaranteed the originality of this building down to the present today.   M. H.

PETER BEHRENS

1868	Born on April 14 in St. Georg, Hamburg, Germany
1889	Studies art at the vocational college in Hamburg and at the school of art in Karlsruhe, Germany
1890	Moves to Munich, Germany; produces depictions of industrial workers and industrial landscapes
1892	Participates in the Munich Secession
1899	Participates in the artists' colony on the Mathildenhöhe in Darmstadt, Germany
1901	Construction of his own house on the Mathildenhöhe in the context of the Darmstadt exhibition "A Document of German Art"; realization of the idea of the *gesamtkunstwerk*
1903	Teaching and reform work in the Düsseldorf School of Arts and Crafts, Germany
1904	Karl Ernst Osthaus commissions him to design various projects in Hagen, Germany, including the crematorium in Delstern (1905-08), the Schröder House (1908-09), and the Cuno House (1909-10) as a contribution to the Hohenhagen villa colony
1907	Artistic adviser to the AEG, Germany's General Electric Company; commissioned by the founder of the firm, Emil Rathenau, and his successor, Walter Rathenau, to design the entire range of company products; co-founder of the German Werkbund, an association of designers, manufacturers, and people from art and industry
1908-09	AEG Turbine Factory
1911-12	German embassy in St. Petersburg, Russia; works for other large German industrial concerns such as Mannesmann; construction of the firm's administrative headquarters in Düsseldorf
1920	Construction of the administration building of Hoechst AG in Frankfurt-am-Main, Germany
1922	Professor at the Academy in Vienna
1926	Terraced apartment block as part of the Weissenhof Estate, Stuttgart, Germany
1936	Head of the architectural department of the Prussian Academy of Arts, Berlin
1940	Dies on February 27 in Berlin

Adolf Loos

Goldman & Salatsch Building | VIENNA 1909-1911

After a number of conversion and interior design projects, the construction of this housing and commercial block in an inner city location in Vienna was Adolf Loos' first major commission and at the same time the last scheme of this size he was to realize. It is an early work, in which the themes he was later to develop and refine to a high degree of complexity are already evident: the rich aesthetic in the use of materials, which the architect euphemistically referred to as "purism"; the lack of ornament, which was to become his morally defining principle of architecture; and the sequences of linked internal spaces that were a distinguishing feature of his later housing schemes. Loos designed the volume of the building in accordance with his own concept of architectural integrity. The side elevations of the commercial zone at the base reveal the different levels of the spaces within. The entrance to this zone is between four somewhat squat columns. Above the plinth and contrasted with it are the ascetic, white rendered planar facades of the housing stories with their articulation in the form of punched rectangular openings.

During the construction period, a broad critical front developed that rejected the new building. Loos retaliated in his usual sharp-tongued manner in a number of articles and lectures. Criticism was focused above all on the lack of ornamentation to the upper floors. "A building without eyebrows" or a "manhole cover building" were two of the least flattering epithets applied in this context. Even critics who were favorably disposed to the scheme adopted this imagery; the "lack of eyebrows" became a pioneering feature, a guarantee of architecture devoid of ornamentation for an architect whose pamphlets against decoration — and in particular the article "*Ornament und Verbrechen*" (Ornament and Crime), dating from 1908 — were received with such euphoria that Loos saw himself obliged to tone them down 20 years later. It was not just the lack of orchestration that his adversaries condemned. His contemporaries were particularly offended by shortcomings of this kind in such an important location — immediately opposite the Hofburg, the imperial palace in Vienna. It was an affront to decorum. It was something unbefitting in such close proximity to the imperial apartments.

Loos' building is of a monumental scale, from the proportions of the two lower floors, with the monolithic columns in Cipollino marble, to the squat form of the roof. Even the window openings, deeply incised in the facades of the housing stories, suggest a firm, immovable quality. The building seeks to communicate the solidity of a well-run department store. What is more, it possesses the concentrated strength of a bourgeois culture that now faces up to the imperial palace opposite with a great degree of self-assurance. Loos' building is monumental not only in its dimensions and proportions, but in terms of its demeanor. It is no coincidence that the Goldman & Salatsch development enjoys a prominent position in the "Città Analoga" collage (1973) suggested by Aldo Rossi, the great theoretician of urban monumentality.   R.H.

ADOLF LOOS

1870	Born on December 10 in Brno, Moravia
1885–89	Attends the Imperial and Royal State Technical School in Reichenberg, Bohemia, and the department of architecture and engineering of the Imperial and Royal German State Technical School in Brno with Josef Hoffmann
1889–90	Occasional student at the Royal Saxon University in Dresden, Germany
1892–93	Further studies in Dresden
1893–96	Travels to the U.S.; visits Philadelphia, the World Exposition in Chicago, and New York
1896	Returns to Brno and later moves to Vienna
1899	Interior design of Café Museum in Vienna
1903–06	Conversion of the Villa Karma in Clarens near Montreux, Switzerland
1908	Interior design of the American Bar in Vienna; publishes the article "*Ornament und Verbrechen*"
1909–11	Goldman & Salatsch Building erected on the Michaelerplatz, Vienna
1910	Hugo and Lilly Steiner House in Vienna
1912	Helene Horner House in Vienna
1912–13	House for Dr. Gustav Scheu and Helene Scheu in Vienna
1914	Anglo-Austrian Bank II, Vienna
1921–24	Head architect of the Housing Development Office of the City of Vienna
1922	Josef and Marie Rufer House, Vienna
1925	Moves to Paris
1926	Town house for Tristan Tzara in Paris
1927–28	Hans and Anny Moller House in Pötzleinsdorf, Vienna
1928–30	House for the engineer Frantisek Müller and Milada Müller in Prague
1930–32	In collaboration with Heinrich Kulka, erects two two-family houses as part of the Viennese Werkbund estate (overall planning: Josef Frank)
1933	Dies on August 23 in Kalksburg near Vienna

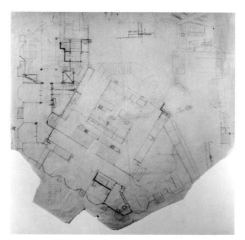

GOLDMAN & SALATSCH

GOLDMAN & SALATSCH

1 | Layout sketch
2 | Michaelerplatz facade
3 | First-floor salesroom
4 | Staircase

3

4

1

2

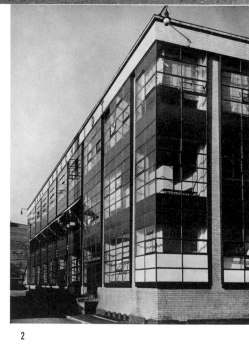

3

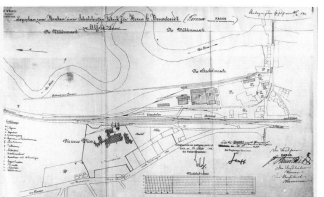

4

Walter Gropius with Adolf Meyer

Fagus Factory | ALFELD–AN–DER–LEINE (GERMANY) 1911–1913

With his first major commission, which he received at the age of 28 through the agency of his uncle from the industrialist Karl Benscheidt, the young architect Walter Gropius succeeded in creating an early masterpiece. The historical significance of the Fagus Factory lies in its remarkable modernism compared to the standard office building of the times. Begun in 1911 and extended in 1913, it has shaped the image of the shoe-tree factory down to the present day. After the functional concept for the various parts of the complex had been drawn up by an architect versed in the technical requirements of the plant, Benscheidt made Gropius responsible for the "artist building design" and requested him "to give the entire plant a stylish appearance." With the experience he had gained in the office of Peter Behrens, the artistic adviser to the AEG, Germany's General Electric Company, Gropius was ideally equipped for this task.

To lend the factory a "worthy appearance," Gropius chose a leathery, yellow brick commonly used for industrial buildings. Against all expectations, however, he did not design a solid brick block, but a dematerialized, transparent enclosure. The stability of the reinforced concrete structure of floor slabs and internal columns enabled Gropius to dissolve the facade as he wished. The openings he formed in the traditional brickwork were so large that the remaining wall areas represent little more than a skeleton framework, and the building is reduced to its bare outlines. The solid external structure, consisting of a low plinth, slender piers, and a horizontal parapet wall at the top, is closed with panels of glazing that extend over all three stories.

In his first factory building, Gropius emancipated himself from his mentor, Peter Behrens. The Fagus works can be seen as the architectural antithesis of the latter's best-known building, the AEG Turbine Factory in Berlin. Gropius did not build a temple of labor, but a regular cubic block in which work is objectified. The various functions of the building and the internal production processes are made visible. Nevertheless, the factory has a number of different faces, depending on the viewpoint. Gropius designed a structure with an outer skin that, seen from an angle, as it normally is when one approaches the building, congeals to a glazed curtain wall. Viewed frontally, on the other hand, it is articulated by a row of receding piers. Gropius thus reverses the concept of the

Turbine Factory. For a moment, one has the impression of a self-supporting curtain wall wrapped around the corners. Here, for the first time, the facade provides some indication of the great degree of transparency that skeleton-frame structures were to make possible in the future. At the corner, where the observer would expect the greatest loading to occur, the building gives an impression of weightlessness.

Although iron floor girders had long enabled structures to be cantilevered out at the corners, Gropius was the first architect to draw formal conclusions from this. Where Behrens resorts to architectural history, Gropius is radically modern. On being attacked in the press for his daring, Gropius replied that by leaving out the corner pier, he had saved not merely a column, but money, too.   M.H.

WALTER GROPIUS

1883	Born on May 18 in Berlin
1903	Studies architecture in Munich, Germany
1905–07	Studies architecture in Berlin
1906–07	Design and execution of estate buildings in Pomerania
1907–10	Assistant in the office of Peter Behrens, Berlin; designs buildings for the AEG, Germany's General Electric Company
1910–14	Own architectural practice in Berlin — from 1911, with Adolf Meyer; member of the German Werkbund; edits the Werkbund yearbooks for 1912, 1913, and 1914; spring of 1911, lectures on industrial building in the Folkwang Museum, Hagen, among other places
1911–13	Fagus Factory, Alfeld-an-der-Leine, Germany
1914	Model factory and office building at the German Werkbund exhibition in Cologne, Germany
1914–18	Wartime military service
1919	Head of the Working Council for Art; director of the Grand Ducal School for the Visual Arts, including the former arts and crafts school, in Weimar, Germany, renamed the "State Bauhaus in Weimar"; Adolf Meyer again becomes an assistant in his office
1919–28	Director of the State Bauhaus until 1924 in Weimar, and from 1925 on in Dessau, Germany

1925	Own architectural practice in Dessau
1925–26	Bauhaus building, Dessau
1926	Awarded the title of professor by the State of Anhalt, Germany
1928–34	Own architectural practice in Berlin
1932	Dissolution of the Bauhaus in Dessau by the Nazis
1934–37	Goes to England; works with Maxwell Fry
1937	Emigrates to the U.S.
1937–52	Professor of architecture at Harvard University, Cambridge, Massachusetts
1938–42	Collaboration with Marcel Breuer
1946	Founds joint practice, The Architects' Collaborative
1956	Member of the Academy of Arts in Berlin
1960	Collaborates in founding the Bauhaus Archive in Darmstadt, Germany; design of museum building — project is moved to Berlin in 1971 and realized in 1979
1969	Dies on July 5 in Boston, Massachusetts

1 | Main building with entrance
2 | View of main building from southeast
3 | Site plan
4 | Overall view of works: historical photo

Albert Kahn

River Rouge Plant | DEARBORN, MICHIGAN 1918–1934

Henry Ford's Model-T transformed the automobile from a work of high craftsmanship suitable only for an elite class to a mass-produced product economically accessible to almost everyone. Similarly, Ford's River Rouge plant, a few miles southwest of the center of Detroit, Michigan, realized Henry Ford's dream of taking Model-T mass production techniques to a scale that at the time seemed extraordinarily vast. Ford's architect, Albert Kahn, designed several projects at the 2,000-acre site that remain among the most elegant essays in twentieth-century industrial architecture. They successfully integrated light and ventilation in structures of enormous technical and visual economy.

At the Rouge site in 1918, Ford began a 16-year process of creating a huge integrated complex with the capacity to process raw materials, which would in turn be assembled into finished automobiles.

Albert Kahn's first building at the Rouge site, the Eagle Plant, was a final-assembly building for ships. Ford had been directed by the government to mass-produce submarine-chasing ships for the war effort. The assembly building would be one long single-story building, basically a shed framed in steel. Kahn laid out five equal bays, three of which carried the continuously moving assembly lines and two that contained railroad tracks for conveying subassemblies and parts. The roofs of the bays were framed in simple steel trusses with additional framing projected upward to allow more glazed area, improving visibility on the factory floor. Where most earlier factories were filled in with glazing between the concrete framing, continuous curtain walls of steel-sash operable glazing were fixed to the exterior sides of the columns in the Eagle plant. At 255 by 1,700 feet (78 by 518 meters), it was an enormous industrial building, and was completed only five months after authorization in mid-1918.

Buildings were rapidly added in the early 1920s as automobile production took off. To organize operations on such a vast scale, Ford and Kahn divided the site into large square superblocks. Each subsequent plant (many of which were much larger than Eagle) was far longer than it was wide, and ran parallel to rail tracks and a shipping channel. The buildings were spaced well apart to permit ample rail or road access and rapid alteration and expansion. It was a simple site idea, but its discipline permitted the continuous alterations that made operation viable long after Ford's dream of a vast integrated complex was abandoned.

By the time the complex was complete, Kahn had built a glass-making plant, a foundry, a cement plant, a spring and upset building, a mill for rolling steel into sheets, a pressed steel building, a motor assembly building, and structures for ovens and open-hearth furnaces which were used for manufacturing steel. The result is a stripped-down expression of pure industrial power. Each succeeding structure became simpler and more prismatic, deriving its visual power from the sheer scale of its repetitive, minimal form. These projects presaged the far greater refinement Kahn would bring to industrial buildings in the 1930s for both the automobile and the nascent aircraft industries.   J.S.R.

ALBERT KAHN

1869	Born on March 21 in Rhaunen, Germany
1880	Moves with his parents to Detroit, Michigan
1885	After apprenticing in several architectural firms, Kahn is promoted to draftsman at the offices of Mason and Rice
1896	Founds a firm with George W. Nettleton and Alexander Trowbridge; completes his first major commission for a children's hospital in Detroit
1901–02	Builds the Palms Apartment House in Detroit with his former boss and new partner, George D. Mason
1903	Hires his brother, Julius Kahn, as the firm's chief engineer, and together they develop the concrete structural system for the Engineering Building at the University of Michigan, Detroit
1905	Building No. 10 for the Packard Motor Company, Detroit
1910–16	Completes the Highland Park Plant, Detroit, for the Ford Motor Company

1918	Begins work designing and building the Ford River Rouge Plant in Dearborn, Michigan, completed in 1934
1928	Builds the Plymouth Factory in Detroit for the Chrysler Corporation
1930–32	Supervises the building of a tractor factory in Stalingrad; receives several more commissions in the Soviet Union, and with his brother, Moritz, trains Russian workers to design industrial complexes
1937–41	Further refines the steel-framed industrial building, including an assembly building for the Glenn L. Martin Airplane Co. (Middle River, Maryland; 1937), the Curtiss-Wright Airport Corporation Building (Buffalo, New York; 1938), and the Chrysler Corporation Tank Arsenal (Detroit; 1941)
1942	Dies on December 8 in Detroit
1998	Albert Kahn Associates still serves the auto industry; its latest project is an assembly plant recently completed for Mercedes Benz in Tuscaloosa, Alabama

1

3

2

1 | Glass factory
2 | Eagle Works; aerial view
3 | River Rouge complex; aerial view
4 | Eagle Works

4

Erich Mendelsohn

Einstein Tower | POTSDAM 1919-1924

"Organic!" Albert Einstein is alleged to have exclaimed on seeing the Einstein Tower on the Telegrafenberg near Potsdam, Germany. The new solar observatory erected for the venerable Astrophysical Institute for the practical testing of Einstein's theory of relativity was soon famous beyond Germany's borders as a building with a distinctive identity and a tremendous aura. It is the symbol of Expressionism become form.

The origins of the Einstein Tower go back to the trenches of World War I, long before the building was actually commissioned. It was there, during lulls in hostilities, that Erich Mendelsohn put his architectural visions on paper in small-scale sketches drawn with a sure hand. The bold curves of his perspective drawings were to become the distinguishing feature of all subsequent designs. The organic, self-contained form of the tower can already be recognized in the soft con-

tours of the sketched "astronomical observatories" and "factory for optical instruments." Mendelsohn was assured of receiving the commission in a letter dated July 2, 1918, from Einstein's assistant Dr. Erwin Finlay-Freundlich, in which the functional requirements of the observatory were precisely laid down. In a series of exchanges that took place before the end of the war and the actual granting of the commission in 1919, the two men, who were good friends, agreed upon the main details between the two poles of functionalism and aesthetics, fusing them into a most successful synthesis.

Formally, the Einstein Tower is Mendelsohn's own personal creation, not based on any previous models. He depicted in pure, unadulterated form an architectural organism that, in its molded, sculptural design represents a unity that can be neither divided nor extended. A dynamic quality pervades the volume of the building, intensifying its expression and the space around it. Nothing could better focus — in a metaphorical sense — the rays of the sun that enter here than this compact archetype that reflects matter, energy, space, and time in a relative play of forces.

During the construction work, the three-dimensional concept soon revealed its limitations. Formwork problems meant that the specified material, in situ concrete, could be used only for the entrance portal and the topmost ring of the tower. The rest of the flowing form was built conventionally in brickwork. It was, however, covered with a thick layer of cement rendering to lend the surface a uniform appearance.

On a number of occasions, Mendelsohn described the Einstein Tower, in contrast to his later work, as having a form derived from a mystic-cosmic emotion, a form that for him resulted in a unique and inimitable maiden work. None of his later buildings adopts the formal language of the Einstein Tower again. It remains *the* icon of Expressionist architecture.   C.B.

ERICH MENDELSOHN

1887	Born on March 21 in Allenstein, East Prussia, Germany
1908-12	Studies architecture at the University of Technology in Charlottenburg, Berlin
1914	Makes the acquaintance of the astrophysicist Dr. Erwin Finlay-Freundlich, the future assistant of Albert Einstein
1915-18	Called up for military service
1918	Own architectural practice in Westend, Berlin
1919	Commission from Dr. Finlay-Freundlich to build the Einstein Tower, Potsdam, Germany, completed in 1924
1921	Basic structure of the Einstein Tower; planning of a hat factory in Luckenwalde, outside Berlin (1921-23); employs Richard Neutra in his office and converts the Mosse House in Berlin-Mitte
1923	First visit to Palestine; villa for Dr. Walter Sternefeld, Berlin
1924	First visit to the U.S.; meets Frank Lloyd Wright; Einstein Tower taken into service; building for Herpich furriers in Berlin-Mitte
1925	Visits the U.S.S.R.
1926-30	Major department store designs for Schocken in Nuremberg, Stuttgart, and Chemnitz; further stores in Duisburg, Breslau, and Berlin, all in Germany
1930-32	Administrative headquarters of the German Metalworkers Union, Kreuzberg, Berlin; Columbus Building in Potsdamer Platz, Berlin
1933	Emigrates to Britain
1933-39	Lives in London; joint practice with Serge Chermayeff; De La Warr Pavilion in Bexhill-on-Sea, England
1935-	Opens an office in Jerusalem; villa for Professor Chaim Weizmann (1935-36) near Tel Aviv and the Hadassah University Hospital Medical Institute (1936-39) in Jerusalem
1939	Moves to Palestine
1941	Emigrates to the U.S.
1945	Moves to San Francisco; opens an office there
1946-53	Maimonides Hospital, San Francisco (1946-50); Russell House, San Francisco (1950-51)
1953	Dies on September 15 in San Francisco

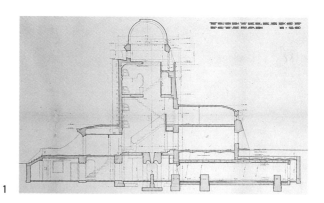

1

4

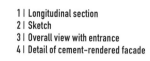

1 | Longitudinal section
2 | Sketch
3 | Overall view with entrance
4 | Detail of cement-rendered facade

3

Gunnar Asplund

Municipal Library | STOCKHOLM 1920-1927

Since the erection of the famous reading room of the British Museum in London, the rotunda has been regarded as a symbol of the knowledge of the world. It reappears in the municipal public library of Stockholm in a prominent position. As the centerpiece of the building, it defines its heart and forms a crowning element flanked on three sides by elongated horizontal tracts.

These linear structures, laid out in the form of a "U" in the plan, enclose the central drum like a bastion, screening it from the road. Towering above the clean cubic volume at its base, the cylinder nevertheless forms a landmark that is visible from afar. It houses the central lending hall, which may be reached via two axial routes that intersect at right angles to each other. The hall is flanked by reading and study spaces and offices. The layout of the staircases reveals a clear hierarchy of primary and secondary routes: two pairs of stairs, one straight, the other curved, are complemented by a straight-flight staircase in the center. Whereas the straight external stairs make contact with the rotunda at only one point, the double internal stairs hug the curve of the drum. The third flight of stairs rises radically toward the center of the cylinder and leads directly to the central booklending facilities.

The main axis, which ends at this point, begins outside the building in a long ramp and leads through the darkness of the outer sheath of walls up into the high, light-filled space of the hall, which is lined at the base by three floors of bookshelves. The main entrance to the building is framed by a monumental, Egyptian-looking portal that rises above a rusticated plinth zone and dominates the entire three-story facade. Apart from the continuous frieze courses, the portal is the only historical stylistic quotation that Asplund used, applied like some object from antiquity to the otherwise plain front of the building, which is punctuated by rectangular window openings. The pale gray stone faces of the portal are strikingly contrasted with the rust-red external rendering. The industrially prefabricated grid-like entrance glazing, on the other hand, echoes that of the unornamented window openings. The ascetic stance of modernism triumphs over the stylistic urge.

Although Asplund's design is regarded as a crowning achievement of Scandinavian neoclassicism, in its formal restraint it heralds the change to functionalism that was to be accomplished only a short time later in the buildings for the Stockholm Exposition in 1930. The classicism of the library is evident in its symmetrical layout, in its predominantly axial circulation system, and its rigorous formal reduction to basic geometric volumes: a cube penetrated by a cylinder. The architect's preliminary designs reveal his overwhelming inclination to simplification. Asplund did not hesitate to omit the glazed dome originally foreseen over the central reading room. In its place, he designed the tall cylinder one knows today, with windows punched in its walls to allow the direct ingress of daylight from the sides and partial views to the sky above.

M.H.

GUNNAR ASPLUND

1885	Born on September 22 in Stockholm, Sweden
1905–09	Studies at the Royal University of Technology, Stockholm, where he obtains his diploma
1910	Study trip to Germany
1912–18	Secondary school in Karlshamm, Sweden
1913–14	Study trip to Italy
1915	Together with Sigurd Lewerentz, wins the competition for a cemetery in Stockholm; chapel erected 1918–20; working buildings 1922–24
1915–24	Karl-Johann School in Göteborg, Sweden
1917	Competition entry for Götaplatsen, Göteborg; kitchen designs for "Homes Exhibition," Stockholm
1917–18	Snellmann Villa in Djursholm, Sweden
1917–20	Works on the editorial staff of *Arkitektur* magazine

1917–21	Law courts, Lister in Sölvesborg, Sweden
1920–27	Municipal Library, Stockholm: leading work of Swedish classicism in the 1920s
1922–23	Skandia Cinema, Stockholm
1930	Principal architect responsible for the Stockholm Exposition; breakthrough to functionalism
1931	Professor of architecture at the Royal University of Technology, Stockholm
1933–35	Bredenberg Department Store, Stockholm
1933–37	State Bacteriological Laboratory, Stockholm
1934–37	Town Hall extension in Göteborg
1935–40	Crematorium in Stockholm
1937	Designs his own summer house in Sorunda, Sweden
1940	Dies on October 30 in Stockholm

1

2

1 | Staircases to library hall
2 | Main facade
3 | Longitudinal section
4 | Second-floor plan
5 | Circular library hall

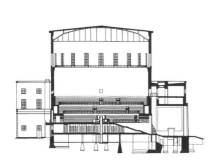

3

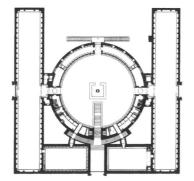

4

5

Fritz Höger

Chilehaus | HAMBURG 1921-1924

FRITZ HÖGER

1877	Born on June 12 in Bekenreihe, Schleswig-Holstein, today Germany
1895-96	Apprenticeship as carpenter and bricklayer
1897-99	Studies at the school of building crafts in Hamburg, Germany
1901-05	Draftsman in the Hamburg architectural practice of Lundt and Kallmorgen
1907	Sets up his own practice; Rappolt Building, Hamburg (1911-12) and the Klöpper Building, Hamburg (1912-13)
1910-14	Supporter of the Home Protection Movement for the protection of traditional regional culture, a group close to the German Werkbund
1920-21	Sasel Housing Estate, Hamburg
1921-24	Chilehaus, Hamburg
1922-23	Stormarn Building (today the Wandsbek Town Hall), completed in 1923; numerous housing developments and villas, mainly in Hamburg, Schleswig-Holstein, and Berlin, through 1945
1925-36	Publishing house for the *Hamburger Fremden-blatt* daily newspaper (Broschek Building)
1926	Scherk Perfume Factory, Berlin
1926-29	Extension of the Reemtsma Cigarette Factory in Wandsbek, Hamburg
1927-28	Publishing house for the *Hannoverscher Anzeiger* daily newspaper in Hanover; housing scheme near Hamburg airport; Leder-Schüler Works Factory Building, Hamburg; Dransfeld Housing Block, Hamburg; Sprinkenhof Office Building, Hamburg (jointly with the Gerson brothers), completed in 1943
1928-33	Ecclesiastical buildings in northern Germany
1933	Member of the Combat Order of German Architects and Engineers (KDAI); his hopes to be appointed master-builder to Hitler are disappointed
1934-36	Professor of architecture at the Nordic University for Art in Bremerhaven, Germany
1935-41	Siebethsburg Estate in Rüstringen, Wilhelmshaven, Germany
1949	Dies on June 21 in Bad Segeberg, Germany

"On a narrow tongue of land, drawn out over hundreds of meters, culminating at one end in the most acute of angles, attached at the other, broader end to existing buildings, rises the trunk of a building that positively strains towards its pointed tip: elongated like a trout, slender as a ship, rippling away like a wing, uninterrupted, unending like a stream of stars, incredibly light and incredibly strong, like the quill-feathers of an eagle, and unfurling like a banner in the wind. . . ."

With this expressive tribute, the writer Rudolf G. Binding sang the praises of the Chilehaus, a striking example of a regional manifestation of Expressionism. Completed in 1924, it became the second landmark of Hamburg after the famous "Michel," the Late Baroque church of St. Michael. It is difficult to resist the popular metaphors used to describe the building: a "flagship of stone" that has "dropped anchor in the harbor." Its architect, Fritz Höger, had nothing of the kind in mind, however. There can be no doubt that he shrewdly recognized the opportunity to place a building with an unusual form on this irregularly shaped site on Buchardplatz with a road running through the middle. With the 17 requested changes that he managed to implement, he carried the design to an extreme and truly made his point — in a literal as well as a metaphorical

sense. In this way, he was, therefore, in no small part responsible for the image of an ocean liner that came to be attached to the building. The pointed bow with a cormorant — the Chilean state emblem — as a figurehead; the three stepped back stories at the top that take the place of the roof, each with broadly cantilevered balcony cornices like the decks of a ship; the triangular pilasters of the facade that, when viewed obliquely, cause the windows to vanish as in the flank of a ship's hull; the S-shape curving south facade that owes its elegance to Höger's abandonment of two vertical projections; the Gothic-like pointed arch decoration to the projecting structures and arcades; and many other ornamental details developed from the brickwork — all these elements suggest the curving bow of a ship.

The Chilehaus was the first large-scale building to be erected in what was soon to be a famous office district of the city between the new Mönckebergstrasse (1908–13) and the unique warehouse area of the free port (1888–1906). It was erected on the cleared site of a once densely populated neighborhood dissected by narrow lanes, which had been afflicted by a cholera epidemic in 1892. The Chilehaus was built with a reinforced concrete structure and with 4.8 million dark, colorfully shimmering Oldenburg engineering bricks.

The Chilehaus is a tremendously high-spirited building — thanks to its varied and exciting form and its ingenious brick decoration, to which the ceramic depictions of animals and figures by the sculptor Richard Kuöhl also belong. As a result, the interplay of vertical and horizontal lines is augmented by diagonals, and one has the impression that it is not oneself who is moving, but the building, in a kind of a kinetic spectacle. The Chilehaus heralded a new metropolitan density: over an area of approximately 65,000 square feet (6,000 square meters) it stacks up a floor area some six times as vast.   M.S.

1

2

1 | Aerial view
2 | Historical photo of elevation
3 | Detail of decorative brickwork
4 | View of the "bow"

3

4

Rudolph Michael Schindler

Lovell Beach House | NEWPORT BEACH, CALIFORNIA 1922–1926

The Lovell Beach House, the summer residence of the well-known doctor Philip Lovell and his family, is a central work in Rudolph Michael Schindler's architectural development. Erected in Newport Beach on the Balboa peninsula, south of Los Angeles, it occupies a splendid site bounded to the north by 13th Street and to the west by the beach promenade. The distinctive form of the structure is visible from a great distance, and by raising the house on columns, it was possible to retain a large part of the site as a play area. The elevated position of the living areas also ensures a good view of the sea and affords a degree of privacy from the public beach promenade. "The motif used in elevating the house was suggested by the pile structures indigenous to all beaches," Schindler explained in 1926.

The salient features of the north-facing entrance front are the cantilevered horizontal volume at the top level and the five reinforced concrete supporting frames beneath, which establish a distinct structural rhythm. The diagonal lines of the two external staircases also represent an enrichment of the rectilinear facade forms. The west face is dominated by the horizontal strips of the balcony and the roof parapet, and by the large window openings in the two-story living space. In comparison, the south and east faces are relatively restrained and contain few openings.

The entrance staircase on the north side, with its comfortable proportions, leads up to a balcony at the second-floor level, where visitors have a magnificent view of the beach and the ocean below. After entering the house via one of the two doors, visitors immediately find themselves in the double-height living room, which extends over the full depth of the house and receives natural light from three sides. The entire house is laid out about this generous hall space. The top-floor gallery leads to four small changing rooms with open "sleeping porches" beyond. Sleeping outdoors, however, proved to be a wet experience on occasion, which was why the sleeping porches were enclosed after a short time. The

roof is used as a terrace area, part of which is divided off for sunbathing.

In this masterpiece, Schindler was able to realize his spatial concepts of architecture and living. In the beach house, Schindler also expressed his theoretical ideas on the "Care of the Body," which he was to formulate in 1926 in six articles in the *Los Angeles Times*. With this new and unconventional approach, Schindler implemented his own architectural and social ideas, which may be seen as an undogmatic interpretation of the main axioms of modern architecture. In the American context, his preoccupation with the European avant-garde occurred at a very early date. Nevertheless, his Lovell Beach House was not included in "The International Style" exhibition staged by the Museum of Modern Art in New York City in 1932. Today, the house is regarded as an important contribution to the Modern Movement in the United States.   P.S.

RUDOLPH MICHAEL SCHINDLER

1887	Born on September 10 in Vienna	1932	"The International Style" exhibition, Museum of Modern Art, New York City; Frank Lloyd Wright's and Rudolph Schindler's works are not exhibited
1906–11	Studies building engineering at the Imperial and Royal University of Technology in Vienna		
1910–13	Studies architecture under Otto Wagner at the Academy of Visual Arts in Vienna	1933	Prototypes for filling stations, and design of the "Schindler Shelter" — prefabricated dwellings in reinforced concrete
1913	Forms the "architectural school" of Adolf Loos		
1914	Emigrates to the U.S.; works as a draftsman for Henry A. Ottenheimer, Stern and Reichert, Architects, Chicago	1934–37	Designs the Buck House, 1934; Walker House, 1935; McAlmon House, 1936; Rodakiewicz House, 1937 (all in Los Angeles)
1917	Begins working in Frank Lloyd Wright's studio in Oak Park, Chicago	1939–40	Lectures at the Art Center School, Los Angeles; design critic for student work
1920	Moves to Los Angeles	1944	Bethlehem Baptist Church, Los Angeles
1921	Founds his own architectural practice; designs his house at 835 N. King's Road, Los Angeles, in collaboration with Clyde Chase; meets Leah and Philip Lovell	1947–48	Visiting critic at the University of Southern California, Los Angeles
1922–26	Lovell Beach House, Newport Beach, California	1948	Publishes his *Collected Papers*
1923	Pueblo Ribera holiday houses, La Jolla, California	1953	Dies on August 22 in Los Angeles
1926	Publishes "Care of the Body" in the *Los Angeles Times*; Richard Neutra's family moves into the house on King's Road		
1930	Lectures on spatial architecture		

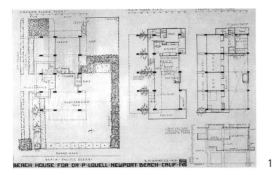

BEACH HOUSE FOR DR·P·LOUELL·NEWPORT BEACH·CALIF·

1

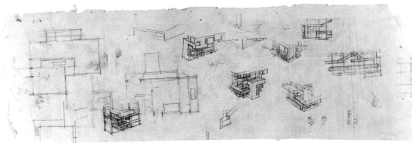

1 | Plans and section
2 | Entrance front; present state
3 | Design sketches
4 | Gallery
5 | View from northwest, showing the
    originally open sleeping porches
6 | Living hall

Gerrit Thomas Rietveld

Rietveld-Schröder House | UTRECHT (THE NETHERLANDS) 1924

Against the last blind side wall at the end of a peaceful Dutch street lined with otherwise unassuming houses for "respectable citizenry" stands a small and fragile family house which represents a visual and conceptual break in the history of twentieth-century architecture. In 1924, this place marked the spot where the open countryside met the town. Since then the town has claimed it for its own.

The Rietveld-Schröder house could be seen as a personal provocation by the self-assured client, Truus Schröder. It is also the declaration of a new artistic conception by a young architect in what was the first house he built. Until this time Rietveld had been primarily involved in making furniture — including the famous red/blue chair — and designing residential and shop interiors to be executed in his own workshop. The Schröder commission provided him with a new kind of challenge: Truus Schröder had very definite ideas as to how she wanted to live in this house. It was her wish to have the first floor designed as an open space with no dividing walls. As this was to be used as both a sleeping and living area for her and her three children, a layout solution was not easy to

come by. Building regulations also stood in the way of such an open layout. The problem was neatly circumvented by officially calling the upper floor "the attic."

Client and architect devised a system of sliding and revolving dividing walls so that the story could be adapted to each required function. Schröder's notions of a clean usage of materials and a simple finish equated with Rietveld's own working methods. They both regarded decoration as a misguided attempt to imitate nature. Instead they allowed nature to enter the house by including windows that revolved outwards and a glass skylight.

The house is small and yet commands the space around it effortlessly. The architecture is not an expression of the materials used, but of the space itself. The interior is a reflection of the orderliness of the modernistic town. It forms a microcosm of pronounced lines which navigate across color surfaces, alongside and around pieces of furniture, which in turn comprise permanent features on the interior landscape. And just as each architectural element of a modernist town reflects a particular function, there are separate areas for movement, storage, sitting, sleeping, and working.

All of Rietveld's designs are references to the machine aesthetic and are therefore often designed to permit serial production. In principle, this is also true of his architecture. His concepts are always clearly and functionally presented, and yet, through his use of economical and modest materials and their often careless finish, everything he creates acquires an aura that stands in contrast to the very precision and stringency of the design. It is a sort of personal aesthetic of imperfection that mitigates its intellectual strictness. Rietveld always transformed his concepts into individual images which hence stand counter to the collectivist ideal of modernism. It is this very paradox that lends Rietveld's work its human scale. His designs are for normal people with human emotions.

R.K.

GERRIT THOMAS RIETVELD

1888	Born on June 24 in Utrecht, the Netherlands
1900	Goes to work in his father's furniture workshop
1904–08	Takes evening classes at the Industrial Art School of the Foundation "Het Utrechts museum van Kunstnijverheid te Utrecht"; is employed at C.J.A. Begeer's gold and silver workshop
1906	Takes evening classes from the architect P.J.C. Klaarhamer in Utrecht
1909–13	Works in C.J.A. Begeer's workshop
1917	Starts his own furniture workshop in Utrecht
1921	First commission: Truus Schröder-Schräder employs him to design the interior of her living room
1923	Meets Bruno Taut, Kurt Schwitters, and El Lissitzky
1924	Designs and constructs a new house for Truus Schröder-Schräder; sets up his architectural practice in the Schröder House, which subsequently becomes known as the Rietveld-Schröder House
1926–27	Meets Mart Stam, El Lissitzky, László Moholy-Nagy; exhibits in Moscow and Stuttgart, Germany

1929	He and Mart Stam are the Dutch delegates to the famous Congrès Internationaux d'Architecture Moderne (CIAM) symposium "Die Wohnung für das Existenzminimum" in Frankfurt-am-Main, Germany
1931	Honorary member of the Kyoto Architects' Association, Japan
1934	Interior decoration for the model apartment in Rotterdam's (the Netherlands) Bergpolder flats by W. van Tijen, J.A. Brinkman, and L.C. van der Vlugt; a realization of the concept of minimalist living
1946–60	Works as an architect, but continues to design furniture and interiors; travels extensively; several international exhibitions on his work take place; he participates in numerous design juries and on consulting commissions
1961	Establishment of the Rietveld, van Dillen, and van Tricht architectural office
1964	Honorary doctorate from the Technical University in Delft, the Netherlands; becomes an honorary member of the Dutch Architects' Association; dies on June 25 at the Rietveld-Schröder House

1 | Living and dining area on upper floor
2 | Upper floor plan: open layout
3 | Upper floor plan with partitions
4 | Outward-opening windows
5 | View of house in urban context

1

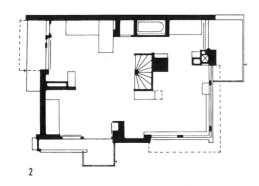

2

4

3

5

1

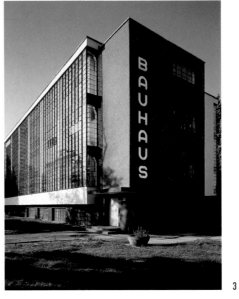

2

3

4

5

The State Bauhaus was founded in 1919 as a union of the Grand Ducal College of Visual Art and the Grand Ducal Arts and Crafts School in the city of Weimar, Germany, which at that time was governed by a social-democratic council. In 1925, however, conservative forces compelled the Bauhaus to leave Weimar and move to Dessau, Germany, where Walter Gropius planned a complex of new buildings in which his architectural teachings were to assume manifesto-like form.

The irregular layout of the Bauhaus buildings can best be seen from an aerial view. The three L-shape tracts interlock with each other spatially like the vanes of a windmill. The complex has little in common with conventional university buildings. In its asymmetrical grouping of different functional realms, it bears a certain resemblance to a modern factory complex. Gropius did indeed see this place of instruction, of which he was "master builder" and the first director, as a laboratory, in which art, arts and crafts, and industrial design were to be unified. Based on the model of the medieval stonemasons' lodges, architecture was here regarded as the mother of the arts.

The institution has gone down in architectural history as the incarnation of functionalism and of the white aesthetic of the Modern Movement. The highlight of this ensemble is the fully glazed four-story workshop wing, which faces on to the public road. The developments heralded in the office tract of the Fagus Factory in Alfeld-an-der-Leine, Germany, also by Gropius and Adolf Meyer, here come to fruition. Any hint of a load-bearing wall or column is denied by the facade. The glazed curtain wall construction that encloses the building on three sides was made possible by the internal reinforced concrete skeleton frame structure.

In his Bauhaus manifesto published in 1919, Gropius wrote: "Let us create together the new building of the future that will represent everything in a single form: architecture, sculpture, and painting; that, created by the hands of millions of craftsmen, will one day rise up to heaven as a crystalline symbol of a newly dawning belief." The integration of all artistic disciplines is demonstrated most convincingly in the interior design. Decorations by the mural painting department were used; lamps and tubular steel furniture were made in the metal workshops; and the inscriptions and lettering were provided by the Bauhaus printing shop.

While the suspended curtain walls to the collectively used workshop tract deliberately mask any indication of story divisions, in the adjoining sections of the complex, the lines of the floors are given prominence. The horizontal dynamics of the low-rise blocks are echoed by the dark-framed strips of fenestration set in the pale facades. The studio building to the rear of the development represents the only vertical note. Sixteen separate balconies on its west face indicate the individual student apartments within and provide them with light, fresh air, and sunshine. The balconies project like springboards from the wall of the snow-white tower block and cast a lively pattern of changing shadows over the taut, sail-like facade. Together with the balustrade railings, they evoke an image of nautical architecture — of an ocean liner beached in the middle of Dessau.   M.H.

WALTER GROPIUS
Architect's biography on p. 33

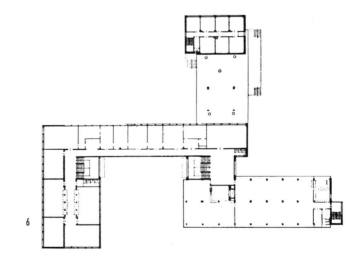

6

1 | Studio building
2 | "Technical teaching establishment,"
     administrative and workshop tracts
3, 4 | Workshop tract
5 | Staircase
6 | Plan

1 | View of curved facade and glazed
    bridges
2 | Detail of glass facade
3 | View from south
4 | View from southeast
5 | Axonometric of site layout

Van Nelle Factory | ROTTERDAM 1925-1931

Situated on the outskirts of Rotterdam, the Van Nelle Factory continued to fulfill its original purpose, the production and packaging of coffee, tea, and tobacco, until 1996. The factory complex, which was built in stages, was designed by the office of Brinkman & Van der Vlugt, one of the foremost Dutch exponents of functionalism. However, the elegance of this structure sets it apart from the sometimes rather spartan products of this straight-lined movement.

The commission to build the Van Nelle Factory was in fact awarded to architect Michiel Brinkman. After his death in 1925 the commission passed to his son, civil engineer J.A. Brinkman, who for this purpose and at the insistence of the Van Nelle chairman, C.H. van de Leeuw, entered into partnership with L.C. van der Vlugt. The design of the Van Nelle Factory can in large part be attributed to Van der Vlugt. Some architectural historians attach great significance to the presence in the office of Mart Stam, who had recently made a name for himself with his dwellings at the Weissenhof Estate in Stuttgart, Germany. The role of Stam remains unclear, but it is certainly true that in the course of his career he was often present on occasions of ground-breaking significance. There can be no doubt, however, of the important role played by the Van Nelle chairman, C.H. van de Leeuw. He was a pro-

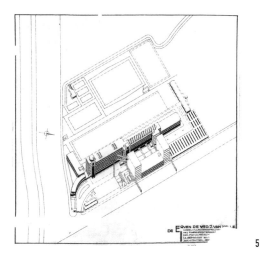

5

gressive employer who took an interest in the welfare of his employees and who was therefore receptive to the functionalist ideals of light, air, and space.

The Van Nelle Factory is a largely transparent building, whose graceful curve and glazed aerial walkways with conveyor belts express the dynamics of modern factory production. It is a concrete structure in which the floors are supported by columns while the facade is a non-supporting curtain wall of glass and steel, a quintessentially functionalist feature for modern architects. The dividing walls are likewise made of glass and steel and the offices were originally fitted out with equally functional tubular steel furniture. An integral part of the architecture are the huge illuminated letters on the roof which advertise the factory's name far and wide. For strictly orthodox functionalists the rooftop chocolate box (as the conference room was called) was a superfluous frivolity. Nonetheless, viewed as part of the three-dimensional composition, this round box provides a very effective termination to the building. In fact, Van Nelle board meetings were not the only gatherings held in the conference room. Van der Leeuw was active in numerous social organizations in Rotterdam and on more than one occasion he allowed the chocolate box to be used by the working parties, committees, and boards of which he was a member. During World War II, for example, meetings were held there to discuss the future reconstruction of the severely damaged city of Rotterdam.

The factory complex has been extended several times by Van den Broek & Bakema, the office that carried on the work of Brinkman & Van der Vlugt after the war. The office's most recent involvement with the Van Nelle Factory concerned the construction of a coffee silo in 1991 and the circumspect renovation-cum-reconstruction of the circular rooftop conference room in 1993. H.I.

J.A. BRINKMAN AND L.C. VAN DER VLUGT

1894	L.C. van der Vlugt is born on April 13 in Rotterdam, the Netherlands; trains at the Rotterdam Academy of Arts and Technical Sciences; sets up on his own practice
1902	J.A. Brinkman is born on March 22 in Rotterdam; studies civil engineering at Delft Technical College, the Netherlands, while working for his father, the architect Michiel Brinkman
1919-22	Technical Secondary School in Groningen, the Netherlands, Brinkman with J.G. Wiebenga
1925	Brinkman takes over his father's practice and enters into partnership with the architect L.C. van der Vlugt
1925-31	Van Nelle Factory, Rotterdam
1927	Various villas in Rotterdam: Van der Leeuw's House (1927-28), the Boevé Residence (1932-34), and the Sonneveld Residence (1932-33)

1931	Van der Vlugt and Brinkman design the telephone booth that enhances the Dutch street scene for 50 years
1932-34	Bergpolder Apartment Building in Rotterdam in collaboration with W. Van Tijen
1935-36	Ypenburg Airport, Rotterdam; Feyenoord Football Stadium in Rotterdam-Zuid
1936	Van der Vlugt dies on April 25; Brinkman enters into partnership with J.H. van den Broek
1939	Brinkman retires; the practice continues to bear the name Brinkman & Van den Broek for another 12 years, when it is renamed Van den Broek & Bakema
1949	Brinkman dies on May 6 in Rotterdam

Ludwig Mies van der Rohe and others

Weissenhof Estate | STUTTGART 1927

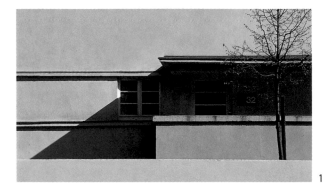

1

Overall planning and artistic direction: Ludwig Mies van der Rohe
Project management: Richard Döcker
Participating architects: Peter Behrens, Richard Döcker, Josef Frank, Walter Gropius, Ludwig Hilberseimer, Pierre Jeanneret and Le Corbusier, Ludwig Mies van der Rohe, Jacobus Johannes Pieter Oud, Hans Poelzig, Adolf Rading, Hans B. Scharoun, Adolf G. Schneck, Mart Stam, Bruno Taut, Max Taut.

The Weissenhof Estate was presented to the public on July 23, 1927, as the centerpiece of the German Werkbund exhibition, "The Dwelling," in Stuttgart, Germany. Under the artistic direction of Ludwig Mies van der Rohe, 16 internationally known architects from various countries were invited to present their ideas on the subject of the dwelling of the future in single- and multi-family housing developments. The participants were supported by a team of architects and interior designers who had been commissioned to draw up model proposals for the furnishings and fitting out of the 63 housing units. The outcome was a compendium of modern architecture built on a sloping site above the city. The development also provided a superb illustration of the different architectural approaches of the time and a hitherto unparalleled presentation of the architectural avant-garde of the 1920s.

Unlike the large-scale housing developments being built at the same time on the outskirts of large cities, where architects like Bruno Taut, Ernst May, or J.J.P. Oud sought to formulate model urban and architectural solutions for socially acceptable small dwellings in mass housing schemes, the Weissenhof Estate consisted largely of detached single-family houses. The participating architects were able to present their formal and functional ideas of the design and layout of dwellings, rationalization, and typification to a comprehensible, individual

scale and in a relatively free arrangement. Only Mart Stam and Oud built single-family terrace houses in which they addressed the theme of the small dwelling in what Oud termed a "segment of a large-scale housing scheme."

Peter Behrens' moderately modern housing block consisted of a series of stepped-down volumes, one to four stories in height, articulated by simple rectangular window openings. The roof areas were to be used as terraces for the dwellings. Mies van der Rohe, in contrast, propagated a concept of alternative layouts in his elongated block of flats, which rises impressively above the detached houses scattered over the slope of the site. His freely divisible, flexible layouts within a load-bearing, steel-skeleton frame structure were meant to allow adaptations of the plans to the changing needs of future tenants. The two elegant houses Le Corbusier built are given prominence by being raised on slender columns, or pilotis. They were designed to demonstrate the essential points of his new concept of architecture. Bruno Taut, on the other hand, wished his contribution to be seen as the "proletarian among the single-family houses."

The Weissenhof Estate was the subject of heated controversies and defamation on the part of conservative architects. Although the Nazis declared it to be an "eyesore" and a disgrace in the 1930s, the development managed to escape their plans for its conversion or demolition. The houses in the central part of the estate suffered the heaviest damage from wartime bombing and conversions and demolition in the postwar years. The buildings that have survived and are now protected by conservation orders have been rehabilitated, and today convey a vivid impression of the original quality and appearance of the Weissenhof Estate.   A.G.

LUDWIG MIES VAN DER ROHE
Architect's biography on p. 56

2

3

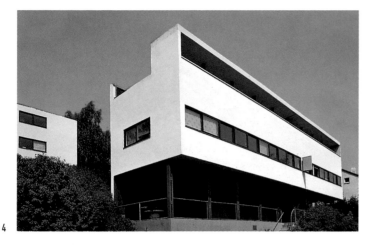

4

5

6

8

1 | Entrance to house 32 by Peter Behrens
2 | View of development from northeast; present state
3 | Overall plan of development
4 | View from southeast of blocks 14–15 by Le Corbusier
5 | Courtyard face of houses 5–9 by J. J. P. Oud
6 | Rear face of blocks 3–4 by Mies van der Rohe
7 | Entrance front to blocks 1–4 by Mies van der Rohe
8 | Entrance to house 33 by Hans B. Scharoun

Konstantin Melnikov

Rusakov Workers' Club | MOSCOW 1927–1929

"Everything is in a state of flux in this city," the author Franz Carl Weiskopf reported from Moscow in 1932. "Where a little church might have stood during your previous visit, a huge workers' club is now going up." In the mid-1920s, the Soviet capital was in the grip of a building boom, which had been made possible by the "New Economic Policy" propagated by Lenin. Particularly striking in the urban context at that time were the new building types that were being erected for revolutionary education, public services, recreation, and housing for the "socialist people." In addition to the buildings for the communes with small housing cells, there were large-scale communal developments like libraries and dining halls, together with central kitchens and large garages, public baths, and department stores. One building type in particular was to become the architectural symbol of the new society: the workers' club.

As an important instrument of the cultural revolution, the club was meant to serve the needs of political, aesthetic, and physical education. The workers' clubs were built by the unions or by individual industrial works. In Moscow, the club buildings, which are of great significance in the history of architecture, were designed mainly by one architect, Konstantin Melnikov, who had achieved international recognition with his Soviet Pavilion at the World Exposition in Paris in 1925. This glazed building with boldly colored elements and a timber skeleton frame was like a signal banner of the new age.

In Moscow, Melkinov built five workers' clubs. In their spatial and volumetric composition, they were strikingly different from each other. The Rusakov Club for Municipal Workers, completed in 1929, was a masterpiece of functionalism. Located on an arterial road near Sokolniki Park, this building's exciting form is recognizable from afar. Three prominent balcony-blocks are cut like wedges into the symmetrical volume of the building, the main facade of which is in concrete and glass. The courtyard face, in contrast, is in brickwork. The blocks contain three small auditoria for 200 people apiece. These were to be used either individually or in combination with the halls and stalls area below to form a single large space for 1,200 people. As a result of problems with the electro-mechanical movement of the dividing screens, however, the simultaneous use of the halls for different purposes had to be abandoned after only a short time.

As a member of the Soviet avant-garde, Melnikov belonged to the constructivist group, which took the precision of the machine as an architectural model. Selim O. Chan-Magomedov, an expert on the Soviet pioneers, places Melnikov's work in a different formal category from Expressionism, because it was motivated "not by external dynamics, not by the explicitness of the structure and not by untroubled statics, but by the inward tensions of the architectural form." If one sees the clubhouse today, which is still used for cultural and sporting events, one will understand why Melnikov compared his building to a "tensed muscle." W.J.S.

KONSTANTIN MELNIKOV

1890	Born in Moscow
1905–17	Studies at the Moscow School of Painting. Sculpture, and Architecture, initially painting. then architecture
1921–24	Teacher at the VchUTEMAS, Higher State Studios of Art and Technology in Moscow
1927	Bus garage, Moscow
1927–29	Rusakov Workers' Club, Moscow
1929	Kautschuk Rubber Workers' Club, Moscow: his own house and studio in Moscow
1930	Burevestnik Workers' Club
1933–38	Head of one of the architectural workshops of Mossoviet and teacher at MARChl, the Moscow institute of architects
1936	Garage of the State Planning Commission, Moscow
1974	Dies in Moscow

1

1 | Side view
2 | Main front
3 | Courtyard face
4 | Longitudinal section and plans

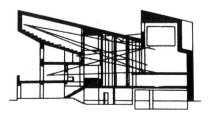
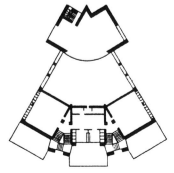
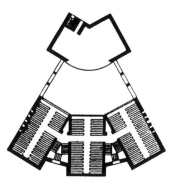

William Van Alen

Chrysler Building | NEW YORK CITY 1928-1930

While hubcaps, mudguards, hood ornaments, and radiator caps may be essential components of any Chrysler automobile, they are also indispensable as decorative elements of William Van Alen's Chrysler Building. Once the tallest building in the world at 1,046 feet (319 meters), the structure was built at the command of Walter P. Chrysler of the Chrysler Motor Company after he bought the site and Van Alen's designs from New York City real estate speculator William H. Reynolds in 1927.

The Chrysler Building made Van Alen famous, and much of its popularity was due to its innovative Art Deco style. The building's iconic image, however, comes from its stainless steel spire, a testament to Chrysler's relentless drive to build the world's tallest skyscraper. This battle for height was already an essential element of New York City skyscraper construction and Van Alen took it up to compete with his former partner, H. Craig Severance. At the time, Severance was at work on the Bank of Manhattan at 40 Wall Street, and upon its completion it topped out at 927 feet, two feet taller than the Chrysler Building's intended height. Nevertheless, Van Alen had a plan. The vertex, the series of sunbursts punctuated by triangular windows, was secretly assembled in the fire shaft of the Chrysler Building. Van Alen's team then hoisted it into place as one 27-ton piece, raising the building's height to 1,046 feet, 119 feet (36 meters) taller than the Bank of Manhattan.

The interior of the building is just as breathtaking as its exterior. A three-story-high portal of black Georgian marble on Lexington Avenue is a lavish prelude to the lobby, which provides easy access to the four banks of elevators to the 65 floors of offices. More impressive than its functional success, the lobby boasts a striking and colorful finish: adorning the surfaces are exotic woods, nickel, chrome, and steel, as well as Moroccan red marble walls and a yellow sienna floor, all trimmed with amber onyx and blue marble. The indirect lighting on these materials makes the space even more dramatic.

Shortly after its completion, the architectural critic Kenneth Murchison said of the building and its architect: "And as it is a commercial proposition, embodying the emblazonment of automotive progress, why should the architect have hesitated a moment in being the Ziegfeld of his profession?" Indeed, Van Alen's theatrical building is, more than anything, a personal projection of Walter P. Chrysler and his corporation. Today, the building is seen as more than Chrysler; it is the quintessential image of New York City, with its illuminated summit capturing the elegance and excitement of the Big Apple.   V. M. Y.

1

WILLIAM VAN ALEN

1882	Born on August 10 in Brooklyn, New York
1908	Attends classes at the Pratt Institute in Brooklyn but never graduates; works for the firm of Copeland and Dole, then Glinton and Russell; wins the Paris Prize and a scholarship to the Ecole des Beaux-Arts in Paris
1908–11	Studies in the atelier of Victor A.F. Laloux at the Ecole des Beaux-Arts; returns to New York; forms a partnership with H. Craig Severance
1911–24	Bainbridge, Bar, Gidding, and Prudence Buildings, New York City
1925	Van Alen leaves Severance and practices architecture independently
1926	Fifth Avenue Child's Restaurant Building, New York City
1927–28	Reynolds and Delman Buildings and 555 Madison Avenue in New York City
1928	Structures on the Chrysler Building site are razed on October 15
1929	Foundation work is completed by March 25 and building begins two days later
1930	The building is officially opened on May 27; Van Alen moves into offices on the 65th floor; Chrysler refuses to pay Van Alen, accusing him of taking bribes from subcontractors; Van Alen sues Chrysler for his fees and wins, but his career was virtually over
1936–54	Van Alen completes designs for a House of a Modern Age and builds Defense Housing in Newport, Rhode Island; a diminished practice leads him to a greater involvement in various architectural organizations such as the Beaux Arts Architects and the Beaux Arts Institute of Design
1954	Dies on May 24 in New York City after virtually abandoning architecture for real estate

1 | Overall view
2 | Interior of elevator
3 | Elevator doors with Art Deco ornamentation
4 | Spire

Ludwig Mies van der Rohe

Tugendhat House | BRNO (TODAY CZECH REPUBLIC) 1928–1930

"Can one live in the Tugendhat House?" Justus Bier asked in 1931 in *Die Form*, the journal of the German Werkbund. With this question he sparked off a debate that ended only when the occupants of the house spoke out themselves. Bier's words were not aimed at architect Mies van der Rohe personally. They were a criticism of the application of his concept of flowing space to a residential building. At the end of the 1920s, when the Modern Movement had established itself, a series of buildings was created that was meant to be the expression of an absolute idea. Villas and single-family houses in particular had always been ideal testing grounds for new concepts in spatial composition. With the Villa Savoye by Le Corbusier, Adolf Loos' Müller Villa, and the Tugendhat House by Mies van der Rohe, three buildings of a similar sort were created at roughly the same time, each of which was a built manifesto.

Immediately before he built the Tugendhat House, Mies van der Rohe had designed the German Pavilion for the World Exposition in Barcelona, in which he realized for the first time his concept of continuous, flowing space. In the Tugendhat villa, he applied the same idea to a house. As in the Barcelona Pavilion, he used a steel skeleton frame structure that permitted the free layout of the non-load-bearing walls. As a result of the sloping site, the house was not oriented to the street, but to the garden. The street face is relatively modest, whereas the garden aspect, with its continuous glass front, conveys an impression of a spacious, privileged lifestyle. The dualism of the facades is also reflected in the different semantic content of the two stories of the house. The lower floor is the principal level, while the more intimate spaces are located on the upper floor oriented to the street. In contrast to the traditional villa layout, in the Tugendhat House one does not ascend to the main living area; one descends to it. This main level comprises an approximately 2,400-square-foot (223-square-meter) space articulated into four functional realms (music room, library, dining room, and salon), which are, however, not divided by continuous walls. The open expanse and light transparency of this space seemed to meet the demands for a "liberated form of living" that were prevalent at that time.

Although it breaks with convention, the Tugendhat House does not forgo all elements of a grand lifestyle. Extremely fine materials were used to ennoble the bare rooms and lend them a certain pathos. The fear that the occupants would be forced to live a kind of "model life" that would allow no scope for privacy and intimacy or for personal development, as Justus Bier surmised, was not shared by the Tugendhats. They were to enjoy their home for only a few years, however. In 1938, they were forced to emigrate, and since then, the house has not been used as a private residence. Nonetheless, the open plan proved suitably flexible for other uses. At the beginning of the 1980s, the villa underwent an extensive restoration and has served since then as a venue for formal occasions and to provide accommodation for guests of the mayor. Justus Bier would probably see himself confirmed in his opinion that the Tugendhat House is, after all, best suited as a showplace for living.   M. J.

LUDWIG MIES VAN DER ROHE

1886	Born on March 27 in Aachen, Germany
1899–	Draftsman for stucco and ornamental work in Aachen workshops until 1903
1905–07	Apprentices with furniture designer Bruno Paul; studies at the school of arts and crafts in Munich, Germany
1908–11	Assistant in Peter Behrens' office in Berlin
1911	Own architectural practice in Berlin
1921–24	Four major ideal designs for high-rise buildings, villas, and offices
1927	Director of the Werkbund exhibition "The Dwelling" in Stuttgart (Weissenhof Estate), Germany
1928–30	Tugendhat House in Brno, today Czech Republic
1929	Construction of the German Pavilion at the International Exposition in Barcelona (today known as the Barcelona Pavilion), Spain
1930–33	Last director of the Bauhaus
1938	Emigrates to Chicago
1938–58	Director of the architectural faculty of the Armour Institute (later Illinois Institute of Technology); at the same time, runs his own office in Chicago
1946–51	Farnsworth House, Plano, Illinois
1948–51	High-rise apartment blocks: 860–880 Lake Shore Drive, Chicago
1954–58	Seagram Building, New York City
1962–67	New National Gallery, Berlin
1969	Dies on August 17 in Chicago

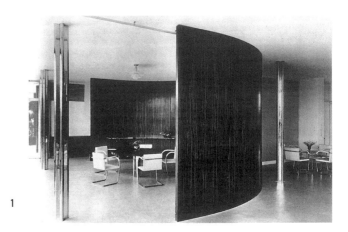

2

3

5

4

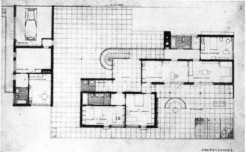

6

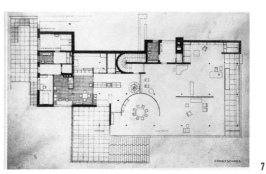

7

1 | Dining area
2 | Garden aspect
3 | Stairs down to main living area
4 | Entrance at street level
5 | Street face
6 | Upper-floor plan
7 | Lower-floor plan

1

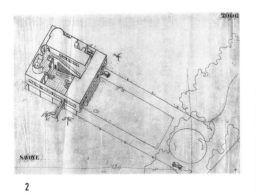

2

3

4

1 | External view
2 | Axonometric drawing
3 | Internal staircase
4 | View of ramp to roof garden

Le Corbusier with Pierre Jeanneret

Villa Savoye | POISSY (FRANCE) 1928-1931

In 1929, Le Corbusier described the Villa Savoye as "a box suspended in the air in the fields over an orchard." The house, designed for the Savoye family, was erected 20 miles (30 kilometers) by road from their Paris home. The use of the car as a link between the two homes was fundamental to the design of the villa. The semicircular form of the ground floor plan was based on the turning radius of a limousine: "About the house, between the pilotis, is a vehicular route ...; the curve encloses the entrance, the vestibule, the garage, and the servants' and utilities rooms. The cars drive up, are parked or drive away again — all beneath the house." In the entrance area, the theme of circulation is again encountered in the expressive forms and dialectic arrangement of the primary and secondary routes up to the living quarters: in the form of a curving staircase and a gently rising ramp. The changing course of the ramp, which ascends through the entire height of the building, reveals an array of visual attractions as one progresses upwards. It is a "*promenade architecturale*," as the architect termed it.

Situated about a hanging garden, the living rooms are laid out in an L-shape form along two edges of the main living area. Strip windows drawn around all four sides frame the views out of the building to the surrounding landscape. Emerging into the open air at the top, the ramp culminates in a roof garden with a solarium, an area screened from outside view and from the wind by high and partly curving walls. Aligned with the axis of the ramp, an opening in these walls marks the end of the "promenade." At the same time, it provides a visual continuation of the route by forming a framed view of the landscape and leading the eye out across the valley beyond.

The Villa Savoye is a summary of the vocabulary, ideas, and methods that Le Corbusier had developed in his work during the previous five years. The pilotis, the horizontal strip windows, the roof garden, the "open layout" and the flexible treatment of the facades had all been formulated in the architect's "Five Points of a New Architecture" in 1926. The free layout (*plan libre*) and the variable facade forms were made possible by the separation of load-bearing columns and internal partitions. The derivation of the formal criteria from functional needs and the use of standardized, industrially fabricated elements are in accordance with Le Corbusier's concept of the house as "a machine for living in."

The aesthetic, too, is influenced by the world of machines: by ocean liners, for example, with which the architect had illustrated his 1923 book, *Vers une architecture*. The forms of the solarium are reminiscent of a ship's funnel and of the Platonic ideal volumes contained in the chapter "The Lesson of Rome" in the same book; they also recall the shapes of the bottles, glasses, and jugs that Le Corbusier depicted in his purist paintings. The *promenade architecturale* was the outcome of his interpretation of space in Arab architecture.

The Villa Savoye is an ode to modern life. At the same time, it is Le Corbusier's elegant homage to antiquity: "It will seem [to the people who come to live here] as though their domestic life formed part of a poem by Virgil."　　M.-T.S.

LE CORBUSIER

1887	Born on October 6 in La Chaux-de-Fonds, Switzerland, as Charles Edouard Jeanneret	1927-31	Villa Stein in Garches and Villa Savoye, Poissy, both in France
1900-04	Training under Charles L'Eplattenier	1928	Co-founder of the Congrès Internationaux d'Architecture Moderne (CIAM) in La Sarraz, Switzerland
1907	Villa Fallet, La Chaux-de-Fonds; meets Josef Hoffmann in Vienna		
1908	Moves to Paris and works in the studio of Auguste Perret	1928-35	Centrosoyus building, Moscow; Salvation Army building and Pavillon Suisse, Paris
1910-11	Studies in Germany; works with Peter Behrens	1929	Furniture design for the Salon d'Automne in Paris with Charlotte Perriand
1914	Project for Domino Houses		
1916	Villa Schwob, La Chaux-de-Fonds	1935	"La ville radieuse" plan
1917	Moves to Paris; he and Amédée Ozenfant publish *Après le cubisme*	1941	Offers his services to General Pétain for reconstruction work
1920-25	Co-editor of the journal *L'Esprit Nouveau*	1947	Project for the United Nations Headquarters, New York City
1922	Begins work with his brother, Pierre Jeanneret; house in Vaucresson; develops "Contemporary City for Three Million Inhabitants" plan	1947-52	First Unité d'Habitation apartment building, Marseilles, France
1923	Publishes *Vers une architecture* under the pseudonym Le Corbusier; two-family house La Roche-Jeanneret, Paris	1950	Publishes *Le Modulor*; begins Notre-Dame-du-Haut Chapel, Ronchamp, France, completed in 1955
1925	Pavillon de l'Esprit Nouveau at the Exhibition des Arts Décoratifs in Paris	1952-65	Buildings in Ahmedabad and planning of a governmental complex in Chandigarh, India
1927	Shares first prize in the competition for the League of Nations Headquarters, Geneva, Switzerland; two houses in the Weissenhof Estate exhibition, Stuttgart, Germany	1957-60	Sainte-Marie-de-La-Tourette Monastery, Eveux, near Lyon, France
		1965	Dies on August 27 in Roquebrune-Cap Martin, France

Pierre Chareau with Bernard Bijvoët

Maison de Verre | PARIS 1928-1932

PIERRE CHAREAU

1883	Born on August 3 in Bordeaux, France
1900-08	Studies at the Ecole des Beaux-Arts in Paris
1908-14	Apprentices in furniture design at the firm of Waring and Gillow
1914-18	Serves as a soldier in World War I
1918-19	Designs interiors for the Dalsace apartment in Paris; furniture later shown at the Salon d'Automne
1923-32	Member of the Société des Artistes Décorateurs
1925	Exhibits a "Suite for an Ambassador" at the Exposition Internationale des Arts Décoratifs et Industriels Modernes, Paris
1925-35	Associated with the architect Bernard Bijvoët
1927-28	Collaborates with Bijvoët on a golf club at Beauvallon, France, near Saint-Tropez, which was unusual for its reinforced concrete construction; Chareau designs its metal and wood furnishings
1928	Interiors for a hotel in Tours, France
1928-32	Maison de Verre, Paris
1931	Joins the Union des Artistes Modernes (UAM); exhibits with them until 1937
1934	Interior of the Compagnie du Téléphone, Paris, which includes furnishings in exotic woods
1937	Djemel Anik Country House near Paris; office interiors for the Ministry of Foreign Affairs
1940	Emigrates to the U.S.; organizes and designs exhibitions in New York for the French Cultural Center; Chareau House, East Hampton, New York
1948	Studio for painter Robert Motherwell constructed of army surplus materials
1950	Dies on August 21 on Long Island, New York

In 1933 Paul Nelson wrote in the magazine *L'Architecture d'Aujourd'hui* that entering the Maison de Verre, or "House of Glass," in Paris was like being transported to "another planet." For contemporary viewers, the house seemed to invert all expectations of domestic architecture, such as obvious comfort and distinct traditionalism. Instead, the Maison de Verre suggested a new path for domestic design that would incorporate modern materials in inventive ways. Yet the building was not the "machine for living" that Chareau's contemporary Le Corbusier imagined the house would become. Instead of using modern materials mechanistically, Chareau used them in an original way to produce what Pierre Vago characterized as a "charming fantasy."

During the late 1920s and '30s, domestic architecture in France was subject to a highly politicized debate. Some architects and critics called for a return to the forms of traditional houses, such as steeply-pitched roofs and massive stone walls, to enforce a recovery of conservative social and political values. Others demanded that domestic architecture be profoundly reconsidered, and made to incorporate materials like metal and glass as an inexpensive way to meet the critical need for housing. The Maison de Verre was an important model for how the architecture of private residences could be reconceptualized. While Chareau's design made use of modern materials, it was not as severe as some modernist houses of the 1920s. Moreover, the dramatic effects produced by light on the building emphasized the subjective element of architecture.

1

The Maison de Verre was conceived to include the family residence as well as Dr. Dalsace's medical office. As a result of its program incorporating a variety of functions, and its construction within the courtyard of an eighteenth-century private residence, the Maison de Verre constituted a complex space. Nonetheless, a degree of openness was achieved by the use of moveable partitions made of metal or glass, as well as curtains to subdivide the interior. Among the most celebrated spaces within the Maison de Verre was its three-story living room and library with a soaring wall comprising a metal grid filled with glass block.

The fame of the Maison de Verre has developed primarily as a consequence of its glass wall that faces into the courtyard. The wall of glass block served to filter natural light into the interior during the day; at night this function continued as the wall was flooded with artificial light from the exterior. Indeed, it is this dramatic and glowing wall of glass that has made the Maison de Verre one of the canonical houses of the twentieth century. It has continued to inspire architects concerned with generating new aesthetic qualities from modern materials up to the present day. K.D.M.

2

3

5

4

1 | Courtyard face
2 | Facade at night
3 | Living room
4 | View from hall up to private quarters
5 | Doctor's consulting room

Giuseppe Terragni

Casa del Fascio | COMO (ITALY) 1928; 1932–1936

The Casa del Fascio (Fascist Party Building) in Como, Italy, is not only Giuseppe Terragni's undisputed masterpiece: it is quite simply the most perfect example of Italian rationalist architecture to be created in the 1920s and '30s. At the same time, it is also the building in which the contradictions of architecture in totalitarian states are most clearly evident.

There is an immediate (and dialectic) spatial relationship between the Fascist Party Building and the magnificent late-medieval cathedral of Como. Although it was conceived as a distinct entity, the Casa del Fascio was meant to line a broad, newly created square, the central axis of which would have continued that of the historic basilica.

Depicted in an early sketch as a traditional Lombard town hall with an open central court and a tiled roof, in accordance with the requirements of the party, this administration building was gradually transformed into a precisely drawn, abstract cube laid out about an enclosed, glass-roofed courtyard. The footprint of the building is a square approximately 108 by 108 feet (33 by 33 meters) in extent, and the approximately 54-foot (16.6-meter) height is almost exactly half the side length. The proportions of the four elevations, each of which has a different composition, are based on the golden section. This pure cube is devoid of ornamentation and reveals its structural framework in part. Clad entirely in white Botticino marble, however, it appears dematerialized. The entrance facade is dissolved into a series of overlapping layers of marble, glass, and glass blocks. Solids and voids, which manifest themselves as values of light and shade, are strikingly juxtaposed. Internally, pure geometric planes and

subtle mirror effects confound one's sense of top and bottom, right and left, and create an enigmatic space that can be read many different ways.

The Casa del Fascio is not just a manifesto of the Italian avant-garde of the times, however. It is, above all, an utterly Fascist building. Its elegant transparency embodies the concept of the "house of glass" with which Mussolini was fond of comparing his, in truth, anything but transparent regime. The smooth marble face, closed on one side, was conceived as a backdrop for propagandistic collages. Internally, the only exposed concrete column, which is encased in glass like a shrine, stands explicitly for the hard, openly violent aspect of the party. Furthermore, the glass door to the main entrance, the pivoting elements of which could all be opened at the same time thanks to an ingenious mechanism, was not only a hymn to the modernist myth of the unity of internal and external space; whenever necessary, it facilitated a rapid deployment of the Fascist militia stationed in the building.

Not least because of this ambivalence, the Casa del Fascio sparked off a controversial debate as soon as it was completed. Terragni was accused by other architects of having copied German and Czech models; and some of his fellow party members thought that the Fascist movement had not been adequately represented. The intervention of friends such as Alberto Sartoris, who rejected the accusations of plagiarism, and the fact that Terragni's brother Attilio was *podestà* (governor) of Como, protected the architect from the consequences of these animosities.　　　V. M. L.

GIUSEPPE TERRAGNI

1904	Born on April 18 near Milan, Italy	
1921–26	Studies architecture at the Politecnico in Milan	
1927	Founding member of the organization of young architects called "Gruppo 7": signs the manifesto and presents his schemes for a gasworks and a pipe-casting plant at the biennial exhibition in Monza, thus participating in the fierce debate about a new direction for Italian architecture	
1927–29	Novocomum Housing Block in Como, Italy, a pioneering work of Italian architectural rationalism; planning for the Casa del Fascio in 1928	

1932	Interior design of Sala O for the Mostra della rivoluzione fascista, staged in the Roman Palazzo dell'Esposizione to celebrate the tenth anniversary of the Fascists' March on Rome
1932–36	Casa del Fascio, Como
1933–38	Along with partner Pietro Lingeri, builds a number of pioneering housing blocks in Milan: Casa Ghiringhelli, Casa Toninello, Casa Rustici, Casa Lavezzari, and Casa Rustici Comolli
1933–40	Urban planning projects for Como
1935–37	Villa for Amedeo Bianchi in Rebbio, Italy
1936–37	Sant'Elia Kindergarten, Como; Villa Bianca in Seveso, Italy, a brilliant reinterpretation of the

	famous villas Le Corbusier built on the outskirts of Paris
1937–38	Design for the Palazzo dei ricevimenti e dei congressi for the E42 near Rome with Cesare Cattaneo and Pietro Lingeri
1937–39	Casa del Fascio in Lissone near Milan, in collaboration with Antonio Carminati
1938–40	Danteum project in Rome, with Pietro Lingeri
1939	Called up as a soldier
1939–40	Builds the pioneering housing block Giuliani Frigerio in Como
1941	Posted to the Russian front
1943	Dies on July 19 in Como

1

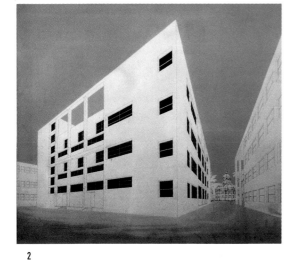

4

2

3

1 | Main facade
2 | Perspective drawing
3 | Internal space: foyer
4 | Party building as unique structure in
   urban fabric

Alvar Aalto

Sanatorium | PAIMIO (FINLAND) 1929-1933

When the still unknown 30-year-old "provincial architect" Alvar Aalto took part in the competition for the tuberculosis sanatorium in Paimio, Finland, he had just returned from a European tour during which he had made a study of new, "modern" architecture. In Finland, no building had been created in the rationalist style up to that time. In January 1929, Aalto won the competition and was thus in a position to realize the first modern architectural forms in his own country and to implement the latest building technology that he had seen abroad only a short time beforehand.

To combat TB in Finland, large sanatoria were built on pine-covered slopes. The means of treating the disease at that time coincided largely with the goals of rationalist building: light, air, and sun. Aalto laid out the various wings of his complex in the woods of Paimio in a fan-shape form. Each wing was allotted a different function, which in turn determined the overall aspect. The south-facing halls open to the air and sunshine were designed as continuations of the patients'

1

rooms. In the middle is a tract that contains spaces for communal activities, such as the dining room, lounges, and library. Facing north and furthest removed from the patients' rooms are the working quarters with the kitchen and laundry. During the period of construction, the project was increased in size by three stories, and as a result the monumental effect of the white sanatorium was accentuated even further, making it a prime example of heroic rationalism.

The free spatial planning in Paimio was made possible by an open form of construction with concrete piers. Concrete was also used for the facades of the open-air wings, the walls, and the flat roofs. Particular care was taken in furnishing the patients' rooms. Aalto was concerned with achieving as positive a psychological effect as possible. He had the soffits painted in warm tones, placed the light sources out of sight of patients lying in bed, and installed the heating and ventilation in such a way that patients were not immediately exposed to radiated heat and received enough ozone and fresh air from the surrounding woods. Aalto also designed a special washbasin that could be used with a minimum of noise. A significant part of the interior furnishings were made of wood and were also designed by Aalto, such as the Paimio chair, which consisted of bent birch plywood. Originally, the chair was shaped anatomically to meet the needs of pulmonary patients. Today, it is one of the most famous and sought-after pieces of furniture Aalto designed.

Even before it opened in June 1933, the building was the subject of international acclaim in the architectural press. The sanatorium represented a breakthrough in Aalto's career. He became world-famous as one of the leading rationalists of his day. Soon afterwards, however, he was to develop his own organic approach to architecture. Although it was later altered to some extent internally, the Paimio Sanatorium remains an undisputed icon of classical modern architecture.   T.J.

ALVAR AALTO

1898	Born on February 3 in Kuortane, Finland; five years later his parents move to Jyväskylä, Finland
1916-21	Studies architecture at the University of Technology in Helsinki, Finland
1923-27	Founds his "Office of Architecture and Monumental Art" in Jyväskylä: designs houses, churches, and buildings in and around Jyväskylä
1927-28	Designs first rationalist buildings, such as the editorial offices of *Turun Sanomat* in Turku; designs the first standard items of furniture in wood
1927-33	Establishes own architectural practice in Turku, Finland
1929-33	Sanatorium in Paimio, Finland
1933	Moves his architectural practice to Helsinki
1935	Inauguration of the Municipal Library in Viipuri, Finland
1938	Villa Mairea in Noormarkku, Finland; first trip to the U.S.
1939	Finnish Pavilion, World Exposition, New York
1943-58	Chairman, Finnish architectural association
1946-48	Guest lecturer at the Massachusetts Institute of Technology, Cambridge, Massachusetts; builds the M.I.T. student lodgings
1949-74	Planning of the University of Technology in Otaniemi near Helsinki
1952	Municipal administration building in Säynätsalo, Finland
1955	Member of the Finnish Academy
1959	Planning of a theater in Essen, Germany, built in 1983-88 after Aalto's death; begins the town center of Seinäjoki, Finland
1961-72	Planning of the city center of Helsinki; only the Finlandia Building is realized
1963-68	President of the Finnish Academy
1976	Dies on May 11 in Helsinki

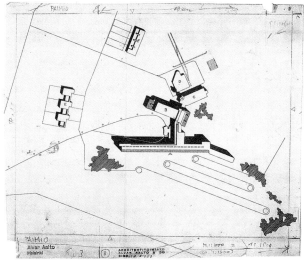

1 | Paimio chair
2 | Overall view from north
3 | View of patients' tract from
northwest
4 | Site plan

Shreve, Lamb, and Harmon

Empire State Building | NEW YORK CITY 1930-1931

On a foggy morning in July 1945, Air Force Colonel William F. Smith crashed his B-25 bomber into a Manhattan skyscraper. But even without Smith's mishap or King Kong's cinematic wrath, the Empire State Building would still be the best known building in New York City. Since then it has become the icon of the metropolis, a symbol of stability, durability, and hope during the uncertain times of the Great Depression and years of corporate rebuilding thereafter.

The architects of the Empire State Corporation speculative project were the New York City firm of Richmond Shreve, William Lamb, and Arthur Harmon: Shreve was responsible for solving production and administrative problems, and Harmon and Lamb were the designers. The firm was famous for its corporate, commercial, and institutional buildings in the Art Deco, and later, functional style.

The Empire State design was a response to practical requirements with added modernist Art Deco detailing. The exterior of limestone, granite, aluminum, and nickel created a streamlined appearance that was enriched by ornamental features cast in aluminum, such as the window spandrels and the Fifth Avenue grand entrance. Rising 102 stories above the ground, the building is skillfully massed: its five-story base occupies the entire site, above which rises the tower with its mass broken by indentations, a crown of set backs, and an uppermost pinnacle, originally designed as a mooring station

for dirigibles. Its Art Deco exterior hides a steel frame whose construction was an unrivaled feat of engineering. The finished skyscraper broke records not only for its height of 1,250 feet (381 meters), but also for speed of construction with workers erecting an average of four and a half stories per week.

The interior is divided into a modernistic, yet welcoming entrance lobby and a functionalist concourse leading to the elevator banks from West 33rd and 34th Streets. The lobby is a long, high, narrow rectangular space covered with German marbles in gray and red tones. Beyond this lies a vertical core of circulation and mechanical equipment placed in the center of the building, surrounded by a perimeter of office space 28 feet (8.5 meters) deep. The 86th- and 102nd-floor observation decks, which provide the best views in Manhattan, kept the building prosperous during the 1930s when 25 percent occupancy left some calling the skyscraper the "Empty State."

But the Empire State Building, rented or not, was for New York City a symbol that hard times could be overcome and that man could triumph in all situations. On opening day, Alfred E. Smith summed up the reasons that the powerful image of the building would endure, calling the Empire State Building, "the greatest monument to ingenuity, to skill, to brain power, to muscle power, the tallest thing in the world today produced by the hand of man."   V.M.Y.

1

RICHMOND SHREVE, WILLIAM LAMB, AND ARTHUR HARMON

1877	Richmond Harold Shreve is born on June 25 in Cornwallis, Nova Scotia, Canada
1878	Arthur Loomis Harmon is born on June 13 in Chicago
1883	William Frederick Lamb is born on November 21 in Brooklyn, New York
1898–02	Shreve studies architecture at Cornell University, Ithaca, New York
1901	Harmon, after studying at the Art Institute in Chicago, graduates from the School of Architecture at Columbia University, New York City
1902–11	Harmon works in the office of McKim, Mead and White in New York City
1903	Lamb graduates from Williams College; studies architecture at Columbia University and at the Ecole des Beaux-Arts in Paris
1906–20	Shreve works in the office of Carrère and Hastings, New York
1911	Lamb graduates from the Ecole, returns to New York City; works for Carrère and Hastings
1913–29	Harmon practices architecture independently

1920	Shreve and Lamb become partners in the firm of Carrère and Hastings, Shreve and Lamb
1924	Shreve and Lamb form an independent firm
1925–27	Shreve and Lamb complete the General Motors Building in New York City
1928	Shreve and Lamb are put on retainer for the Empire State project; Harmon becomes Shreve and Lamb's partner during the final designs for the Empire State Building
1930–31	Empire State Building, New York City
1931	Alfred E. Smith opens the Empire State Building
1932	The Empire State Building is awarded the American Institute of Architects' Gold Medal
1939–40	The firm completes Hunter College, New York City (with Harrison and Foulihoux)
1946	Shreve dies on September 10 at his home in Hastings-on-Hudson, New York
1952	Lamb dies on September 8 in New York City
1958	Harmon dies on October 17 in White Plains, New York

3

4

1 | Detail of facade
2 | Overall view
3 | Entrance hall on opening day,
   May 1, 1931
4 | Aerial view shortly before
   completion
5 | Floor plan

5

1

3

2

4

5

George Howe and William Lescaze

PSFS Building | PHILADELPHIA 1931

The Philadelphia Savings Fund Society Building, designed by George Howe and William Lescaze, is considered to be the first International Style skyscraper erected in the United States, and a work which permanently altered the course of skyscraper design in America.

The PSFS departed radically from previous tall buildings in America, such as Cass Gilbert's Gothic-inspired Woolworth Building (New York City, 1911–13), and the beaux-arts-influenced, stepped-back "slabs" designed for Rockefeller Center (New York City, c. 1928–40). Howe and Lescaze conceived a streamlined 32-story rental office tower, combined in an off-center T-shape with a 36-story service tower. The finest polished black granite, glazed brick, and combination of copper, brass, and stainless steel were used in the construction, making PSFS one of the most scrupulously and lavishly appointed buildings in the country.

The towers, cantilevered out over the lower floors, express the unadorned functionality and volumetricity characteristic of the European International Style. But the building's massing, with the curved granite-clad retail and banking floors at and just above street level, the decorative quality of the materials, and the complex articulation of the facade, with its pronounced horizontal spandrels and projecting vertical columns, all suggest that its relationship to International Style modernism is more complex than one might suspect. The departure from consistent rectilinearity distances the PSFS Building from the strict conventions of European modernism as defined by Henry-Russell Hitchcock and Philip Johnson in their International Style exhibition of 1932 at the Museum of Modern Art, and links it to the Expressionism of 1920s German architecture.

Perhaps most reminiscent of German modernism is the enormous billboard-like sign in block letters announcing the identity of the company: PSFS. Angled across the top of the office tower, the giant sign is visible from a distance of 20 miles (30 kilometers) and also fulfills an architectural function, since it balances the asymmetry of the cooling towers and the penthouse atop the building. Not until Mies van der Rohe's Seagram Building of the late 1950s would there be such a daring statement in skyscraper design.

Beyond their goal of creating a truly modern image, Howe and Lescaze were motivated by "ultra-practical" concerns. These included ensuring the building's economic viability in downtown Philadelphia by making the radical decision to place the banking floors on the second level and attracting customers to the retail businesses at street level. Furthermore, they conceived a total image for the building by designing the furniture and various other elements within. An advertisement from the *Philadelphia Inquirer* of July 14, 1932, invites any and all to visit the PSFS Building during the honest part of the day: "Sniff the bracing atmosphere," the ad urges. "When you've done all this, then celebrate, in your own way, the modern office building!"
E. P.

GEORGE HOWE AND WILLIAM LESCAZE

1886	George Howe is born on June 17 in Worcester, Massachusetts
1896	William Lescaze is born on March 27 in Geneva, Switzerland
1914-16	Howe practices architecture in Philadelphia, Pennsylvania, with the firm of Furness, Evans and Company, and then enters a 13-year partnership with Walter Mellor and Arthur I. Meigs
1923	Lescaze starts his private practice in New York
1924	Howe renovates the PSFS Main Office
1929-34	Howe and Lescaze enter into a partnership
1930-31	Museum of Modern Art, New York City; PSFS Building, 12th and Market Streets, Philadelphia
1934	Howe and Lescaze dissolve their partnership; Lescaze becomes principal, William Lescaze and Associates, New York, until 1969
1935-40	Howe in private practice
1937-38	Lescaze builds the CBS Radio Building, Hollywood, California (with E.T. Heirschmid)
1939	Lescaze designs the Aeronautics Pavilion and the Swiss Pavilion, World's Fair, New York
1941	Howe in partnership with Louis I. Kahn
1944-45	Howe is Deputy Commissioner for Design and Construction, Public Buildings Administration, Federal Works Agency
1950-54	Howe is Chairman, Department of Architecture, Yale University, New Haven, Connecticut
1955	Howe dies on April 16 in Cambridge, Massachusetts
1959	Lescaze designs the Chancellery, Swiss Embassy, Washington, D.C.
1969	Lescaze dies on February 9 in New York City

1 | Perspective view from below
2 | Design sketch
3 | Banking hall on second floor
4 | Stairs and escalators to banking hall
5 | Corner detail

Frank Lloyd Wright

Fallingwater | BEAR RUN, PENNSYLVANIA 1936-1937

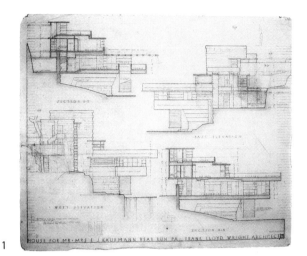

1

FRANK LLOYD WRIGHT

1867	Born on June 8 in Richland Center, Wisconsin
1885–87	Studies at the University of Wisconsin School of Engineering, Madison; draftsman for Allen O. Conover, Madison; and Lyman Silsbee, Chicago
1888–89	Assistant architect, Adler and Sullivan, Chicago
1889	Frank Lloyd Wright House, Oak Park, Illinois
1889–93	Head of the Planning and Design Department, Adler and Sullivan
1893–96	Partnership with Cecil Corwin, Chicago; then private practice until 1909
1894	Winslow House, River Forest, Illinois
1900	Select projects published in *Ladies Home Journal*
1904	Larkin Company Administration Building, Buffalo, New York
1906	Unity Temple, Oak Park, Illinois
1909	Robie House, Chicago
1909–11	Travels in Europe with Mrs. Mamah Bortwick Cheney
1911	Builds first Taliesin house and studio and works in private practice, Spring Green, Wisconsin
1912	Reopens Chicago office
1914	Taliesin destroyed by fire, rebuilt as Taliesin II
1915–20	Works on the Imperial Hotel, Tokyo
1916	Hollyhock House (Barnsdall House), Los Angeles
1921–24	First concrete "textile" block houses, California; La Miniatura (Millard House); Ennis-Brown House
1925	Taliesin II burns down, rebuilt as Taliesin III
1933	Broadacre City utopian plan
1936	Johnson Wax Administration Building, Racine, Wisconsin
1936–37	Fallingwater, Bear Run, Pennsylvania
1938	Builds Taliesin West, Paradise Valley, Scottsdale, Arizona
1956	Price Tower, Bartlesville, Oklahoma; begins building the Solomon R. Guggenheim Museum in New York City (originally planned in 1943)
1957–66	Marin County Government Center, San Rafael, California
1959	Completes the Guggenheim Museum, New York City; continues to practice in Wisconsin and Arizona until his death on April 9 in Phoenix, Arizona

Fallingwater has been described as the most famous house in the world not owned by royalty. Perched directly over a waterfall on Bear Run, a stream that flows through the woodlands of western Pennsylvania, the structure is an eloquent extension of its environment — the ultimate embodiment of Wright's concept of the "natural house."

When the Kaufmann Family, owners of a department store in Pittsburgh, invited Frank Lloyd Wright to build a weekend retreat for them, the career of the world-famous architect had been in eclipse for some 15 years. At a time when the International Style dominated, Wright's organic designs seemed dated; he was called the greatest architect of the nineteenth century! But Edgar Kaufmann Jr., later curator of architecture at New York's Museum of Modern Art, admired Wright's brilliant works, including his prairie houses, and convinced his parents to hire him.

The Kaufmanns were astounded when they saw Wright's drawings for the house. Having shown the architect their beloved waterfall, they assumed that he would place the house across from it so it would remain in constant view. But Wright, in his genius, sited the house directly on top of it. In order to do so, he designed a system of cantilevers so that the house and its large balconies would project out over the stream from the rocky banks with no visible supports.

By the fall of 1937, some $50,000 over budget, Fallingwater was completed. Wright's desire to emphasize the theme of nature and the porousness between interior and exterior is expressed in virtually every facet of the program. The house is composed of three levels of concrete, painted steel, and irregularly layered stone that mimics the natural ledges. Vertical columns of windows counterpoint the stuccoed balconies, or trays. The rocks where the Kaufmanns once sunned form the floor of the living room, and the original boulders of the waterfall sit in front of the central hearth. The combined living room-dining room is decorated with furniture designed and installed by the architect. A glassed-in stairway leads down from the living room directly to the water below; when open, the breezes waft up from the stream into the house. Wright's characteristic ribbon bands of windows, set directly into the walls, their frames painted in his signature cherokee red, capture and organize the views of forest landscape on all sides. The never-ending music of the water rushing under the house and over the falls becomes an integral feature of the experience of the house. Thus, as part of the continuum of the flowing stream, the house no longer is engaged with space alone, but with time as well. Fallingwater still rests in its woodland setting today, reflecting the eternal cycle of life as seasons and the river flow by. E.P.

2

1 | Elevations and sections
2 | View of house over waterfall
3 | Living room
4 | Stairs to river
5 | View of house at dusk

3

4

5

Adalberto Libera

Casa Malaparte | CAPRI (ITALY) 1938-1943

1

The unique quality of this house lies in its form and location. Jean-Luc Godard was so impressed with it that he shot his film *Le Mépris* here. Like a stranded ship, its clear cubic contours lie stretched out on a rock on the east coast of the Isle of Capri, a few miles off the shore of Naples, Italy. The house, with its provocatively red rendered facades, is set with its longitudinal axis at right angles to the coastline, as if it were a ship ready to be put to sea.

The client, Curzio Malaparte (1898–1957), was a writer, journalist, and political adventurer with strong connections to top members of the Fascist movement. During a visit to Capri, he discovered the remote Punta Masullo with its remarkable landscape, which he recognized as an ideal setting for a house. It lay in an area, however, where building was not allowed. That presented no problem for Malaparte. He obtained permission to build a cistern, on top of which he then proceeded to erect a villa of not exactly modest dimensions.

Malaparte commissioned Adalberto Libera, one of the leading rationalist architects in Italy, to design the basic concept of the house. This took the form of an elongated cubic structure, pointing out to sea, with an open roof terrace on top. It was Malaparte's own modifications to the design, however, that lent the house its theatrical magic. On the island of Lipari, the writer had once noted a monumental flight of steps

leading up to a church, and he reproduced this on Capri in the form of an open staircase that broadens as it rises and leads onto the roof of the house. The roof terrace is a stage, surrounded on all sides by a remarkable natural panorama. The unity of staircase, roof terrace, and landscape evokes images of ceremonial structures of the past — Greek theaters, altars, sacrificial tables, stepped pyramids, or Indian calendar structures. The gleaming white, curving concrete wall that rises from the roof serves to provide shade from the sun and creates a sharp contrast with the red brick pavings of the roof and the stairs.

Libera had no hand in the design of the interior. Among the surprising features here are the lavish carpentry of the timber staircase and the wood-paneled parlor with its tiled stove. Highly unusual in this part of the world, these were reminiscences of Malaparte's service on the front in the Alps during World War I. A living room with an open fireplace forms the main space, which is of vast dimensions. It receives daylight through undivided windows 13 feet (4 meters) wide and is fitted out with cyclopean furnishings such as extremely heavy wooden tabletops on simulated truncated columns.

Even when he was dying, the headstrong owner continued to surprise the world. He bequeathed his house to the People's Republic of China as a token of thanks to the Chinese doctors who had treated him during one of his last journeys. The will was contested, however, and this extraordinary house passed into the hands of the Ronchi Foundation, which for some time now has been successfully restoring the building.   W.V.

ADALBERTO LIBERA

1903	Born on July 16 in Trentino, Italy
1923-25	Studies at the State Institute of Art in Parma, Italy
1925-27	Moves to Rome; attends the Royal School of Architecture
1927	Travels to Germany to study Modern Movement building; becomes a member of the avant-garde "Gruppo 7" at the invitation of Gino Pollini
1928	Author of manifesto "Arte e razionalismo"; participates in the first exhibition of rationalist architecture in Rome
1930	General secretary of "Miar" union of architects
1931	Holiday camp in Portocivitanova, the Marches, Italy
1931-34	Primary school in Trient, Italy
1932	Designs the jubilee exhibition of the Fascist revolution in Rome
1933-34	Post office on the Aventine, Rome; Palazzo del Littorio competition, Rome
1935	Italian Pavilion at the World Exposition in Brussels, Belgium
1937-42	Congress hall of the E42 in Rome
1938-43	Casa Malaparte, Capri, Italy
1949	Director of design office of "Ina Casa," state institute for publicly assisted housing, Rome; Ina housing in Trient
1950-54	Ina housing in Tuscolano, Rome
1953	Professor for design in the faculty of architecture, University of Florence, Italy
1956-58	Office block in Via Trentino, Rome
1956-69	Cathedral in La Spezia, Italy
1957-60	Olympic Village in Rome
1959	Pharmaceutical laboratory, Latina, Italy
1959-61	Works housing for Italsider in Piombino-Salivoli, Italy
1960-66	Incis housing in Decima, Rome
1963	Dies on March 17 in Rome

2

3

1 | Drawing: northeast elevation
2 | View from southwest
3 | View of roof staircase
4 | View of house from cliff path

4

Arne Jacobsen with Fleming Lassen

Town Hall | SØLLERØD (DENMARK) 1939-1942

When the mayor greets the people from his balcony, he does so as *primus inter pares*, first among equals. Arne Jacobsen's town hall in Søllerød, Denmark, is a democratic building for the people. With its unobtrusive elegance, it not only invites the public to enter; it also stimulates public debate.

Located in a fashionable residential district in the conurbation of Copenhagen, the town hall consists of two staggered blocks set in front of each other and intersecting at one corner. The main staircase is situated where the rectilinear tracts meet. Laid out about a glazed lift shaft, the stairs create an internal link that is at first not visible from the outside.

Approaching the complex via the curved forecourt, one notices the differences between the two blocks from a distance. These contrasts culminate at the top in the different heights of the two volumes, which give rise to the distinctive roofscape. Since the front block is framed by the rear tract — which is also taller by the height of its roof — one expects there to be a gap between the two parts, although in fact there is not. At first sight, the two tracts appear to be two independent volumes, separated by a narrow passageway.

Even if this separation did exist, one would still attribute the two blocks to the same architect. The unity of the design is obvious. It manifests itself in the silver-gray Solvag marble facade cladding, in the green patina of the copper roofs, and in the recurring form of the square windows, fixed flush with the outer face and arranged in horizontal rows. The compositional strength of the design lies in the tension created between distance and proximity, foreground and background, center, and periphery.

The stately character of the section used for formal functions is contrasted with the restrained grid-like arrangement of the set-back office tract. The architect avoids all tokens of monumentality. He places emphasis not on the center of the facade, but on the edges, where groups of elegantly proportioned, two-story-high windows allow views into the eastern council chamber and into the western entrance hall. The sense of symmetry is upset. Axiality is called into question. The official balcony to the right of the hall modestly conforms to the articulation of the row of windows that mediates between the vertical bays of glazing. The eccentric position of this balcony signals a playful, almost ironic denial of architectural expressions of power.

Like the town hall in Århus, built a few years earlier, that in Søllerød was the outcome of a competition design. Both buildings mark important milestones on the way to Danish functionalism. Whereas the citizens of Århus were dissatisfied with the plain character of their town hall scheme and insisted on their right to monumentality until a tower was added to the building, the people of Søllerød were always receptive to Jacobsen's modern ideas.   M.H.

ARNE JACOBSEN

1902	Born on February 11 in Copenhagen, Denmark
1924	Completes studies at the Technical College in Copenhagen
1924-27	Studies at the School of Architecture of the Royal Academy of Arts in Copenhagen; friendship with Swedish architect Gunnar Asplund
1925	Study trips to France and Italy; participates in the World Exposition in Paris
1927	Villa for Professor Sigurd Wandel in Gentofte, Copenhagen; is awarded a prize for good building; further single-family houses in Gentofte
1927-28	Travels to Berlin; studies the architecture of Mies van der Rohe and Walter Gropius
1928	Gold medal for the design of the National Museum in Klampenborg, a beach area near Copenhagen
1928-29	Builds own house in Klampenborg in white Modern Movement style

1929	"House of the Future" at the Danish Building Exhibition, Copenhagen
1930-35	Bellavista Estate in Klampenborg, followed by numerous single-family houses, factories, and administration buildings in and around Copenhagen
1934-35	Novo Terapeutiske Laboratory, Copenhagen
1937	Town Hall in Århus, Denmark
1939-42	Town Hall in Søllerød, Denmark
1943	Exile in Sweden
1954-56	Town Hall in Rødovre, Denmark; breakthrough to the International Style of postwar modernism
1960-64	St. Catherine's College, Oxford University, England
1962-70	Administrative headquarters of the Hamburg Electricity Works, Hamburg, Germany
1970-73	Town Hall in Mainz, Germany
1971	Dies on March 3 in Copenhagen

2

3

4

1 | Site plan
2 | Main entrance
3 | Staircase with glazed elevator
   shaft
4 | Facades clad with Solvag
   marble
5 | Elevation of entrance front

5

Frank Lloyd Wright

Solomon R. Guggenheim Museum | NEW YORK CITY 1943: 1956–1959

It is said that Frank Lloyd Wright hated museums. He also hated cities. Yet it was in the Solomon R. Guggenheim Museum, after years of architectural experimentation, that Wright realized the ultimate symbolic image for organic architecture — the circle, and the spiral that derived from it. On this basis Wright created the era's most daring structure to exploit the sculptural possibilities of reinforced concrete, and, as a result, perhaps his most famous building of all.

The Baroness Hilla Rebay, curator of mining magnate Solomon R. Guggenheim's collection of non-objective art, contacted Wright about a museum commission in the summer of 1943. The utopian aspirations embodied in the collection perfectly coincided with Wright's own fascination with symbolic form. Despite Wright's enthusiasm for the project, the realization of the complex and elegant structure he designed was long and difficult. Plans were submitted in 1943 but not approved until 1945, when the project was delayed because of the uncertainties of the postwar economy. Construction did not begin until 1956, and was completed in the fall of 1959, six months after Wright's death.

On the exterior, the museum consists of a monumental mass of angles and curves, with few visible windows and a continuous, horizontal set of interlocking concrete bands that, in contrast to nearby skyscrapers, serve to divert attention from its actual height. Wright acknowledged in 1945 that the basic idea of the building came from the ziggurat of the ancient Middle East, which he inverted and otherwise adapted to suit the museum commission.

The important experience of the Guggenheim Museum occurs within. One continuous tilted ramp winds upward around a great central space toward a majestic glass dome. The simplicity of this design concept was deceptive, and posed formidable technological problems during construction. The great skill and know-how needed to create the molds for the poured concrete, to construct the circular ramp, and to place the vertical "webs" that support the ramp and separate the space into galleries frightened off a number of contractors before George Cohen finally took on the job. Working in collaboration, architect and contractor solved the almost insuperable challenges of creating an apparently unsupported, ever-widening curve from reinforced concrete. The result, an unprecedented building feat, represented a good approximation of Wright's original intention.

When finally completed, the Guggenheim Museum was heartily disliked by many, including artists and critics who recalled Wright's contention that pictures spoiled architecture. They also resented the way in which the building rejected previous assumptions about galleries, such as that level floor and wall planes were an absolute necessity for viewing art. Strolling down the ramp provides a vertiginous adventure and may well distract the visitor from the art on exhibit. However, the Guggenheim Museum, a triumph of inventive design and construction, remains one of the greatest architectural experiences ever created, and if art must bow to architecture in this instance, then so be it.   E.P.

FRANK LLOYD WRIGHT
Architect's biography on p. 70

1

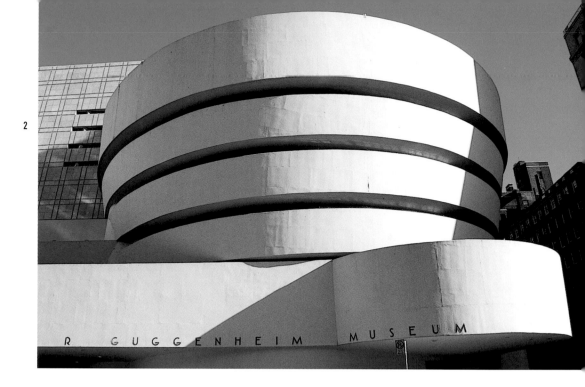

1 | Spiral ramp
2 | Horizontal articulation of drum
3 | View to glass dome
4 | View from Fifth Avenue

Lev Rudnyev

Lomonosov University | MOSCOW 1947-1952

In the period of reconstruction in the Soviet Union after World War II, the socialist urban utopia was visualized as a city of skyscrapers. This ideological concept first assumed form in Moscow on January 13, 1947, when the Council of Ministers of the U.S.S.R. ordered the erection of eight tower blocks in the center of the Soviet capital. These high-rise buildings were meant to complement the unfinished Palace of the Soviets, which stood isolated in its urban surroundings, and to link up with other buildings in the city center to create a visually unified urban silhouette. The foundation stones were laid in 1947 to mark the 800th anniversary of the founding of Moscow. The new urban concept thereby acquired a historical dimension based on national tradition. By 1952, seven of the eight tower blocks had already been completed, although Stalin had the external design of a number of them altered by personal decree.

Within this ensemble of prestigious state buildings, the Lomonosov University, conceived by a collective of architects under the leadership of Lev Rudnyev, assumed an almost symbolic importance. The mighty complex rises on the Lenin Hills, the highest point within the metropolitan area of Moscow, and creates a visual axis along the Moskva to the Kremlin. The ensemble comprises a number of elements, the centerpiece of which is an approximately 790-foot (240-meter) high tower flanked by various ancillary structures. The complex is laid out on a strict axial plan and rises in a series of steps to the main vertical volume. The crowning structures on the towers, ordered by Stalin, are decorated with neoclassical motifs and a phalanx of sculptures of the heroes of Socialism. They recall the many towers of the Kremlin and thus reflect the reciprocal relationship that existed between these two state complexes.

The Lomonosov University building was enthusiastically acclaimed in official architectural circles as a "triumph of vertical composition"; but underlying it is a rigid schematism that seeks to convince the observer of the righteousness of its ideological origins through the sheer mass of stone that goes to make up its innumerable individual volumes. Greater emphasis was laid on the outward appearance than on the functional needs and the internal spatial program. The exaggerated overall form is a prime example of the hypertrophic attitude of official regime architecture during the Stalinist era. The architectural line that was followed without exception consisted of a monumental and decoratively overladen neoclassicism that caused major state projects to degenerate into perfunctory expressions of pathos.   S.K.

LEV RUDNYEV

1885	Born on March 13 in Novgorod, Russia
1915–	Teaches at the St. Petersburg Academy of Art, Russia, where he is later appointed professor
1919	Monument to the Victims of the Revolution in Petrograd, U.S.S.R.
1925–32	Chairman of the architectural committee of the City of Leningrad Department for Economic Affairs, U.S.S.R.
1930	Government building in Minsk (unrealized project), U.S.S.R.
1931	Palace of Culture in Moscow (competition scheme)
1931–37	Frunze Military Academy in Moscow
1933	In charge of the project for the People's Commissariat for Defense in Moscow
1934–55	Ministry of Defense building in Moscow
1947–52	Lomonosov University in Moscow
1951	Government building in Baku, U.S.S.R.
1955	Palace of Culture in Warsaw, Poland
1956	Dies on November 11 in Moscow

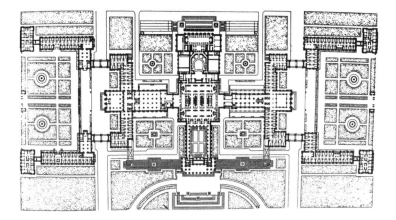

1

2

3

4

1 | Layout plan
2 | Overall view
3 | Main portico
4 | Drawing. 1948

Kenzo Tange

Peace Center | HIROSHIMA (JAPAN) 1949–1950

On the morning of August 6, 1945, the American Air Force dropped the first atomic bomb on the Japanese town of Hiroshima. Three days later, a second bomb was dropped on Nagasaki. With the use of these weapons, the potential for human destruction attained a new dimension. Many attempts were made during the ensuing decades to justify the use or possession of such weapons as the means of having brought World War II to an end, or of maintaining the balance of power in the world through the threat they implied; but none of these arguments was able to fill the void of something that exceeded human comprehension. Hiroshima and its aftermath have engraved themselves traumatically and indelibly on the history of the twentieth century.

This collective memory called for a special place where the suffering caused by these acts of destruction as well as hopes for lasting peace could manifest themselves symbolically. The town of Hiroshima, therefore, decided to convert its historic center, which had been destroyed by the atomic bomb, into a monument to peace. In 1949, after winning the competition for the Hiroshima Peace Center, Kenzo Tange was commis-

sioned to execute his design. The idea of the project was to create a park of peace on the site where the bomb had fallen — a piece of land between the two arms of a river. The ruins of a building destroyed by the bomb formed a visual axis on one side of the water, and remained in place as a monument. Access to the Peace Center is via a bridge with a dynamic concrete balustrade, designed by Isamu Noguchi. The three buildings forming the actual center are laid out in a line at the top edge of the park, parallel to the bridge and at right angles to the visual axis. In the middle is the commemorative museum, which is raised on concrete columns and thus allows a view through to the park and the monuments beyond. To the right of this is the community center, and to the left, the hall and hotel, which were planned by Tange, but subsequently begun by another architect. In the middle of the park, the parabolic arch of the memorial to the dead of Hiroshima straddles the visual axis. It combines Japanese forms that symbolize the house and the grave with the expression of the International Style, to which the other buildings are particularly indebted.

Raised on pilotis, the transparent commemorative museum in reinforced concrete, with its sunscreen installation, is an evident homage to the architecture of Le Corbusier; yet it also has a specifically Japanese character. Many Japanese architects practicing at that time had worked with Le Corbusier in Paris, among them Kunio Maekawa, in whose office Tange had been an assistant after completing his studies. Tange, however, was not interested in adopting the architectural language of the West. Through his approach to space and the structure of a building, he attempted to achieve a synthesis of traditional Japanese elements and the international architecture of the Modern Movement. His sensitive urban design for the Peace Center in Hiroshima, which he presented to the 8th Congrès International d'Architecture Moderne (CIAM) in 1951, was not simply the first major scheme he realized as an architect; it also marked the beginning of his international role in design.   A.S.

KENZO TANGE

1913	Born on September 4 in Imabari on Shikoku, Japan
1935–38	Studies at the architecture department of the University of Tokyo; subsequently enters the office of Kunio Maekawa, a former assistant in Le Corbusier's office
1942–45	Studies at the Graduate School of the University of Tokyo; doctorate in 1959
1946–61	Studio Kenzo Tange
1946–74	Professor at the University of Tokyo, department of architecture and urban planning
1948–52	Plan for Hiroshima, Japan
1949–50	Hiroshima Peace Center
1952–57	City Hall, Tokyo
1955–58	Administration building for the prefecture of Kagawa, Takamatsu, Japan
1959–60	Visiting professor at the Massachusetts Institute of Technology, Cambridge, Massachusetts
1960	Plan for Tokyo as one of numerous urban projects
1960–64	Stadia for the 18th summer Olympic Games, Tokyo
1961–64	St. Mary's Cathedral, Tokyo
1961–85	Kenzo Tange & URTEC, Urbanists & Architects
1962–66	Yamanashi Press and Broadcasting Center, Kofu, Japan
1964–	Informal association with the Metabolists

1965	Gold Medal, Royal Institute of British Architects
1965–66	Plan for Skopje; first prize in a competition with a group of Yugoslavian architects
1966–70	Design of Expo '70, Osaka, Japan
1970–	Numerous projects outside Japan, especially in the Middle East, Africa, and Europe; visiting professorship at Harvard University, Cambridge, Massachusetts (1972)
1983–89	Museum of Art, Yokohama, Japan
1985–	Kenzo Tange Associates; winner of numerous competitions and awards, including the Pritzker Architecture Prize (1987)
1986–91	City Hall, Tokyo

1

2

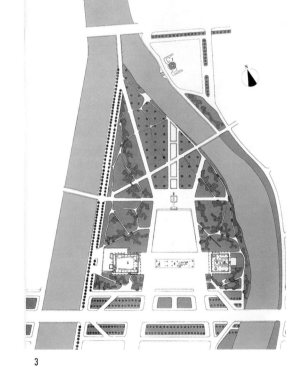

3

4

1 | Museum with memorial and
ruins of domed structure to rear
2 | Memorial
3 | Site plan
4 | Side view of museum

Le Corbusier

Notre-Dame-du-Haut Chapel | RONCHAMP (FRANCE) 1950-1955

Paradoxically, the most famous and influential architectural work built for the Roman Catholic Church in the twentieth century, the Notre-Dame-du-Haut Chapel in Ronchamp, France, was created by an architect who had been brought up as a Protestant of Albigensian origin and who had a tendency to pantheism. In his interpretation of the design task, Le Corbusier was not thinking primarily of the pilgrims who came to this holy place, which had been venerated for centuries. "When I built this church, I wanted to create a place of silence, of prayer, of peace, of inner joy. The sense of being blessed inspires our endeavors. Some things are blessed; others are not, whether they be of a religious nature or not."

The initial point of reference for the design was the broad, hilly landscape of the Belfort Gap between Belfort and Dijon. The topography is echoed in the dynamic lines of the facades in the form of an *acoustique paysagiste.* The most frequently photographed "expressionist" view of the chapel, seen obliquely from the east, shows the raking south wall with the main tower and entrance portal to the rear, and the concave curve of the east wall, which on fine days can be used as the choir of an outdoor church. The broad cantilevered roof, raised slightly above the outer walls, has the form of a wind-filled sail, and was inspired by a shell Le Corbusier found on the beach of Long Island, New York, in 1946. The north facade is dominated by the twin towers between which the entrance for everyday use is situated. The interplay of vertical, horizontal, and square window openings and the steep, open staircase that leads to the sacristy enlivens the overall form. There are no windows in the west face. The sloping edge of the roof falls to meet a gargoyle whose shape is reminiscent of the nostrils of a horse.

The raking, curving walls, the floor that slopes down toward the choir, and the suspended roof all form an "organic" spatial enclosure, the plasticity of which is accentuated by the dramatic lighting and polychrome coloration. The embrasured window openings are filled with both colored and clear glass, and the light entering this space reflects off of the painted white walls. Critics and adherents of Le Corbusier reacted to the finished building with expressions of irritation, and reproached the architect — some triumphantly, others apprehensively — for having betrayed his own principles. Nikolaus Pevsner described the chapel as the "manifesto of a new irrationalism"; Peter Meyer referred to it as a "romantic, ultra-subjective project"; and many other epithets of this kind were applied to it. On closer examination, however, it is evident that Ronchamp can be understood only as a continuation and a synthesis of the architect's earlier work.

Pevsner warned against a repetition of this unique experiment — in vain, as we know today. The spatial, sculptural event that Ronchamp represents became the most influential model for the wave of church building that took place in the 1950s and '60s. As a result of its wealth of visual metaphors, it also became an object for subsequent appropriation by postmodernism. It was James Stirling who pointed out this characteristic, and it may indeed explain why the chapel is arguably the most popular building of the twentieth century, rivaled only by Utzon's Sydney Opera House.   B.M.

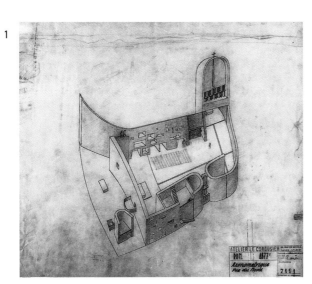

1

LE CORBUSIER
Architect's biography on p. 59

1 | Axonometric drawing
2 | View from north
3 | Internal space
4 | Detail: south face
5 | View from southeast

2

3

4

5

1

2

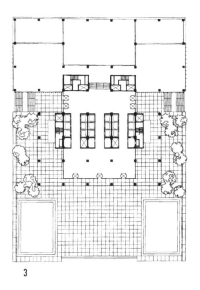

3

4

"It is not a building; it is *the* building."

More than almost any other structure, the Seagram Building in New York City is the symbol of skyscraper architecture in the twentieth century. It is one of the most frequently copied structures to have been built after World War II, and its influence can be seen throughout the world. Nevertheless, the Seagram Building marks the end of a line of development rather than a beginning. As early as 1921, Mies van der Rohe designed a glass skyscraper for the Friedrichstrasse Station competition in Berlin. It was the starting point in his lifelong fascination with skyscrapers, although he was able to build them only after emigrating to the U.S.

In 1954, the Seagram whiskey concern declared its intention of erecting its own building on Park Avenue in New York City, to mark the company's centenary in 1958. The architects Luckman & Pereira were awarded the commission, but when Phyllis Lambert, the daughter of the company president, found out about this, she intervened to stop the "mediocre" design and consulted Philip Johnson, the head of the architectural department at the Museum of Modern Art. After the work of many of the best-known architects of the day had been considered, including that of Marcel Breuer, Walter Gropius, Le Corbusier, Eero Saarinen, and Frank Lloyd Wright, a decision was made in favor of Mies van der Rohe's design.

It is hard to imagine now what a revolution the Seagram Building represented in those days. Up to that time, in response to city building regulations, skyscrapers in New York had a typically stepped-back form that tapered toward the top, while the footprint of the building covered the entire site

area so as to ensure a maximum exploitation of the land. For Mies van der Rohe, whose famous maxim was "less is more," a solution of this kind was out of the question. He designed a simple 515-foot (157-meter) high slab, of which Henry-Russell Hitchcock said: "I've never seen more of less." Furthermore, Mies did not set the building along the site's street edge, but drew it back from the building line and created a forecourt in front of it. The effect he achieved becomes clear if one can imagine that at that time there was no comparable open square in the center of New York City, with the exception of the Rockefeller Plaza.

The unadorned elegance of the Seagram Building conveys no impression of the lengths to which Mies went to achieve this result. The aphorism often attributed to Mies, "we build simply — regardless of the cost," is probably true in this case. The bronze T-sections over the entire facade, which make the building shimmer like a fine Seagram whiskey, are a prime example of this. The Seagram Building, in contrast to its innumerable successors, is not an impoverished box, but one of the most luxurious high-rise office blocks of its age.   M.J.

LUDWIG MIES VAN DER ROHE
Architect's biography on p. 56

5

BBPR

Torre Velasca | MILAN 1956-1958

BBPR: Gian Luigi Banfi, Ludovico Barbiano di Belgiojoso,
Enrico Peressutti, and Ernesto Nathan Rogers

The Torre Velasca, or Velasca Tower, soars above the narrow streets of the city center of Milan. Instead of adhering to the existing urban street block structure, the building is situated in the middle of the site. By setting a broad volume over a more slender shaft, it was possible to create a public open space at the first-floor level. The cantilevered section at the top signifies the termination of the tower and defines the space below. The building is anchored to the ground by an exhibition hall that extends out from the base of the tower. A continuous vertical load-bearing structure links the volumes stacked on top of each other. In the bays between the pilasters are wall panels with reflecting areas of glass, and loggias.

The two basement stories house car workshops, garages, and spaces for mechanical services. The first floor is reserved for shops and business premises, the second floor for exhibi-

tion uses. Above this are ten stories of offices and seven further floors of offices combined with dwellings. The projecting upper section of the building is reserved exclusively for housing purposes. The set-back 26th and 27th stories contain six two-floor flats. By constructing this building to accommodate a broad range of uses, the architects attempted to halt the trend to zoning and the segregation of functions in the city center.

Ultimately, however, the architects did not adopt the typical form of a modern skyscraper, nor did they create a new prototype. The building is not an autonomous structure that could be located anywhere. According to G.M. Kallman, it is an example of the neglected art of inserting modern architecture into a historical built continuum, within which it seeks its own status. The building was designed at a time when the architects were engaged in an examination of the past. The concept of the Torre Velasca is, therefore, inspired by the "poetry of the existing environment," although it does not explicitly quote the historical structures of the city. The projecting top section, supported by raking struts, is reminiscent of a medieval defensive tower; and the external pilasters remind one more of the nearby Gothic cathedral than of a modern skeleton-frame structure with a curtain-wall facade. The proportions, the massive volumes, and the steeply rising line of the roof all seem far removed from the Modern Movement of the twentieth century. These historicist features are contrasted with other associations, such as certain points of resemblance to agricultural structures or naval architecture.

The tower in the Via Velasca sparked off a protracted polemic. People complained that the building had a negative impact on the cathedral, for example. On the other hand, the BBPR team of architects was criticized for abandoning the rationalist stance it had assumed during the interwar years, since the tower design was viewed as a step backwards in the development of modern architecture. The goal of the Milan architects — to subsume the complexity of modern life, the challenge of new technologies, and the continuity of time and place in a formally and structurally coherent solution — may not have been fully realized. Nevertheless, the bid to achieve a synthesis of this kind makes this building, if not wholly beautiful, at least of great significance. M.-T.S.

BBPR

1908	Enrico Peressutti is born on August 28 in Tagliamento, Italy	1945	Banfi dies in the Mauthausen, Austria, concentration camp; Belgiojoso, Peressutti, and Rogers continue the practice; co-founders of the Movimento di Studi per l'Architettura (MSA); planning work; zoning plans for Milan in collaboration with the Italian CIAM group
1909	Ernesto Nathan Rogers is born on March 16 in Triest, Italy; Ludovico Barbiano di Belgiojoso is born on December 1 in Milan, Italy		
1910	Gian Luigi Banfi is born on April 2 in Milan		
1932	The four complete architectural studies together	1946	Monument for the victims of German concentration camps in the memorial cemetery of Milan
1932-	Studio BBPR, Milan; first prize for the design of a Casa del Fascio prototype		
1934	Project for the Palazzo Littorio, the Fascist Party headquarters in Rome, with Luigi Figini and Gino Pollini	1954	Showroom for Olivetti, New York City; pavilion at the 10th Triennale di Milano
1934-38	Collaboration with the journal *Quadrante*	1954-63	Restoration and installation of museums in Castello Sforzesco, Milan
1935	Join the Congrès Internationaux d'Architecture Moderne (CIAM)	1956-58	Torre Velasca, Milan
1936	Zoning plan for Aosta Valley, Italy, with Piero Bottoni, Figini, and Pollini; exhibition spaces at 6th Triennale di Milano	1959	Housing and commerical building, Piazza Statuto, Turin, Italy
		1963	Gratosoglio residential district, Milan
		1965	Building for Hispano-Olivetti, Barcelona, Spain
1938	Holiday colony in Lignano, Italy (demolished in 1956)	1967	Monument at the Mauthausen concentration camp
1942	Exhibition pavilion for the 1942 World Exposition in Rome	1969	Commercial building, Piazza F. Meda, Milan; Rogers dies on November 7
		1976	Peressutti dies on May 3

1

2

3

1 | Model
2 | The tower in its urban context
3 | View from base to the projecting
   section of the tower

Pier Luigi Nervi

Palazzetto dello Sport | ROME 1956-1958

PIER LUIGI NERVI

1891	Born on June 21 in Sondrio, Italy
1913	Graduates in civil engineering from the University of Bologna, Italy
1913–20	Works for the Società per Costruzioni Cementizie in Bologna
1915–18	Lieutenant in the Italian army's Corps of Engineers
1920	Founds Nervi & Nebbiosi in Rome
1926–27	Designs the Cinema Augusteo, Naples
1929–32	Football stadium, Florence, Italy
1932	Sets up Nervi & Bartoli, Rome, together with his cousin
1939–41	Six aircraft hangars for the Italian Air Force in Orbetello, Orvieto, Torre del Lago, Italy (destroyed in World War II)
1948–49	Exhibition hall (Salone Principale), Turin, Italy
1950	Exhibition Hall C, Turin; beach pavilion with Attilio la Paula, Ostia, Italy
1952	Hall for spa complex, Chianciano, Italy; tobacco factory, Bologna (extension 1954)
1953–56	UNESCO headquarters, Paris, with Marcel Breuer and Bernard H. Zehrfuss
1955–56	Structural design for the Pirelli skyscraper, Milan, with Arturo Danusso
1956–60	Buildings for the Olympic Games, Rome, including the Palazzetto dello Sport, completed in 1958
1959	Savona Railway Station, Italy
1959–61	Palazzo del Lavoro, Turin
1962	George Washington Bridge bus station, New York City; paper mill, Mantua, Italy
1971	Papal Audience Chamber, the Vatican
1979	Dies on January 9 in Rome

Pier Luigi Nervi realized four major works for the 1960 Rome Olympics: the Stadio Flaminio, the Corso Francia viaduct, the vast Palazzo dello Sport, and the more modest Palazzetto dello Sport designed in collaboration with the architect A. Vitellozzi. This "small" sports coliseum in the Flaminio district of Rome is the most architecturally interesting of Nervi's Olympic projects and ranks as one of the highlights of his oeuvre. The Palazzetto, 256 feet (78 meters) in diameter, consists of a huge dome carried on obliquely placed, Y-shaped stanchions. The dome was erected using prefabricated units of prestressed concrete laid over a temporary steel structure and then finished on the upper side with a layer of concrete. Once this had hardened, the auxiliary structure was removed.

Beneath the dome is a sports arena with a sunken floor well below ground level, surrounded by stands seating 5,000 spectators. This column-free space, 171 feet (52 meters) in diameter, is enclosed by a glazed curtain wall above which the dome seems to float. The structure is largely of concrete, the material whose potential Nervi spent his entire career exploring. In his view, "reinforced concrete [was] the most beautiful structural system humanity had managed to discover to date." He used concrete in a wide range of forms: in situ and prefabricated, reinforced, and prestressed. Furthermore, during the period when he was designing the Palazzetto dello Sport, he was also busy experimenting with the now obsolete ferrocement.

Like so many famous names from the history of reinforced concrete, which began in the second half of the nineteenth century, Nervi was active in several fields: those of the civil engineer, architect, inventor, and contractor. He produced independent designs, worked as a consulting engineer, took out patents on the various systems he developed, and acted as contractor for the construction of his own designs. In 1920 he founded the firm Nervi & Nebbiosi, and in 1932 he and a cousin set up the contracting company of Nervi & Bartoli.

In his work, Nervi combined great structural expertise with a highly developed sense of form. He regarded construction as fundamental: "A technically perfect work can be aesthetically expressive, but there does not exist, either in the present or the past, a work of art which is accepted and recognized as excellent from an aesthetic point of view, which is not excellent from a technical point of view." Although he accorded primary importance to construction, he did not believe that the final form was the only possible outcome of a structural problem. Nervi was convinced that an intuitive idea of form preceded every design. Calculations were merely a way of testing the viability of this intuitive idea. In the final analysis, Nervi was quite literally a "form-giver."   H.I.

1

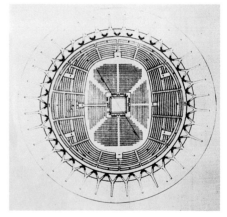

2

1 | View of stadium during construction
2 | Plan of stadium
3 | Interior
4 | Dome structure illuminated at night
5 | Detail: entrance to stands

Eero Saarinen

TWA Terminal | NEW YORK CITY 1956–1962

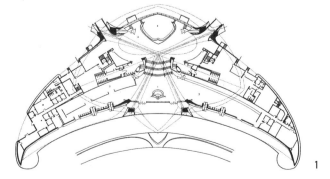

Eero Saarinen always maintained that his air terminal was not intended to resemble a bird with wings outstretched. But surely the exhilaration of flight has never before been rendered so evocatively through the medium of architecture. With its flowing lines and graceful curves, the world-renowned Trans World Airlines Terminal seems perpetually poised to soar, a metaphor for the modern age of jet travel.

The TWA Terminal was commissioned for New York's Idlewild Airport (now Kennedy Airport), which was the first to have terminals representing individual airline companies. The enlightened TWA company was committed to having Saarinen devise a unique corporate image, and they gave him free rein. Completed in 1962, the TWA Terminal signaled a moment of optimism and ambition in American economic and architectural history; not only did it aim to fulfill its public function of processing passengers, but it gave a highly recognizable face to a large company.

Saarinen was a master engineer as well as a master designer. A corrective to engineering problems in his previous works, such as the Kresge Auditorium at the Massachusetts Institute of Technology (1953–55), the terminal structure consists of a shell of reinforced concrete with four segments that extend outward from a central point. Colleague Kevin Roche recounts the "squashed grapefruit" story, noting that, "Eero was eating breakfast one morning and was using the rind of his grapefruit to describe the terminal shell. He pushed down its center to mimic the depression that he desired, and the grapefruit bulged. This was the seed for the four bulges of the shell."

The organic lines of the segments are complemented by vaulted roofs with numerous inset windows. Concrete "wings" unfold on either side of the exterior, lending the traveler a sense of enveloping security. The exterior flows organically into the interior at the same time that the flow of movement continues within; ceilings run continuously into the walls and the walls become floors. This seamlessness of form and style extends to the built-in fixtures throughout the building, including seating and lighting, which results in overall design consistency — a total work of art. The self-contained quality of the terminal and the somewhat overdetermined movement within make a stunning piece of architecture, but it has not proven adaptable to growth and change. It is Saarinen's later terminal, Dulles Airport in Chantilly, Virginia (1958–63), that has emerged as more flexible; Dulles has just sustained a successful expansion without compromising its essential design.

The TWA Terminal has not aged well, and, because of its sculptural design, it has not been able to grow along with the evolving corporate and technological worlds. Nonetheless, it remains a monument of Saarinen's idiosyncratic, anti-Bauhaus modernism, and a testament to his belief in inventive interaction between architect and engineer. Saarinen saw the three principles of modern architecture as "function, structure, and being part of our time." In the TWA Terminal, where concrete bends and twists improbably according to the will of the architect, Saarinen realized those goals.   E.P.

EERO SAARINEN

1910	Born August 20 in Kirkkonumnii, Finland; son of the architect Eliel Saarinen
1923	Emigrates to the U.S.; naturalized in 1940
1934	Studies architecture at Yale University, New Haven, Connecticut
1936–41	Joins his father's architectural practice in Ann Arbor, Michigan
1938	Berkshire Music Center, Tanglewood, Massachusetts (with Eliel Saarinen)
1941–47	Partner with his father and J. Robert Swanson
1942–45	Works in the Office of Strategic Studies, Washington, D.C.
1944–48	Edmundson Memorial Museum, Des Moines Art Center, Iowa (with Eliel Saarinen and J. Robert Swanson)
1947	Civic Center, Detroit, Michigan (with Eliel Saarinen)
1948–56	First Prize, Jefferson National Expansion Memorial Competition, St. Louis, Missouri (1948); General Motors Technical Center, including interiors and furniture, Warren, Michigan (with Smith, Hinchman, and Grylls)
1950	Eliel Saarinen dies on June 1 in Bloomfield Hills, Michigan
1950–61	Principal of Eero Saarinen and Associates, Birmingham, Michigan
1953–56	Kresge Auditorium, Massachusetts Institute of Technology, Cambridge, Massachusetts
1954	Master plan for the University of Michigan, Ann Arbor
1956–62	Trans World Airlines Terminal, Idlewild (Kennedy) Airport, New York City
1957–63	Thomas J. Watson Research Center, IBM, Yorktown, New York, completed 1961; John Deere and Company Administration Center, Moline, Illinois
1958–63	Terminal Building, Dulles International Airport, Chantilly, Virginia (near Washington, D.C.)
1959–64	Jefferson National Expansion Memorial (Gateway Arch), St. Louis, Missouri
1961	Dies on September 1 in Ann Arbor

1

2

3

1 | Plan of building
2 | External view at night
3 | Entrance hall
4 | External view

4

1

2

3

1 | Concert hall
2 | Design sketches
3 | Entrance front
4 | Longitudinal section

Hans B. Scharoun

New Philharmonic | BERLIN 1956-1963

On September 19, 1960, the foundation stone for the New Philharmonic was laid on Kemperplatz in the Tiergarten district of Berlin. This exact site was also where, in 1938, Albert Speer had demolished the first street blocks to create the north-south axis of his new "capital of the world," Germania, and where World War II had left behind an unprecedented wasteland. According to Hans B. Scharoun's concept, the Philharmonic was to form the first element of a "cultural forum" that was to counteract the urban desolation of the southern part of the Tiergarten area and the effects of the newly built Berlin Wall on Potsdamer Platz. Although the decision to replace the war-destroyed Philharmonic had been made in 1956, when 12 architects were invited to submit competing designs for a new building, Scharoun's ideas came to the fore only when the Senate of Berlin decided at short notice to move the location of the hall from a rear courtyard in Wilmersdorf on the Bundesallee to the present site, which at that time lay on the edge of a political no-man's-land.

Despite the radically different nature of the site, Scharoun, the clear winner of the 1956 competition, did not feel constrained to make fundamental changes to his design, which

had been so highly praised by Herbert von Karajan. The building, erected on Kemperplatz within a period of only three years and at a relatively modest cost, is identical in its concept with the scheme Scharoun designed for the rear courtyard site in Wilmersdorf. The genius of the design lies in the way it embodies Scharoun's vision: a design of convincing strength and clarity that would place "music at the center."

The central position of the podium for the orchestra, in the middle of the auditorium, at the heart of the entire building, revolutionized the design of theaters and concert halls throughout the world. This simple gesture not only swept aside the traditional rigid axial alignment of the seating and the podium; it also opened the space for the community and the arts in a non-perspective form. The deep orchestra pit is enclosed on all sides by "vineyard terraces," and in this way Scharoun was able to accomplish the miraculous feat of accommodating 2,218 seats, none of which is more than 105 feet (32 meters) from the source of the music. The sense of spatial intimacy this creates is heightened acoustically by the "heavenscape of the convex, tent-like suspended ceiling."

On leaving the concert hall, a new and unexpected spatial situation presents itself. The stairs and galleries cascade down to the central foyer, which is situated beneath the auditorium. Julius Posener described the impression most aptly when he spoke of the "Piranesian effect" one feels on entering and experiencing this space in all its breadth and complexity.

Scharoun planned the Philharmonic from the inside outwards. The golden anodized perforated sheet-metal cladding on the facade, which was completed between 1978 and 1981, is evidence of this. There is no show facade to help one understand the external form of the building. Scharoun's achievement lies less in a revolutionary form of architecture than in the way he changed the relationship between people and space. C.B.

HANS B. SCHAROUN

1893	Born on September 20 in Bremen, Germany	1945-46	Head of the Department for Building Construction and Housing in Berlin; presents his urban vision for the city of Berlin in the exhibition "Berlin Plans"
1912-14	Studies at the Faculty of Architecture of the Technical University in Charlottenburg, Berlin		
1915-18	Military service as an architect		
1919-25	Own architectural practice in Insterburg, East Prussia, Germany; member of the Expressionist society of artists, the "Gläserne Kette" (Glass Chain) in Berlin, and creates a large number of drawings and watercolors in the style of that movement	1951	Presentation of his "man and space" concept in conjunction with his design for a school in Darmstadt, Germany
		1952-54	State Theater in Kassel, Germany
		1954-59	"Romeo and Juliet" high-rise housing development, Stuttgart
1925-32	Professor at the State Academy for Art and Arts and Crafts in Breslau, Germany; builds lodgings in Breslau (1929) and a house in the Weissenhof Estate, Stuttgart, Germany (1927)	1956-62	Geschwister Scholl Secondary School, Lünen, Westphalia, Germany
		1956-63	New Philharmonic, Tiergarten, Berlin
		1963-64	State Library, Tiergarten, Berlin
1926	Architectural practice in Berlin; housing design in Berlin, such as the Siemensstadt Estate	1965-73	Wolfsburg Civic Theater, Germany
		1968-71	Recital hall of the Philharmonic, Tiergarten, Berlin; design and execution by Edgar Wisniewski
1933-45	Boycotted by the public sector, builds roughly 20 single-family houses for private clients; Schminke House in Löbau, Saxony, Germany	1970	German Shipping Museum, Bremerhaven, Germany
		1972	Dies on November 25 in Berlin

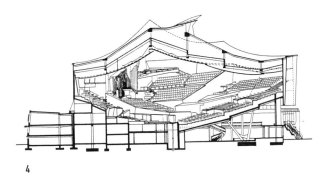

4

Carlo Scarpa

Museo di Castelvecchio | VERONA 1956-1964

The redesign of the Museo di Castelvecchio in the former ducal palace in Verona, Italy, was no simple task for Carlo Scarpa, especially since the original substance of the building was no longer clearly identifiable. The fourteenth-century structure had been subject to repeated alterations in the course of its history; and in the 1920s, it was renovated "true to historical style." Scarpa expressed his verdict succinctly with the words: "Everything about the old castle was false." The only acceptable approach for him, therefore, was "to emphasize certain features in order to break down the unnatural symmetry. The Gothic [structure] required this."

Working in close collaboration with Licisco Magagnato, the curator of the museum, Scarpa began with a series of operations at various points to ascertain the extent and nature of the historical substance and to remove earlier alterations or cover them with his own measures. This process of "clarification" involved not only the Castelvecchio itself, but also its links with the garden and surroundings. Internally, he reorganized the circulation, and, with a number of simple measures,

he drew attention to the existing features of the building. Scarpa designed all the exhibition furniture and supporting elements for the display of objects and determined the positions of the exhibits. All these measures demonstrate his sound judgment in matters of visual art, even if this is not always immediately evident, as in placing the "Cangrande della Scala" sculpture in a seemingly precarious position. On the other hand, the newly created visual links within the complex ensure that the equestrian statue of the Scaligeri prince regains the ubiquitous presence it probably once had in its historical context.

As scarcely any other body of architectural work in the twentieth century, Scarpa's oeuvre contains several designs for exhibitions and museum buildings. He has reorganized a number of leading collections, including those of the Galleria dell'Accademia and the Museo Correr in Venice. He has also worked for smaller regional museums. One particularly successful scheme in this respect was the Galleria Regionale di Sicilia in the Palazzo Abbatellis in Palermo. In his approach, Scarpa developed a strategy that went beyond a neutral presentation of the exhibits, beyond the dramatic staging of their iconographic content. Scarpa's designs for museums are an exploration of the scope for interpretation offered by the aesthetic qualities of a work and its relationship to the actual space in which it is set. As a result of this mental extrapolation of existing conditions, he achieved a balance between dependence and independence. Scarpa's display elements bring out certain innate expressive aspects of an object. The weight of a piece of sculpture, for example, is visually reinforced by a massive plinth; or the sense of lightness of an exhibit might be accentuated by an arrangement of slenderly dimensioned bars. The measures he takes in the building itself are like the careful retouching of a painting: they can always be distinguished from the original work, but they blend well into the overall picture.

R.H.

CARLO SCARPA

1906	Born on June 2 in Venice, Italy
1926	Diploma at the Accademia di Belle Arti in Venice; assistant at the Istituto Universitario di Architettura in Venice
1927–	Own architectural practice in Venice
1935-37	Refurbishment of the Ca' Foscari in Venice as the seat of the Università degli Studi
1945-59	Refurbishment of the Galleria dell' Accademia in Venice
1948	Designs the Paul Klee exhibition in the context of the 24th Biennale in Venice; Villa Zoppas in Conegliano, Italy
1953-54	Refurbishment of the Galleria Regionale di Sicilia in Palazzo Abbatellis, Palermo, Italy
1953-60	Refurbishment of the Museo Correr in Venice (with Egle Trincanato)
1954-56	Refurbishment of the Uffizi Palace (with Ignazio Gardella and Giovanni Michelucci); Venezuelan Pavilion in the Giardini di Castello in Venice
1955-57	Extension of the Gipsoteca Canoviana in Possagno, Italy

1955-61	Casa Veritti in Udine, Italy
1956	Designs the Piet Mondrian exhibition the in Galleria Nazionale d'Arte Moderna, Rome
1956-64	Redesign of the Museo di Castelvecchio in Verona, Italy
1957-58	Olivetti shop in Venice
1960	Designs the Frank Lloyd Wright exhibition at the 12th Triennale in Milan, Italy; Erich Mendelsohn exhibition at the 30th Biennale in Venice
1961-63	Refurbishment of the Fondazione Querini Stampalia in Venice
1962	Professor at the Istituto Universitario di Architettura in Venice
1969-75	Brion Cemetery, San Vito d'Altivole, Italy
1972-78	Director of the Istituto Universitario di Architettura in Venice
1973-80	Banca Popolare di Verona
1974	Venezia–Bisanzio exhibition in the Palazzo Ducale, Venice
1974-79	Ottolenghi House, Bardolino, Italy
1978	Dies on November 28 in Sendai, Japan

1

2

1 | Exterior of former ducal palace
2 | Detail with view of "Cangrande"
     equestrian statue
3 | Part of exhibition space
4 | View into exhibition halls
5 | Circulation route

3

4

5

Jørn Utzon

Opera House | SYDNEY 1957-1973

JØRN UTZON

1918	Born on April 9 in Copenhagen, Denmark; the son of a shipyard director and yacht designer
1937-42	Studies at the Academy of Arts in Copenhagen
1942-45	Works with Gunnar Asplund in Stockholm, Sweden
1946	Spends several months in Alvar Aalto's studio in Helsinki, Finland
1947-48	Tours Europe, North Africa, Mexico, and the U.S., including Frank Lloyd Wright's studio, Taliesin West, in Arizona
1950	Architectural practice, Copenhagen
1952-53	Utzon House in Hellebaek, Copenhagen
1957	Wins the competition for the Opera House, Sydney, Australia, completed in 1973
1962	Proposes a revised design of prefabricated sphere segments for the Opera House
1964	Wins the design competition for a twin auditorium building for the Zurich City Theater, Switzerland
1966	Resigns as architect of the Opera House and closes his practice in Sydney; architectural practice in the U.S. and Switzerland
1971-83	National Assembly Buildings in Kuwait
1973	The Sydney Opera House is completed by Australian architects, with significant changes to Utzon's design
1976	Bagsvaerd Church in Copenhagen
1978	Wins the Gold Medal from the Royal Institute of British Architects
1983	Parliament, Kuwait
1986	In collaboration with sons Jan and Kim, Utzon completes the Paustian furniture showroom in Copenhagen

Jørn Utzon resigned as architect of the Sydney Opera House in mid-construction. He left its completion in the hands of an Australian firm, and never returned to Sydney to see it completed. In fact, in addition to the various dismissals and resignations that the building brought about, it actually played a significant role in the fall of the governmental administration which originally sponsored the project. The building took 16 years to complete, exceeding original budget projections several times over, and it never really increased the popularity of the opera in Sydney. Yet despite all these events, it is by far the best known building in Utzon's substantial oeuvre, and bears an iconic presence as a symbol of Australia.

The project began when the government of New South Wales announced a competition for an opera house, intended to elevate Sydney's cultural viability and visibility. Architects internationally were invited to submit designs for a program to include two halls, a restaurant, and public meeting rooms. The chosen site was Bennelong Point, a spectacular harbor protrusion, visible from every direction in the city. A total of 234 architects from nine countries submitted entries. Eero Saarinen, an American architect who was beginning to explore large-scale, sculptural concrete forms in his own work, was among the jurors. During the judging, Saarinen retrieved Utzon's design from a group that had already been eliminated

from consideration. "Gentlemen," he announced, "this is the first prize."

Utzon's original scheme consisted of an immense platform containing a car entrance, workshops, dressing rooms, and service spaces, surmounted by a series of monolithic parabolic shells of varying heights containing the auditorium spaces. Unfortunately, even with the collaboration of British structural engineer Ove Arup, who had been recommended by Saarinen, the original structure was too complex to calculate, and the shells threatened to be far too heavy for the platform. To speed the process, construction of the platform began immediately, but Utzon went to work on a revised scheme for the auditorium enclosures. In his second submission, Utzon proposed auditorium shell forms which were segments of a single sphere 300 feet (91.4 meters) in diameter. The shells were designed with concrete ribs as structure, to be enclosed by prefabricated, tile-covered, Chevron-shaped panels.

The resulting building is complex in form as well as provenance. The modernist-expressionist structure recalls Utzon's childhood exposure to shipbuilding as much as it does the designs of Eero Saarinen and Frank Lloyd Wright. The construction on a platform derives from Utzon's interest in the pre-Columbian temples of Mexico, while some of the construction techniques are adaptations from the *Ying Tsao Fah Shi*, a 1,000-year-old Chinese builder's manual. Utzon managed to synthesize a very organic sense of form very advanced techniques of prefabrication. While the result is extremely personal, it also evokes an international trend in modernism that was popular in its time and which endures today as one of the world's most highly acclaimed buildings. C.L.R.

1

2

3

4

5

1 | Design detail: internal face of wall
2 | Overall view with skyline of Sydney
3 | View at dusk
4 | Design sketch
5 | Staircase and part of facade

Oscar Niemeyer

Congress Buildings | BRASILIA (BRAZIL) 1958-1960

Oscar Niemeyer was powerfully influenced by Le Corbusier, whose own work was fundamentally affected by his visits to South America, where he found a new freedom and fluidity of line. Niemeyer has explored the potential of that plasticity extensively in his own work over some 60 years, but never again on such an expansive scale as in the city of Brasilia.

The pilot plan for the city drawn up by Lucio Costa provided a graphic diagram for the new capital and center of governance, which Niemeyer filled out in an almost theatrical manner with a series of dramatic architectural monuments. Among these the Congress Buildings in Brasilia, Brazil, takes pride of place, situated at the apex of the Plaza of the Three Powers at the far end of the central axis through the city. The huge construction, housing the senate, chamber of deputies, and administration, is conceived at one and the same time as a powerful landmark, symbolic of its governmental function, visible within a large radius, and as a vast terrace commanding a magnificent view of the Monumental Axis and the city spreading out around it.

The bulk of the building appears as a flat slab, situated in a slight hollow, with road embankments built up on either side to roof level. On the roof, or terrace, sit a pair of large sculptural objects: a dome, over the Senate, and a saucer, over the Chamber of Deputies, each forming a dramatic cupola over the circular chambers inside. In front a huge ramp leads

from ground level onto the terrace, dominating the entrance elevation — although access for day-to-day business is via the garage in the basement. Behind, a pair of tall, slim towers containing the administrative offices — higher than any other building in the city — soar into the bright sky, casting a long shadow over the square pool at the back of the building.

Brasilia was conceived as a true modernist city, consisting of a collection of free-standing architectural objects in space, related to each other by a traffic circulation system and a consistent aesthetic deriving from the method of construction. Niemeyer himself described the Congress Buildings as representing a combination of engineering expertise with "expression of the spirit . . . made to function in urbanization, in building volumes, in open spaces, in visual depth, in perspective and, particularly, in the attempt to give it an outspoken monumental aspect. . . ." But the suggestion that the building operates at an urban level seems something of a delusion. The architectural group on the Plaza of the Three Powers, which Niemeyer later described more accurately as "a symphony of forms," and its relationship with the city master plan, is inspired by an essentially abstract poetic and aesthetic vision. Although immensely impressive at that level, the subsequent history of Brasilia was to reveal its failings as a context for urban life, and the huge cost of the exercise initially led to recriminations against those involved in the venture.   C.M.

OSCAR NIEMEYER

1907	Born on December 15 in Rio de Janeiro, Brazil
1930	Begins his architectural studies at the School of Fine Arts in Rio de Janeiro
1936	After working for Lucio Costa, he joins the team working on the Ministry of Education building with Le Corbusier
1939	Realizes Costa's winning design for the Brazilian Pavilion at the New York World's Fair
1942-43	Garners a commission from his close friend, Juscelino Kubitschek, mayor of Belo Horizonte, for a series of new buildings around Lake Pampulha, Rio de Janeiro
1946	Boavista Bank in Rio de Janeiro
1954	Industry Palace in the Ibiraquera Park in São Paulo, Brazil
1955	Kubitschek is elected president of Brazil, leading to Niemeyer's prestigious appointment as the director of works for the immense task

of constructing Brasilia, the country's new capital

1958-60	Congress Buildings, Brasilia; political changes force Niemeyer, a lifelong member of the Brazilian Communist Party, into exile
1960-70	Undertakes major works in Algeria and Europe, including the KPF Center in Paris (1967), the Mondadori Administration Building in Milan, Italy (1968), the Renault Administration Building in Paris (1969), and Constantine University in Algeria (1969)
1988	Pritzker Architecture Prize
1989	Memorial da America Latina, an expansive cultural center in São Paulo
1990s	Now in his 90s, Niemeyer has recently received the Golden Lion of the Venice Biennale and the Gold Medal of the Royal Institute of British Architects in London

1

2

3

1 | Ramp to roof terrace, with State
Chancellery towers to rear
2 | Roofscape with dish and dome
3 | Dish over Chamber of Deputies
4 | Overall view

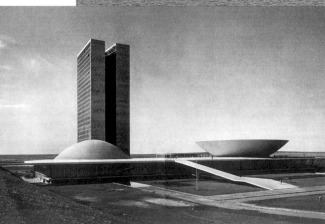

4

1

2, 3, 4

1 | Overall view
2 | Axonometric drawing: view
from southeast
3 | View of building in St. James's Street
4 | Economist Plaza
5 | View of building in Bury Street

Alison and Peter Smithson

Economist Building | LONDON 1959-1964

The Economist Building in London is Alison and Peter Smithson's most accomplished work. Less controversial than their Brutalist school at Hunstanton, England of 1954, it nevertheless proposed the radical concept of breaking up the city block to create a piazza surrounded by a cluster of buildings, a scheme which the Smithsons suggested should be replicated throughout the surrounding area creating a network of public spaces. Despite its departure from the traditional streetscape, the buildings are sensitively designed within the context of St. James's — the heart of London's gentlemen's clubs and a bastion of conservatism.

The commission involved new offices for *The Economist* magazine and the Economist Intelligence Unit, residential accommodation for Boodles' Club, which was already located on the site, and retail space at street level.

A four-story office building and banking hall faces onto St. James's Street and flanks a pedestrian route through to the raised piazza providing access to the 16-story tower and Boodles' Club. The elegant piano nobile surrounds the central core with glazing set back from the perimeter to create an arcade around the base of the building. The tower is square in plan and was originally designed with perimeter offices served by a corridor that wrapped around the core. Daylight enters the corridor via glazed ring ventilation ducts situated along the top of the office partitioning.

The strong verticality of the facades and the concrete structure clad with heavily fossilized roach bed Portland Stone fins sit happily with the classical facades of St. James's and Bury Streets. The chamfered corners effectively reduce the bulk of the building when viewed on the diagonal, and create a sympathetic skyline when seen from the royal palaces nearby.

The Smithsons were lucky to have a sophisticated client in the owners of the Economist Group. At a time when little attention was paid to the quality of commercial development, and International Style blocks ignored their surroundings, the Economist Building stood out as an exemplar of urban development in London. However, it was not until the Broadgate Development, built some 20 years later, that a commercial developer created such a successful mix of new public space and office buildings. The Economist Group still owns the building and has cared for it lovingly. A major refurbishment project was undertaken in the early '90s by Skidmore, Owings & Merrill in consultation with Peter Smithson in order to bring it up to modern office standards. The changes are difficult to decipher, the most obvious being a new canopy above the main tower entrance and changes to the glazing of the Bury Street retail unit. These have been carried out with a sensitivity that reflects the building's importance in the canon of postwar office building, demonstrated by the fact that it was one of the first post-1945 buildings in Britain to be listed as being of historic importance.

The company continues a policy of using the piazza for changing exhibitions of modern sculpture, enlivening the space, and reinforcing its role as a civilizing influence in the modern city.   P.M.

ALISON AND PETER SMITHSON

1923	Peter Smithson is born on September 18 in Stockton-on-Tees, England
1928	Alison Gill is born on June 22 in Sheffield, England
1939-49	Both study architecture at the University of Durham in England; Smithson also studies at the Royal Academy in London
1949	Smithson and Gill marry
1949-50	Both work as technical assistants at the London County Council Architects' Department
1950-	The Smithsons found their own architectural offices in London
1954	Hunstanton Secondary Modern School, Norfolk, England
1956	"House of the Future," ideal house exhibition, Olympia, London
1959-64	Economist Building, London
1960	Exhibition "This is Tomorrow," Whitechapel Gallery, London
1965	Publication of *Team X*
1970	Garden Building, St. Hilda's College, Oxford University, England; publication of *Ordinariness and Light: Urban Theories 1952-1960*
1972	Residential development Robin Hood Gardens, London
1973	Publication of *Without Rhetoric: An architectural aesthetic 1955-72*
1988	Engineering Building, University of Bath, England
1993	Alison Smithson dies on August 16 in London

5

Robert Venturi

Vanna Venturi House | CHESTNUT HILL, PHILADELPHIA 1959-1964

The small house in Chestnut Hill, Philadelphia, designed by Robert Venturi for his mother, was the architect's first building commission — a private, domestic job — but also perhaps his most important theoretical statement. In 1959 the site was purchased and the design process begun, when Venturi was 34 years old; the building was completed five years later, in 1964. The following year it was honored with the Gold Medal Award of the Architectural League of New York, and in 1966 Venturi published a substantial disquisition on the house in his theoretical treatise *Complexity and Contradiction in Architecture*, which was to bring the building international attention and appraisal.

Complexity and Contradiction had an enormous impact on architectural thinking in the 1960s, when the legacy of modernism in architecture was being radically reconsidered. It demanded an end to functionalist dogmatism and a reevaluation of architectural history; today it is widely regarded as the seminal document behind the emergence of postmodernism. Venturi's description and analysis of the Vanna Venturi House elevated the structure to iconic status as a model of the new architecture which he sought to define. "This building recognizes complexities and contradictions," he wrote. "The front, in its conventional combinations of door, windows, chimney, and gable, creates an almost symbolic image of a house."

The building embodies the intellectual agenda and architectural invention which Venturi presented as a powerful challenge to modernism. The flat, cut-out appearance of the front elevation, with its curious split pediment motif above a gaping front door, and prominent chimney stack rising behind, is a striking break with modernist tenets. Behind the facade, the simple rectangular plan is extruded to form a complex volume revealing the influence of the American Shingle Style, or British Arts and Crafts movement, embodied in the work of architects such as Frank Furness and Sir Edwin Lutyens. The main living accommodation is arranged simply at ground level, with an upper level tucked underneath the central area of the large pitched roof. The organization of plan and section hinges on the awkward relationship between the oversized, off-center chimney-piece rising through the house, and the oddly shaped stair, wider at the base and narrowing toward the top, which wraps around the back of the chimney, and is sandwiched between it and the double-height entrance vestibule. On the second floor is the notorious little "stair to nowhere" which was regarded as impossibly whimsical when the house was first unveiled.

The final scheme represented the culmination of a lengthy design process incorporating six different versions of the house. Here Venturi breaks clean of the influence of his teacher and former employer, Louis I. Kahn, and affirms the possibility of a contemporary architecture evolved within a historic framework, a move that profoundly affected a new generation of architects.   C.M.

ROBERT VENTURI

1925	Born on June 25 in Philadelphia, Pennsylvania
1944-50	Studies architecture at Princeton University, Princeton, New Jersey
1951-53	After graduating, Venturi works in the office of Oscar Stonorov in Philadelphia and then for Eero Saarinen in Detroit, Michigan
1954-59	Wins the Rome Prize Fellowship in Architecture; works briefly for Louis I. Kahn
1958	Sets up his own practice, Venturi and Short, with William Short
1959-64	Vanna Venturi House, Chestnut Hill, Philadelphia
1961	His first realized project is the North Penn Visiting Nurses Association Headquarters, Ambler, Pennsylvania
1964	Enters into partnership with John Rauch
1966	Publishes *Complexity and Contradiction in Architecture*, which brings Venturi international acclaim and notoriety
1967	Marries Denise Scott Brown, who later becomes a partner in the practice
1972	Together with Steven Izenour, the couple publishes *Learning from Las Vegas*
1980	The firm Venturi, Rauch and Scott Brown is founded
1986-91	The practice makes a controversial debut in Britain, winning a new competition for the Sainsbury Wing, National Gallery of Art in London
1989	The firm is renamed Venturi, Scott Brown and Associates
1991	Pritzker Architecture Prize

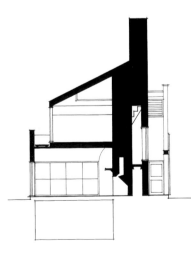

1

2

3

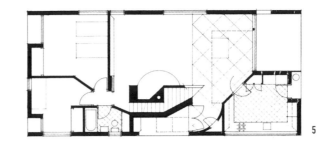

5

1 | Section
2 | Rear face
3 | Bedroom on upper floor
4 | Living room on first floor
5 | First-floor plan
6 | Front elevation

4

6

1 | Swimming hall
2 | Site plan
3 | View of the two halls
4 | Aerial view of site, showing
   the steel roof structures

1

2

3

Throughout his life, the Japanese architect Kenzo Tange has explored the meaning of monumentality. Without copying the forms of buildings, he has attempted to convey to Japan the special sense of "greatness" that he discovered in Western architecture in the course of his many journeys abroad. His buildings for the 1964 Olympic Games in Tokyo are a convincing example of this. Tange's masterpiece consists of two sports halls, or stadia, set diagonally opposite each other and linked by a large platform. Even today, the dramatic roof structures of these halls make them the most memorable buildings in Japan's capital.

Set on a hill behind the urban center of Shibuya, the complex is reminiscent of an acropolis. The large, hand-dressed basalt blocks used in the external works are a reference to an old Japanese building tradition and form a striking contrast to the new structural forms of the stadium roofs. Tange succeeded in creating a location that was, on the one hand, traditionally Japanese in atmosphere and that, on the other hand, employed completely new forms. The scheme signaled to the world that a new and modern Japan had established itself after the inconceivable destruction of World War II. The large curving forms of the steel roofs and the broad cantilevered concrete construction of the stands for spectators possess a breathtaking dynamic. The spacious layout of the whole complex communicates an optimistic and festive sense of a new beginning, which was appropriate to the first major international event to be held in Japan after the war.

The swimming hall provides space for 16,200 spectators. It was possible to cover the 50-meter pool with a structure that could be mechanically raised into position. As a result, the hall can still be used for other sporting events today. In collaboration with the architects, the engineer Yoshikatsu Tsuboi developed a suspended roof structure that was the first of its kind built to this scale. Two tall, dramatically shaped reinforced concrete pylons support a system of steel cables that are anchored in the elegantly curved concrete stands. The network thus created was covered with sheet

steel panels that fit the gently modulating form of the surface. Daylight enters the striking and wholly original internal space through a glazed aperture at the structure's peak.

The second hall, which is much smaller, was built for the Olympic basketball and boxing events, and has a maximum capacity of 5,000 spectators. Again, the load-bearing structure is supported by a cable, but in this case it is suspended spirally from a single, eccentrically positioned pylon. Far removed from the rationalist functional buildings of the immediate postwar years, the architecture reveals its full sculptural effect in the wood-paneled internal space.

Over and above the formal quality of the architecture, Kenzo Tange's extraordinary achievement lay in creating a convincing synthesis of tradition, modernity, and perhaps even a vision of the future in these buildings for the Olympic Games. The work is rightly regarded as a milestone, not only in the history of modern Japanese architecture, but in that of architecture throughout the world.   W.K.

4

KENZO TANGE
Architect's biography on p. 80

Louis I. Kahn

Parliament Buildings | DACCA (BANGLADESH) 1963-1974; 1983

In 1959, the government of Pakistan, under the leadership of Field Marshal Ayub Khan, decided to create two new capitals — in East and West Pakistan. "Sher-e-Bangla" (City of the Bengal Tiger), the new capital of East Pakistan, later Bangladesh, was built near Dacca on flat, open farmland that was subject to flooding. Having first favored Le Corbusier and Alvar Aalto for the design, in 1962 the government contacted Louis I. Kahn, who at that time was at the height of his career and was working on two important public buildings in America: the Richards Medical Research Building for the University of Pennsylvania (1957–65) and the Salk Institute for Biological Studies in La Jolla, California (1959–65). Kahn was acquainted with Le Corbusier's work in Chandigarh, India, which he visited in 1962 and admired, although he criticized the spatial relationships of the buildings. Kahn designed the parliament in Dacca parallel to his work on the Indian Institute of Management in Ahmedabad, India (1962–74).

The two buildings reveal a completely different architectural language from that used by Le Corbusier, achieving a synthesis of Western and Oriental traditions, forms, and, to a certain extent, materials.

The elaborate building brief for the development in Dacca reflected the complicated history of the scheme. In addition to the parliamentary buildings, the Pakistani government required a master plan for the entire area. The plan was to contain other public and administrative buildings as well as housing and infrastructural facilities. Kahn's first designs date from 1963. The construction work for the entire area began in 1964, and the foundations for the parliament were laid in 1965. His scheme is based on the idea of the transcendental nature of assembly. The parliament was seen as a central location for this act, which is regarded as an expression of community and as conducive to a sense of identity. Having studied the importance of the Islamic faith in the daily lives of the people, the architect took the logical step of incorporating a mosque in the building. The parliamentary complex, which consists of a series of individual geometric volumes laid out around the central assembly space, is set beside a lake as a reference to the great importance of water in the local tradition. To achieve the monumentality of a citadel, Kahn isolated the buildings from their surroundings by a series of open spaces, staircases, and grassy areas.

The complex has a seemingly archaic expression. Its walls are in concrete, the broad vertical and horizontal joints of which are accentuated with white marble strips. The walls are further articulated by large, geometric openings that create a strong contrast between areas of light and shade. The greatest problem facing the architect was the roof over the main parliament building, which was originally designed in the form of a pyramid. The issue was finally resolved only in 1971, when a solution was found that incorporated a series of curving structures.

Before its completion, the project was interrupted between 1971 and 1973 by the civil war caused by Bangladesh's declaration of independence from West Pakistan. In 1972, Kahn was involved in negotiations with the new government, and in 1973, he presented a revised master plan, which formed the basis of the contract signed in 1974. After his death a short time later, the designs and construction were executed by David Wisdom & Associates down to the completion of the work in 1983. The National Assembly building was used for the first time in February 1982.   A.S.

LOUIS I. KAHN

1901	Born on February 20 in Kingisepp, Saaremaa, Estonia
1906	Emigrates with his family to Philadelphia, Pennsylvania
1920-24	Studies at the School of Fine Arts at the University of Pennsylvania, Philadelphia; subsequently works in various architects' offices
1925-26	Chief designer for all exhibition buildings for the Sesquicentennial International Exposition, Philadelphia
1935-	Establishes his own architectural practice, working at times in association with George Howe and Oscar Stonorov; numerous unexecuted projects
1935-37	Assistant principal architect for the Resettlement Administration, Washington, D.C.; Jersey Homesteads, in collaboration with Alfred Kastner; maintains a strong interest in settlement projects until long after World War II
1951-53	Yale University Art Gallery, New Haven, Connecticut

1955-74	Professor of architecture at the University of Pennsylvania; numerous distinctions and awards from the 1960s onwards
1957-65	Alfred Newton Richards Medical Research Building, University of Pennsylvania, Philadelphia
1959-61	Margaret Esherick House, Philadelphia
1959-65	Salk Institute for Biological Studies, La Jolla, California
1959-69	First Unitarian Church and School, Rochester, New York
1960-65	Eleanor Donnelly Erdman Hall, Bryn Mawr College, Bryn Mawr, Pennsylvania
1962-74	Indian Institute of Management, Ahmedabad, India
1963-83	Parliament buildings, Dacca, Bangladesh
1966-72	Kimbell Art Museum, Fort Worth, Texas
1974	Dies on March 17 in New York City upon his return from a journey to Ahmedabad

1

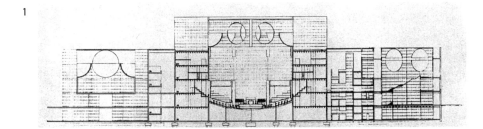

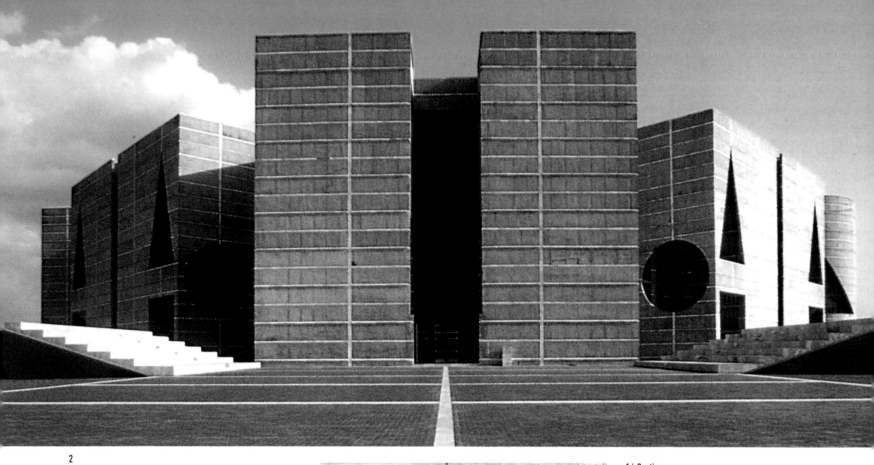

2

3

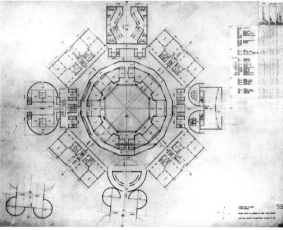

4

5

1 | Section
2 | View of complex from President's Square
3 | Staircase structure
4 | Plan of complex
5 | Accommodation to the east

Richard Meier

Smith House | DARIEN, CONNECTICUT 1965-1967

2

On a rocky outcropping of the Long Island Sound, the Smith House, Richard Meier's first major architectural success, floats like a ghost of modernism past. Its white rectilinear massing is instantaneously recognizable as an echo of the European designer Le Corbusier, whose 1926 "Five Points" founded a social utopianism in architecture that spawned playful villas for the elite as well as misguided mass housing schemes. The Smith House, a residence for a family of four, belongs to the former, and is a stunning example of how modernism's early twentieth-century temperament matured into a light-hearted, elegant aestheticism.

As one of the renowned young architects of the late 1960s known as "The New York Five,"— along with Peter Eisenman, Michael Graves, Charles Gwathmey, and John Hejduk — Meier was one of several East Coast designers reviving 1920s modernism as a style. He adapted the ideas of celebrated early twentieth-century designers and then transformed them. The Smith House is a perfect example of Meier's approach, which makes the most of the house's site, on a hill, and its view, onto the sound, to create a light-infused box framed by woods, water, and clear blue sky.

The main principle of the house's design is the dialectic between public and private spaces. This opposition plays itself out in spatial organization, both vertical and horizontal. The steep front elevation, a closed white plane interrupted only intermittently by windows, acts as an opaque screen to private interior spaces such as bedrooms and bathrooms, which, on all three levels, lie just beyond. The transition through the entryway to the house's southern, public side is sudden: the brilliant blue sound leaps into view, invited by the fully glazed rear elevation. Meier uses glass generously on this side of the house to open the corresponding public spaces above and below the main floor to the spectacular setting.

The building's materials sustain its spatial dynamics. Although often mistaken as a concrete structure in the style of Le Corbusier's Villa Stein, which it resembles, the Smith House keeps to a traditionally American structural system. A wooden bearing-wall and framing system supports the private half of the house, while the glazed public areas rely upon a steel columnar structure.

In 1971 the British magazine *Architectural Design* took stock of the fact that the house had been featured in several upscale advertisements, and in a review entitled "Le Corbusier a la Mode," denounced the villa as empty architectural formalism. Meier's colleague Eisenman shot back in a scathing letter to the editor, denouncing the attack as "American muckraking." Despite the controversy at that time, Meier's work has remained popular, especially with large corporations and art foundations. Most of Meier's commissions since the Smith House have been large-scale civic and commercial buildings, such as the recently completed billion-dollar Getty Center in Los Angeles, whose look retains a loyalty to Corbusian functionalism, but whose message is simple: the market is still mad about modern.   C.W.H.

RICHARD MEIER

1934	Born on October 12 in Newark, New Jersey
1953-57	Studies architecture at Cornell University in Ithaca, New York
1958-63	Apprentices in the offices of Davis, Broday & Wisniewski; then Skidmore, Owings & Merrill; and Marcel Breuer & Associates in New York City
1962	Lambert Beach House, Fire Island, New York
1963-	Meier opens his own practice in New York City
1965	House for his parents, Mr. and Mrs. Jerome Meier, Essex Falls, New Jersey
1965-67	Smith House, Darien, Connecticut; this building puts Meier on the map professionally
1970-76	Gains first major public commission, the Bronx Development Center, New York City
1972	Becomes known worldwide through the publication of *Five Architects*, in which he and four other architects are featured
1975-79	The Atheneum in New Harmony, Indiana
1979-85	Museum for Decorative Arts (Museum für Kunsthandwerk), Frankfurt-am-Main, Germany
1980-83	High Museum of Art, Atlanta, Georgia
1982-85	Des Moines Art Center Extension, Des Moines, Iowa
1984	Pritzker Architecture Prize
1984-97	J. Paul Getty Center in Los Angeles
1989	Royal Gold Medal from the Royal Institute of British Architects
1997	AIA Gold Medal from the American Institute of Architects, and the Praemium Imperiale from the Japanese government

1

1 | Entrance face
2 | View from interior
3 | Section
4 | Southern aspect

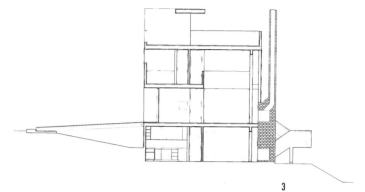

3

4

Skidmore, Owings & Merrill

John Hancock Center | CHICAGO 1965-1968

1

When the John Hancock Center was completed in 1968, a critic wrote the following words and summarized Chicagoans' conflicting emotions toward the building: "Like a fist in the face, the John Hancock Center attacks Chicago's skyline, proclaiming its supremacy despite a backdrop of extraordinary virility." Chicagoans either love or hate the building, affectionately referring to it as "Big John," the true icon of the city, or blaming it for dwarfing the existing urban fabric and providing the impetus for the subsequent high-rise development of North Michigan Avenue.

The John Hancock Center is a monolithic, 1,105-foot (377-meter) tube that tapers elegantly from the base to the top floor. This shape is a reflection of the interior organization — retail, mechanical, and office space on the first 43 floors, and apartments above. An observation deck, a restaurant, and television and mechanical facilities occupy the uppermost floors. The Hancock Center's most salient feature is its cross-bracing, which is actually a structural necessity. This design represented an advancement in the development of skyscraper construction by combining wind-bracing elements with the building's exterior frame. The Hancock's distinctive X-shape braces, each extending across 18 floors, provide stability against the strong gales that blow over Lake Michigan and into "The Windy City." Prior convention called for the construction of separate

framing and bracing systems. In the Hancock Center these systems are merged into one. The cross-braces also allowed SOM to design a building that used significantly less steel than a conventional 100-story skyscraper. There was initial concern, however, that the offices and apartments whose view was partially obstructed by a diagonal brace would be unattractive and difficult to rent. Such fears were unfounded — the "X-apartments" were actually the first to be rented, and have proven to be the most popular over time.

The Hancock Center's location was another source of apprehension. It was built north of the city's downtown core, on a retail street surrounded by residential and cultural areas. Critics thought the Hancock Center's large number of occupants would create serious traffic problems, but instead the building's mixed-use character pre-empted this, since less than half of the total space contained offices. The mixture of uses in the Hancock Center was SOM designer Bruce Graham's idea. His original scheme projected two towers: a 45-story office block and a 70-story residential building. The final scheme combined these separate functions into one 100-story tower. This was a bold step, for at the time there was no precedent for placing apartment space so high off the ground.

Beyond its role as an icon for the city of Chicago, the bold, elegant John Hancock Center was a pioneer for three reasons. First, it demonstrated that a skyscraper need not be an office building exclusively to be successful. Second, the Hancock's structural innovations enhanced, rather than diminished its aesthetic quality. Finally, the Hancock Center proved the skyscraper could grow beyond the rectangular glass box popular in the 1960s to explore new forms of expression. D.A.G.

SKIDMORE, OWINGS & MERRILL

1896	John Merrill is born on August 10 in St. Paul, Minnesota
1897	Louis Skidmore is born on April 8 in Lawrenceburg, Indiana
1903	Nathaniel A. Owings is born on February 5 in Indianapolis, Indiana
1921	Merrill receives a bachelor of architecture degree from the Massachusetts Institute of Technology, Cambridge, Massachusetts
1921-22	Owings attends the University of Illinois, Champaign–Urbana
1924	Skidmore receives a bachelor of architecture degree from the Massachusetts Institute of Technology
1927	Owings attends Cornell University, Ithaca, New York; Skidmore is a visiting scholar at the American Academy in Rome
1936	Skidmore and Owings partnership is formed in Chicago
1939	Merrill joins the partnership, henceforth known as SOM
1942-46	SOM designs Atom City, Oak Ridge, Tennessee for the U.S. government

1949	SOM opens a branch office in San Francisco; subsequent branches are established in Portland, Oregon, Washington, D.C., Boston, Los Angeles, Houston, Texas, and Denver, Colorado
1950	The Museum of Modern Art in New York City runs an exhibition on SOM
1952	Lever House in New York City establishes SOM's reputation as the leading corporate architects in the U.S.
1952-54	Manufacturers' Trust Bank, New York City
1957	Administration Building for the Connecticut General Life Insurance Company, Bloomfield, Connecticut
1962	Skidmore dies on September 27 in Winter Haven, Florida
1965-68	John Hancock Center, Chicago
1971-74	Sears Tower, Chicago; First Wisconsin Plaza Building, Madison, Wisconsin
1975	Merrill dies on June 10 in Colorado Springs, Colorado
1982	National Commercial Bank and airport, Jedda, Saudi Arabia
1984	Owings dies on June 13 in Sante Fe, New Mexico

2

3

1 | View from city
2 | Perspective effect accentuated
    by tapering form
3 | Sky lobby with diagonal bracing
4 | View from Lake Michigan

4

Richard Buckminster Fuller

Pavilion for the World Exposition | MONTREAL 1966-1967

In 1976, when the spherical dome structure of the American pavilion by Richard Buckminster Fuller went up in flames on the former Expo site in Montreal, many observers interpreted it as the end of the futuristic visions of the 1950s and '60s, with their belief in technology, to which Fuller's geodesic domes had lent such paradigmatic expression.

Fuller had developed and tested a wide range of column-free spatial structures derived from the icosahedra that had been patented in 1954. He experimented with various forms and combinations of materials for both civil and military uses, designing a "single-family dome" and serially built accommodation for students, an Arctic research laboratory, military housing and functional enclosures, radar domes, planetaria, workshops, and buildings for representative purposes for large U.S. concerns, as well as the exhibition halls that became a symbol of America at international trade fairs. The U.S. Expo pavilion in Montreal, however, was the largest and most spectacular structure of this kind to be realized. Based on a lightweight demountable or foldable space-frame of steel or aluminium tubes — and occasionally of timber — it allowed structures of unlimited span to be erected. According to needs, these could be covered with plastics or alumi-

num, with polyester-fiberglass, fabrics, or even cardboard. The translucent acrylic-glass skin used in Montreal, fitted with photoelectric cells, proved to be the undoing of this structure when sparks from welding work set it on fire. With a diameter of almost 250 feet (76 meters), the Expo dome was one of the largest of its kind. With a structure weighing 800 tons, it was also one of the lightest.

In using the principles of the geodesic dome, Fuller's aim was not merely to create flexible, mobile spatial elements that could be easily transported, assembled, and adapted to various purposes. He also wanted to create "climatically controlled environments" that, through their low energy use, would make a contribution to saving "Spaceship Earth." In addition, their potential function as gigantic climatic skins was seen as a means of permanently securing the habitability of the earth, both in metropolitan areas of high population density and in less hospitable regions such as the Arctic. As a pragmatic visionary and Utopian with a comprehensive and inexhaustible gift for invention, Fuller developed from a constructor and self-made technologist inspired particularly by practical military applications of his designs — a man who paid innovative tribute to the Modern Movement's functionalist belief in technology — to become an environmental philosopher and engineer who recognized a global responsibility toward the natural resources of the earth. Over and above their technological rationalism, his dome projections were poetically and philosophically enriched by the elevation of their spherical space into a cosmic metaphor. It was not least for this reason that he became the architectural idol of the American hippy generation of the 1960s, which saw the round dome structure as an alternative to the primacy of rectilinear geometry in the architectural conventions of the Western world.   A.G.

RICHARD BUCKMINSTER FULLER

1895	Born on July 12 in Milton, Massachusetts
1913-15	Studies at Harvard University, Cambridge, Massachusetts; after being suspended twice for "lack of interest and irresponsibility," he continues his studies autodidactically
1917	Volunteers for service in the U.S. Navy; is accepted when he places a family motor boat at the disposal of the Navy for use as a patrol boat under his own command
1922	Founds a construction company with his father-in-law, the architect J.M. Hewlett; production of filling materials and lightweight construction elements based on Hewlett's own patent
1927	Forced to withdraw from the company; begins developing the Dymaxion concept; the Dymaxion House becomes a central model of a fully equipped, industrially prefabricated "machine for living in"

1933	Founds the 4D company, later renamed the Dymaxion Corporation; prototype of the Dymaxion car; various projects for prefabricated dwelling units as part of the Dymaxion program; his preliminary studies in the geometry of energetics later form the basis of the development of geodesic domes
1944-47	Planning and development of the Wichita Housing Machine
1947	Begins to develop geodesic domes
1954	Patents a geodesic dome construction system
1957-	Lecture tours and publications
1962	Visiting professor at Harvard University
1963	Adviser to NASA
1966-67	American Pavilion for the World Exposition in Montreal, Canada
1983	Dies on July 1 in Los Angeles

1

2

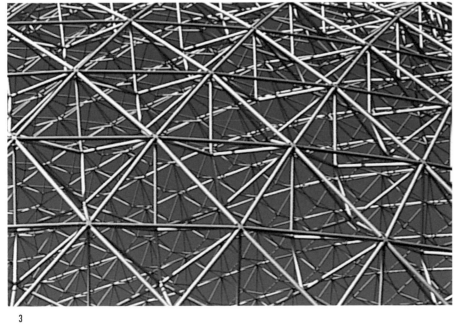

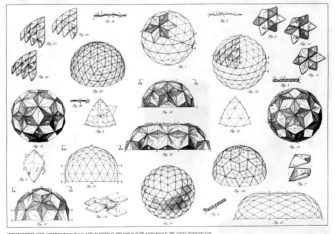

LAMINAR GEODESIC DOME, United States Patent Office no. 3,205,144, filed May 27, 1960, serial no. 32,268, granted August 31, 1965, inventor: Buckminster Fuller

4

1 | Interior view
2 | Pavilion today
3 | Detail of dome structure; present state
4 | Drawings of geodesic dome forms

3

Günter Behnisch with Frei Otto

Olympic Games Complex | MUNICH 1967–1972

1

GÜNTER BEHNISCH

1922	Born on June 12 in Lockwitz, now Dresden, Germany
1947–51	Studies architecture at the University of Technology in Stuttgart, Germany
1952–	Establishes his own office; since 1966, Behnisch and Partners, with changing team members
1963	Technical College, Ulm, Germany
1967–87	Olympic Games Complex, Munich, Germany (completed in 1972); professor for planning, industrial building, and building design at the University of Technology in Darmstadt, Germany
1977	Home for the elderly and nursing home, Reutlingen, Germany
1987	Library of the Catholic University, Eichstätt, Germany
1990	Museum for Post and Communications, Frankfurt-am-Main, Germany
1992	General Assembly of the German Bundestag, Bonn, Germany
1996	St. Benno's School, Dresden, Germany

At one point, the decision hung by a thread. If Egon Eiermann, the chairman of the jury, and various politicians had not intervened on behalf of the tent-roof concept, the competition for the structures for the 20th Olympic Games in Munich, Germany, would have been won by a conventional stadium design. The support given to Günter Behnisch's courageous idea was an expression of the political and intellectual reorientation that was taking place in the 1960s, even in the Federal Republic of Germany. On the other hand, a tried and tested example for the proposed roof structure already existed: the German Pavilion designed by Rolf Gutbrod in collaboration with the structural engineer Frei Otto for the World Exposition in Montreal in 1967.

The West German National Olympic Committee and its president, Willi Daume, had given the participating architects the brief to present the world with a completely different picture of Germany from that staged by the Nazis in Berlin in 1936. Behnisch created this antithesis in ideal form. His design complied both conceptually and architecturally with the motto of the Munich Games: "Olympic Games in green natural surroundings, with short routes; a festival of the muses and sport." Behnisch enjoyed the support of outstanding specialists in various fields: Frei Otto as the structural planner, Günther Grzimek as the landscape architect, and Otl Aicher as the

graphic designer. The Olympic site in Munich is not the work of a single person, but rather an outstanding example of teamwork.

As a piece of "situational architecture," Behnisch's design reflects the conditions of the location and boldly accentuates them by means of various strategic interventions and modifications. What had been a flat area of land — with the exception of a hill created from the rubble of the war — was remodeled into a landscape of gently rolling hills. In contrast to the 951-foot (290-meter) high television tower, the ensemble of buildings was bedded in this newly created park, and the Nymphenburg Canal was dammed up to form a small lake. The transparent, outwardly open sports arenas — the stadium, the Olympic Hall, and the swimming hall — the flowing transitions between architecture and nature, and the experience of alternately constricted and expanding external spaces all helped to create the appropriate setting for the "serene and happy Games" that Munich's government wished to host.

Suspended from 12 steel pylons, the transparent tent roof that extends over all three structures has become emblematic of the entire complex. Above the stadium, the cable network with its perspex sheet covering serves solely as a protection against the rain. Over the two halls, in contrast, it forms the actual roof structure. The hall facades beneath the roof are structurally independent elements designed to balance out fluctuations in temperature and to absorb wind loads. Initially, the tent roof was a highly controversial structure. In the meantime, it has become an internationally acclaimed architectural symbol — not just of the modern city of Munich, but of a new and democratic Germany.   W.J.S.

2

3

1 | Olympic Stadium at night
2 | View into the stadium
3 | Tent roof suspended from steel pylons
4 | Beneath the transparent tent roof
5 | Detail of perspex sheet covering
6 | East–west section through site

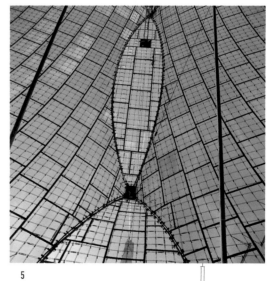

4

5

6

OLYMPISCHES
FEUER

AUFWÄRMHALLE   STADION   ZENTRUM   SCHWIMMHALLE   LIEGEWIESE   RESTAURANT

Herman Hertzberger

Centraal Beheer Office Building | APELDOORN (THE NETHERLANDS) 1968–1972

Around 1960, as a reaction to the increasing desolation that the Modern Movement seemed to exhibit, one of the basic tenets of Dutch structuralism was postulated: a building should be like a miniature town with inviting architecture that would provide people with a hospitable environment for their activities. Since man behaves in an archetypical manner, it was incumbent on architects, the structuralists argued, to create intimate, private spaces as well as communal areas. Alongside Aldo van Eyck, Herman Hertzberger was the leading figure of this movement, the various projects of which exhibited epoch-making significance.

With his administrative headquarters for the insurance company Centraal Beheer in Apeldoorn, the Netherlands, Hertzberger garnered international applause. What was completely new about his design for a large-scale office building was its form — a high-density, low-rise building — and the absence of any hierarchical order or formal, prestigious elements in the spatial organization. The top-lit inner zones, with their eventful sequences of alternately widening and constricted spaces, also contributed to the special character of this "work-ship for a thousand people."

Hertzberger designed the complex as "a kind of settlement." It consists of a series of tightly interlocking volumes based on a square unit plan and rising to a peak at the center. The diagram of the plan structure reveals a cellular layout divided into four quadrants. The groups of black-hatched office units and the lower eastern tract with roof gardens are linked by a communal area that dissects the building in a cruciform system of arcades, passageways, and small squares, with the various entrances located at the ends of these routes. The plan form of this linking area resembles the four vanes of a windmill.

The planning itself began with a question. How could a building in which the staff spent half of its waking time be designed to provide a congenial "domestic" atmosphere? The solution lay in creating a series of interlocking "office islands" that could be used in a flexible manner. Each of the islands has four corner zones, which are fully glazed along their outer edges. They are separated from each other internally, yet at the same time they are linked by voids that extend over the full height of the building. Horizontal access to the office islands is via a regular grid-like network of routes, with glazed bridges across the voids. Subsequent changes in the organization of the building may be implemented without impairing the structure.

Even though this crowning achievement of structuralist architecture remained without a direct sequel, Herman Hertzberger's social concept has been proved sound by the great degree of acceptance it has found among users: "A building must be able to accommodate personal and common activities, meanings, and links; and it must also be able constantly to re-evoke these for everyone."   W.J.S.

HERMAN HERTZBERGER

1932	Born on July 6 in Amsterdam, the Netherlands
1958	Completes studies at the University of Technology, Delft, the Netherlands; own architectural practice
1959–63	Co-editor, Dutch architectural journal *Forum*
1965–69	Lectures at the Academy for Architecture in Amsterdam
1966	Montessori School and Kindergarten, Delft
1968–72	Centraal Beheer Office Building, Apeldoorn, the Netherlands
1970	Professor at the University of Technology, Delft (now the University of Delft)
1978	Music Center, Vredenburg, Utrecht, the Netherlands
1983	Montessori School and Willemspark School, Amsterdam
1986	Housing development in Kreuzberg, Berlin
1990–95	Chairman of the Berlage Institute, Amsterdam; numerous visiting professorships and awards
1992	Ministry for Social Affairs, The Hague, the Netherlands
1995	Chassé Theater, Breda, the Netherlands

1

1 | Eastern section with roof gardens
2 | View between "office islands"
3 | Plan structure: cellular layout
4 | Interior view
5 | Exterior view

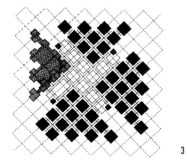

3

4   5

I.M. Pei

East Building of the National Gallery of Art | WASHINGTON, D.C. 1968-1978

I.M. PEI

1917	Born on April 26 in Canton (today Kuang-chou). China
1935	Moves to the U.S.
1940	Bachelor's degree in architecture at the Massachusetts Institute of Technology, Cambridge, Massachusetts
1946	Master's in architecture from Harvard's Graduate School of Design, Cambridge, Massachusetts
1948	Meets New York real estate developer William Zeckendorf and signs on as the director of Webb & Knapp's architectural division
1951	Tours Europe for four months
1952	Mile High Center in Denver, Colorado, and other Denver projects with Zeckendorf
1955	Founds I.M. Pei & Associates along with Henry Cobb and Eason Leonard
1961-68	National Center for Atmospheric Research near Boulder, Colorado
1964-79	John F. Kennedy Library on Columbia Point, Massachusetts, by Boston Harbor
1966	Changes the firm name to I.M. Pei & Partners
1968-78	East Building of the National Gallery of Art, Washington, D.C.
1977-86	West Wing, Museum of Fine Arts, Boston, Massachusetts
1979-82	Fragrant Hill Hotel in Beijing, China
1982-90	Bank of China in Hong Kong
1983	Pritzker Architecture Prize
1983-93	Pyramid and extension, Le Grand Louvre, Paris
1987-95	Rock 'n' Roll Hall of Fame and Museum, Cleveland, Ohio
1988-92	Regent Hotel (Four Seasons), New York City
1989	Firm name changes to Pei, Cobb, Freed & Partners
1991-97	Miho Museum, Shiga, Japan

I.M. Pei's graceful and monumental East Building, an extension of the National Gallery of Art, is a museum addition as refined in its detail as it is unconventional in its space. The elegant surfaces, clear massing, and triangular forms animate the northeast corner of the Mall in Washington, D.C.

The trapezoid formed by the intersection of Constitution and Pennsylvania Avenues provided a challenging site on which to build the addition, particularly since Pei and his clients agreed that the new building should follow the axis of the original museum, John Russell Pope's earlier building, the West Wing of the National Gallery. A conventional, rectangular structure would not efficiently utilize the space of the new site. Pei's brilliant solution, sketched out on a piece of paper during a flight from Washington, D.C., to New York in 1968, was to divide the trapezoid diagonally forming two triangles, a right and an isosceles. The isosceles triangle became the public museum, and the midpoint of its base lined up on axis with the West Wing while the right triangle became the library and research center. This seemingly simple geometric solution created a series of unique places.

The central area of the museum, lit by sunlight streaming in through a glass ceiling of triangular forms, includes open spaces to accommodate large artworks. Several small hexagonal galleries provide intimate settings and offer flexibility in the arrangement of

exhibitions. The acute corners of the building house utilities and provide storage. The research center has its own entrance, and the access points between the museum and the research center are largely hidden from view, so that the visitor has little perception of the activities in the other half of the building. The East Building is connected to the original museum by a subterranean passageway which also houses a restaurant, gift shop, 442-seat auditorium, lecture hall, and parking lot. This concourse is illuminated by natural light from glass sculptures in the courtyard, and water splashes down a glazed wall from a fountain above.

The East Building is a good example of Pei's rigorous detailing. The marble-clad exterior features specially-hewn corners which cut precise 17.5-degree angles. Since the building's opening in 1978, one of these narrow edges near the entrance has been routinely cleaned to remove the stains from the thousands of visitor's who touch the building's edge in awe of its sharpness. On the interior, Pei has refined the use of cast concrete so that it blends harmoniously with the cut stone. The architect's attention to detail can also be observed in the sculptural effect of the scooped-out recesses in the stone around the escalators. In order to match the pink marble of Pope's building, the original Tennessee quarry was reopened, and Pei and the clients carefully selected the slabs of stone by hue and shade.

The museum's clear and graceful geometry, imaginative spaces, and sumptuous details make it one of the most popular monuments of modern architecture. The East Building secured a level of international fame for Pei that would only be surpassed by his Pyramid at Le Grand Louvre in Paris.   J.G.

1

2

1 | Aerial view, showing East and
   West Wings
2 | Entrance front
3 | Aerial view with Capitol Hill in
   background
4, 5 | Views of interior

4

3

5

Sverre Fehn

Archaeological Museum | HAMAR (NORWAY) 1968-1988

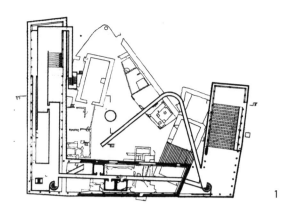

1

In the words of Sverre Fehn, Norway's leading archaeological museum, the Hedmarksmuseum, was conceived as a "floating" structure. It consists of a protective skin inserted within the ruins of a medieval castle near Hamar. Ramps, walkways, and bridges inside and outside the building lead visitors over the excavations and exposed sections of the old structure and past the archaeological objects on display. The route becomes a *"promenade architecturale"* through what would seem today to be a mythical age. The seemingly provisional character of the museum's architecture succeeds in conveying the working atmosphere of the archaeological excavations and brings the visitor a little closer to the period in question. For example, alongside the remains of the old walls, Fehn has set a timber frame structure that supports the roof and evokes the impression of a noble barn-like building; or again, in front of the large, irregularly shaped openings in the walls, he has hung single panes of glass without frames. New elements are constructed in exposed concrete with a rough formwork surface, and are inserted independently within the existing structure, as if they could be removed at any time.

The attraction of this museum lies in the contrast and interaction between past and present, between the irregular historical ruins and Fehn's calm, precise architecture. Using archaic forms of construction in timber, concrete, and glass, the architect creates subtle spatial structures that are mysteriously lighted and that tell a mythical, historical story — like the remains of time in which they are enclosed.

Christian Norberg-Schulz, a leading expert on Scandinavian architecture, has identified a "search for origins" in the architect's approach to the museum: Fehn wanted to reactivate architecture's "basic forms." These elements ap-

pear simple, but they maintain a strict order and are executed with the perfection that modern machinery makes possible.

Fehn himself says that only by building for the present can one enter into a dialogue with the past. He borrows certain features from traditional Norwegian building — the varied forms of construction that are possible with timber, for example — without his architecture becoming "typically Norwegian." In fact, it reveals the influence of various international models.

The oeuvre of this Pritzker Prize-winner contains few large-scale structures. He has kept to a consistent line of thinking in regard to design throughout his life, and this is clearly revealed in the museum building in Hamar. He first became known with his design for the Norwegian Pavilion in Brussels (1958), and the Nordic Pavilion in Venice (1959–62), both of which are clearly indebted to Mies van der Rohe. In the late 1960s and in the '70s, his formal range became broader, and his solutions more complex. The Hedmarksmuseum, the design of which dates from this time, is now regarded as a major work of modern architecture and is recognized far beyond the borders of Norway.

Currently, Fehn is creating works with a bold formal identity, such as the Glacier Museum in Fjaerland, Norway, and his design for the extension to the Royal Theater in Copenhagen. S.S.

SVERRE FEHN

1924	Born on August 14 in Kongsberg, Norway
1949	Registered architect
1958	Norwegian Pavilion for the World Exposition in Brussels
1958-62	Nordic Pavilion, Venice
1968-88	Archaeological Museum, Hamar, Norway
1971-	Professor of architecture at the School of Architecture in Oslo, Norway
1980	Carnegie Distinguished Professorship at Cooper Union, New York City
1981-89	Tutor at the Architectural Association School of Architecture, London
1986	Saarinen Professorship at Yale University, New Haven, Connecticut
1997	Awarded the Pritzker Architecture Prize

2

3

4

1 | Plan of third level
2 | Outdoor area with ramp
3 | Juxtaposition of old stone walls and
    new concrete elements
4 | Large panes of glass over irregular
    openings in walls
5 | Internal ramp

5

Minoru Yamasaki

World Trade Center | NEW YORK CITY 1970-1973

When Minoru Yamasaki was selecting exterior wall material for the World Trade Center, Fritz Close, then the chairman of Alcoa, offered to show him samples of aluminum alloys. Among their advantages were different colors, from which Close offered a shade of pink. "You really aren't serious about making these two large buildings pink, are you?" the architect asked, as he selected a tasteful silver example.

The commission came to Yamasaki's office from the regional Port Authority, which hoped to promote trade in New York by uniting offices, transportation links, shopping, and public space. Yamasaki's architectural response was a five-building complex surrounding a five-acre plaza, but its best known and most visible components are the two 110-story towers in offset placement on the plaza. At 1,362 and 1,368 feet (415 and 417 meters), they spent approximately one year as the world's tallest buildings. Their construction, on the banks of the Hudson River, was made possible by an ingenious slurry-wall foundation process, which allowed shoreline digging.

Yamasaki's towers are monoliths, whose slightly chamfered square floors rise without interruption from the sidewalk to the sky. Structurally, they are distinguished by a loadbearing exterior wall. The exterior grid formed by the floors and columns acts as a vierendeel truss, in contrast to conventional steel-frame and curtain-wall construction.

"The architecture we build should give man an aesthetic and emotional fulfillment," Yamasaki once wrote. Commissions such as the Michigan Consolidated Natural Gas Company in Detroit (1958–63) showed him designing with period Miesian rectilinearity, lightened delightfully by diaphanous walls and screens. Whether critics have found the work Gothic, Islamic, or even organic, Yamasaki at his best has tastefully assuaged America's growing desire for something tactile and humane in straightforward modernism.

In the World Trade Center, though, the architect fell short of his goal. He planned the five-acre plaza to promote street-level activity, and designed a lace-like exterior wall to reduce the scale, modulate light and shade, and minimize acrophobia. Unfortunately, the most notable quality of the buildings is still their overbearing size. This is particularly apparent in the barren, windblown plaza, but also at a distance, where the tight columns of the curtain wall seem opaque; any intricacy is overwhelmed by the exterior walls' uninterrupted run through to their full height. These complaints are extreme versions of indictments that have been leveled at many monoliths of the era, but they seem particularly acute here. And none of these problems would have been solved by making the buildings pink.

C.L.R.

MINORU YAMASAKI

1912	Born on December 1 in Seattle, Washington, to Japanese parents
1930–34	Studies architecture at the University of Washington, Seattle
1934–35	Studies architecture at New York University in New York City
1935–36	Teaches painting at New York University
1935–37	Works as a designer with Githens and Keally in New York City
1937–43	Works for Shreve, Lamb, and Harmon, architects of the Empire State Building; culminates in a position as job captain
1943–44	Works for Harrison and Fouilhoux, New York City
1944–45	Work for Raymond Loewy Associates ends when Yamasaki chooses to give up industrial design for architecture
1945–49	Chief architect and designer for Smith, Hinchman and Grylls, Detroit, Michigan
1949–55	Partnership with Joseph Leinweber in Detroit, Michigan, and with Leinweber and George Hellmuth in St. Louis, Missouri
1951–56	Terminal Building, Lambert Airport, St. Louis, Missouri
1958–63	Michigan Consolidated Natural Gas Company, Detroit
1970–73	World Trade Center, New York City

1

2

3

4

1 | View from Hudson River
2 | Lobby
3 | Detail of facade
4 | Site plan
5 | The monolithic towers
   at night

5

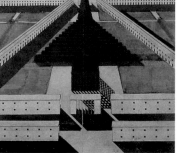

1 | Charnel house: chamber for remains
2 | Interior view
3 | Drawing of overall layout
4 | Drawing of central axis
5 | View through outer enclosure

5

The seemingly banal insight that there is a time for everything — for life and architecture, and for the city, which is a product of the two — is something that Aldo Rossi placed in the forefront of his thinking about design. Before he had realized a single building, he sparked off a process of reorientation with his book, *L'Architettura della città*. The city is the stage on which the theater of life takes place — in its changing face and the enduring qualities of its built fabric, in its architectural images and forms. These themes recur in cities throughout history, even if their underlying function changes. What survives in them is memory, or perhaps more than that, "collective memory."

What might easily have been a routine exercise, namely the planning of a cemetery, became a key project for Rossi: a "city of memories," consisting of "houses for the dead." The shapes of the buildings, familiar archetypes of the dwelling house — or so one always thought — are in fact the forms of ancient graves. Inside, they contain nothing but chambers for the interment of bodies or for urns. Laid out in long rows, they form a double outer enclosure to the cemetery.

Visitors are welcomed by a monumental red cube. Conceived as a charnel house, or chamber for remains, and memorial to the victims of war, it is an "unfinished, deserted house," a built metaphor of death. Beyond this, further graves are planned, increasing in height and culminating in a towering, truncated cone brick that will contain a collective grave for the poor; for it is to them, according to Rossi's proposals, that "the city should build the tallest monument."

Aldo Rossi compared the composition to the layout one might find on the board of a childen's game. He also compared it to the structure of a skeleton. In all events, it has an elemental, seemingly self-explanatory clarity. It is this self-evident quality that roots this location firmly in everyday experience, but that also allots it a special place in life.

Architecture cannot of itself give solace, Rossi says. What determines our image of buildings are the impressions and memories they evoke, both subjective and collective. "To be of any stature, architecture has to forget itself; or it should not create more than a referential image that merges with our memories."

One does not invent memories. It is no coincidence, therefore, if one discovers in this architecture the melancholy of a *pittura metafisica* by Giorgio de Chirico, the enlightening humanity of Ferdinando Fugas's "Cemetery of the 365 Graves" in Naples, or the remoteness of San Michele, the island cemetery of Venice.

In light of this, the incomplete state of the San Cataldo Cemetery hardly matters. The picture of the finished cemetery, as Rossi envisaged it in numerous drawings, can no longer be erased from collective memory or from the history of architecture.   U.M.S.

ALDO ROSSI

1931	Born on May 3 in Milan, Italy
1949–59	Studies architecture at the Polytechnic in Milan
1955–64	Writes regularly for the Italian architectural journal *Casabella — continuità*
1965–71	Lectureship at the Polytechnic in Milan
1966	Publishes the book *L' Architettura della città*
1970	Builds a highly acclaimed housing strip in the Gallaratese II development in Milan
1971	Work begins on the San Cataldo Cemetery, Modena, Italy; Italian teaching authorization withdrawn because of political activities
1972–74	Lectureship at the ETH in Zurich, Switzerland
1973	Makes the film *Ornamento e delitto* (Ornament and Crime)
1975–	Allowed to teach in Italy again; starts teaching architectural composition at the University of Venice
1979	Moors a floating theater structure constructed out of steel and timber off the Dogana al Mare opposite St. Mark's Square in Venice; names it the "Teatro del Mondo"
1981	Publishes his *Scientific Autobiography*
1981–88	Housing block on the Wilhelmstrasse as part of the International Building Exhibition (IBA) in Berlin
1990	Pritzker Architecture Prize
1990–94	Design of the Bonnefanten Museum in Maastricht, the Netherlands
1991–93	Extension of the Linate Airport, Milan
1991–96	Office complex for the Walt Disney Corporation in Orlando, Florida
1992–98	Block on the Schützenstrasse, Berlin
1997	Dies on September 4 in Milan following a road accident

Skidmore, Owings & Merrill

Sears Tower | CHICAGO 1971-1974

The Sears Tower looms over downtown Chicago, an unmistakable symbol of the city's pride in its heritage as the birthplace of the skyscraper. Built in 1974 to a height of 1,468 feet (447.5 meters), the Sears Tower reigned as the world's tallest building until 1996, when it was surpassed by Cesar Pelli's Petronas Towers in Kuala Lumpur by a mere 33 feet (10 meters). It remains a powerful building, merging the achievements of advanced technology with a spare, simple beauty. The Sears Tower epitomizes the aesthetic and functional possibilities inherent in the modern skyscraper form.

In many ways, the Sears Tower is the culmination of Skidmore, Owings and Merrill's (SOM) experimentation with the tall building that began with New York's Lever House in 1952, and included Chicago's other giant, the 1,105-foot (377-meter) John Hancock Center. Sears is a colossus, 110 stories tall and able to accommodate thousands of workers and visitors per day. It also contains staggering services — 102 elevators on eight miles of cable, 25 miles of plumbing, 1,500 miles of electrical wiring, and over 17,000 tons of refrigeration equipment.

The occupants' requirements determined the interior arrangements, which in turn inspired the building's external appearance. The Sears Tower is constructed with a steel frame sheathed in black aluminum and bronze-tinted glass. The structure's most salient features are its setbacks, which seem to refer to the New York skyscrapers of the 1920s and 1930s. Instead of rising straight into the sky, the building's form resembles a series of steps, or as one critic suggested, "staggered stacks of catalogs," referring to Sears, Roebuck and Company's background in the mail-order business. The setbacks are actually byproducts of a structural innovation called the "bundled tube" system. The Sears Tower is a collection of nine framed tubes banded together for maximum support against the gales of the famous "Windy City." Each tube is 75 by 75 feet (approximately 23 by 23 meters) square with no interior columns. All nine tubes rise for the first 49 stories; they then begin systematically to drop off in pairs, leaving seven tubes up to the 65th floor, five up to the 90th floor, and only two tubes to the very top. In addition to providing a distinctive form, the bundled tube construction allowed for a building that was much lighter than the typical Chicago skyscraper. Despite its overwhelming size and scale, however, it remains subservient to nature: in heavy winds, the upper floors of the Sears Tower can rock and sway noticeably off center.

In 1985 SOM remodeled the lobby and commercial concourse levels to make the public spaces more inviting to tourists and shoppers, and more efficient for workers. Another such renovation was undertaken by De Stefano and Partners in the early 1990s when Sears, Roebuck and Company moved out of the building.

The Sears Tower's merger of function, technology, and aesthetics created a memorable building which proudly returned Chicago to the forefront of skyscraper design, and perfectly symbolized the metropolis that the poet Carl Sandburg called the "City of Big Shoulders."   D.A.G.

SKIDMORE, OWINGS & MERRILL
Architects' biographies on p. 110

1

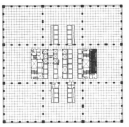

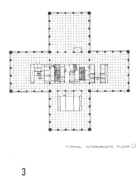

TYPICAL LOWER FLOOR

TYPICAL SKY LOBBY

TYPICAL INTERMEDIATE FLOOR

TYPICAL UPPER FLOOR

3

1 | The tallest building in Chicago
2 | View from Lake Michigan
3 | Floor plans
4 | Reflection of clouds in face of building

4

Renzo Piano and Richard Rogers

Centre Georges Pompidou | PARIS 1971-1977

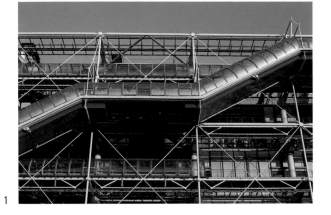

1

The news that two completely unknown, non-French architects had won the first prize in the competition for the Plateau Beaubourg scheme spread like wildfire through the architectural world. Altogether, 681 entries had been received for this international competition which French President Georges Pompidou initiated in 1969 and held in 1971. The site, which had been cleared in the 1930s, lay in the center of Paris, and would host one of the city's most controversial buildings, the Centre Georges Pompidou.

After the presentation of a provocative, radical design for an old Parisian neighborhood, the two young architects were subjected to waves of both enthusiasm and invective. No fewer than seven legal cases were fought with the aim of preventing the realization of the project altogether, or at least stopping the construction work. Without a doubt, the statement contained in the jury report claiming that, "Our age loves the exuberance of life," could not have been more aptly interpreted in all its many meanings.

The great degree of flexibility required by the design brief was taken quite literally by Renzo Piano and Richard Rogers. It called for a cultural center that would be accessible to the public on every floor. Directing the streams of visitors, therefore, had just as great an importance as the layout of the spaces. In response to these constraints, the architects, in close collaboration with the structural engineers Ove Arup & Partners, developed a basic load-bearing framework into which various elements and components could be inserted as required and replaced as needed at a later date.

This economic use of space meant that it was not necessary to build over the whole site, and that it was possible to create a public square to the west of the Centre Georges Pompidou extending almost the entire width of the building. As a result of this open plaza, the architecture can be seen to better advantage — the diagonal line of the escalators, for example. Parisians and visitors alike can also thank the architects for a square in a part of the city that is otherwise not rich in open areas. The public strolls before the backdrop of the building, while jugglers and other entertainers amuse the crowds. No architect could wish for a better location or degree of acceptance.

The visible functional articulation of the building into 13 exposed, load-bearing, steel-frame members is the main architectural highlight. The location of all structural and service elements along the outer edges resulted in an internal space 558 by 157 feet (170 by 48 meters) in extent without intermediate columns. The Centre gains additional space and a depth of almost 20 feet (6 meters) through the cantilevered Gerber girders suspended from the external columns on every floor. These cast-steel elements weigh 9.6 tons and lend the facade, together with the colored tie members and service runs, its characteristic solidity, lightness, and three-dimensionality — qualities that render it both a work of architectural art and an engineering feat of the first order.

The inauguration of the Centre Georges Pompidou in Paris, accompanied by enormous public interest, was like the opening of a second Eiffel Tower; for the "Beaubourg" is every bit as contentious as its famous predecessor, and is regarded as a unique monument to its times.   C.B.

RENZO PIANO, RICHARD ROGERS
Architects' biographies on pp. 169 and 142

1 | Escalators up main facade
2 | Technical installations and service
    runs over the rear face
3 | Section
4 | View over city from escalator
5 | The building in its urban context

2

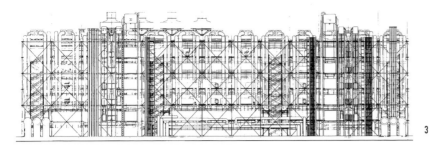

3

4

5

Hans Hollein

Museum Abteiberg | MÖNCHENGLADBACH (GERMANY) 1972-1982

Undoubtedly one of the most irreverent museum designs of the last quarter century, Hans Hollein's Museum Abteiberg in Mönchengladbach, a small city in Nordrhein-Westfalen, Germany, is a celebrated pioneer of postmodernism. Often referred to as an architecture of collage, Hollein's approach to his first large-scale commission was a studied heterogeneity that married a difficult hillside site to a variegated urban context, and generated a modern art museum that is both bewildering and comical.

Set on an east-west axis bounded by a medieval parish church and a modern secondary school, the more than 430,000-square-foot (40,000-square-meter) sandstone-clad steel and concrete structure straddles a slope on the city's southern outskirts that was once inhabited by an abbey complex. The modern plaza around and under which the museum spaces are organized functions as a new town square and hosts the entrance to the main gallery, a hall for itinerant exhibitions, a two-story steel-and-glass administrative tower, and seven titanium-zinc-clad exhibition pavilions.

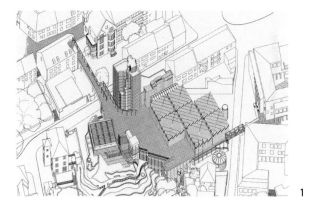

1

HANS HOLLEIN

1934	Born on March 30 in Vienna
1956	Graduates from the Academy of Fine Arts, Vienna, School of Architecture
1958-59	Studies architecture and city planning at the Illinois Institute of Technology in Chicago
1960	Master's degree, University of California, Berkeley, College of Environmental Design
1964	Founds his architecture and design practice in Vienna; Retti Candle Shop in Vienna (completed 1965)
1967-69	Richard Feigen Gallery in New York City; professor of architecture at the Düsseldorf Academy of Fine Arts, Germany
1972-82	Museum Abteiberg in Mönchengladbach, Germany, his first large-scale civic commission
1976-78	Director and teacher at the School and Institute of Design at the Academy of Applied Arts, Vienna (1976); Austrian Travel Bureau in Vienna; Museum of Glass and Ceramics, Teheran, Iran

1979-90	Public School of the City of Vienna, Köhlergasse
1982-90	Museum of Modern Art, Frankfurt-am-Main, Germany
1985	Pritzker Architecture Prize
1985-90	Haas House, Vienna
1988-93	Banco Santander Headquarters, Madrid, Spain, and the Erste Allgemeine Generali Insurance Company, Bregenz, Austria
1994-	Erste Allgemeine Generali Headquarters, Vienna; Vulcania Museum of Vulcanism, Auvergne, France
1996-	Interbank Headquarters, Lima, Peru
1997-	Austrian Embassy, Berlin; Centrum Bank, Vaduz, Liechtenstein; extension to the Museum Abteiberg, Mönchengladbach, Germany
1998-	Museum for the cultural quarter in the new capital of Lower Austria, St. Pölten

To get the full effect of Hollein's playful program, the museum is best approached from the southern base of Abbey Hill. Here Hollein maps out a meandering odyssey of contrasts and collisions: a garden path leads up the slope, slinking its way past serpentine terracing, a deliberate, Gaudíesque parody of adjacent Baroque landscaping. Unexpected encounters with skylights and the artworks revealed below create a confusing sense of not knowing where the garden stops and the museum begins. A flight of stairs meets the path and leads up to the main plaza, but even here no clear architectural hierarchy or visitors' circuit is established. What appears to be the most important building, the administrative block, functions as a folly, an undulating mirrored tower that fails to indicate the entrance. Instead, a white marble slab on the opposite side of the plaza points the way down to the main exhibition hall.

Hollein invites the chaos of the exterior inside, creating a labyrinthine disorder meant to encourage the visitor to wander freely and author his or her own architectural-artistic narratives. Square-plan exhibition chambers grouped in clusters of three and four traverse a matrix stretching from the seven pavilions on the site's northwestern edge around the curve of the hill's southern face. Mute white walls conform to diagonally placed exit and entry portals, and follow topographical nuance with a wanton disregard for the artworks displayed on them.

Instead of achieving a harmonious whole by balancing art and architecture, critics claim that Hollein's design demotes art to a decorative function. But Hollein argues he is staging an architecture that reflects the psychological condition prevalent in today's tangled world of rapidly developing technology and rampant art consumerism. All in all, the building displays the playful opulence of Hollein's previous, smaller commissions, jumbled together in a civic project that is anything but civilized, and confirms its maker as the master of the postmodern.   C.W.H.

2

1 | Axonometric of site layout
2 | Museum square with entrance
    pavilion and administration tract
3 | Aerial view of Abbey Hill
4 | Interior

3

4

1

3

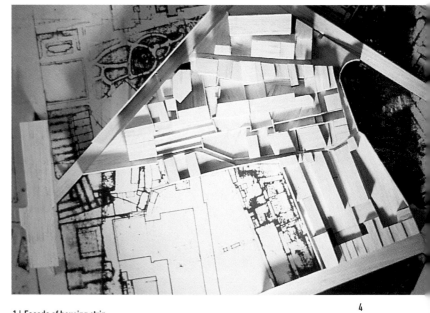

4

1 | Facade of housing strip
2 | View of new facade between old walls
3 | Abutment of new construction with old walls
4 | Model of entire site
5 | Section through dwelling
6 | Street face with passageway through strip

5

Álvaro Siza Vieira is one of the most important Portuguese architects practicing today. With his Schlüterstrasse housing block, built in 1987 as part of the International Building Exhibition (IBA) in Berlin, and a day-care center for children, he has also had an opportunity to realize large-scale works in Germany. From the late 1950s, Siza designed numerous single-family houses and smaller projects, like the Boa Nova Tea House (1958), especially in Portugal. Since the overthrow of the dictatorship in that country in April 1974, he has been intensely involved with social housing schemes.

In collaboration with the architects Tavares and Guedes, Siza was responsible for the rehabilitation and development of the São Victor District of Porto, which comprises a total of 615 dwellings. As one of the first housing projects to be executed after the political revolution in Portugal, it was planned as a step to alleviate the housing crisis that had dramatically worsened during the years of the dictatorship. The scheme was realized partly with public money — it was the first to enjoy the financial support of the state — and partly through self-help measures. It was initiated by the Servicio Ambulatório de Apoio Local, a cooperatively oriented housing aid organization.

The new development was planned for a site where, prior to the overthrow of the regime, a car park had been proposed — a scheme for which a large volume of housing had been sacrificed. The ruined walls and foundations of these demolished buildings were retained in part by the architects and integrated into the new development. The structure designed by Siza comprises a two-story, white rendered strip, the elongated volumes of which assert themselves against the rehabilitated existing fabric. The clear, rhythmically articulated linear form is contrasted with the small-scale, craggy structure of the historical development.

In the IBA scheme, the compact scale of the Berlin street block was translated into an extremely minimal corner development — albeit with a generous curve — possessing a plain facade with punched rectangular openings. This reduction in content earned the block the much-publicized emblematic motto "*bonjour tristesse*," which was sprayed on the walls. The São Victor housing scheme in Porto, in contrast, and the Bouça housing district created at roughly the same time (1973–77), are distinguished by a clearly articulated and differentiated sense of scale. Siza's architectural vocabulary is logically developed from the dialogue between objective, functional form and specific local circumstances. By distilling the essential structural elements, the standard spatial and formal features of the location, such as building heights, entrance situations, proportions, and functional details, he is able to develop architectural elements that are as clearly structured as they are formally restrained, and that avoid all historical allusions. At the same time, they translate the formal language of the Modern Movement convincingly and with a sense of empathy into an architecture that is appropriate to time and place.   A.G.

ÁLVARO SIZA VIEIRA

1933	Born on June 25 in Matozinhos, Portugal
1949-55	Studies architecture and aesthetics at the Escola das Belas Artes in Porto (ESBAP), Portugal; after completing his studies, he works as an assistant to Fernando Távora (until 1958)
1956-63	Competition, planning, and construction of the Boa Nova Tea House in Matozinhos; sets up his own architectural practice
1961-66	De Leca swimming baths, Matozinhos
1964	Casa Alves Costa, Moledo, Portugal
1966-69	Teaches at the ESBAP
1974-	Numerous housing and urban planning projects, including São Victor District Housing in Porto, completed in 1977
1976	Professor for building construction
1977	Overall architectural responsibility for the new Quinta da Malagueira District in Évora, Portugal
1979-	Invitations to participate in international competitions, including the International Building

Exhibition (IBA), Berlin, 1980–87 (Schlesisches Tor housing development, first prize); the rehabilitation plan for Campo di Marte, Venice, 1985 (first prize); the extension of the Salzburg Casino, Austria, 1986 (first prize); La Defensa cultural center, Madrid, Spain, 1989 (first prize)

1983	Urban extension of Macao, Portugal
1983-94	Rehabilitation and public housing in Schilderswijk, The Hague, the Netherlands
1986-93	Teachers' training college, Setúbal, Portugal
1987	Schlüterstrasse housing block, Berlin
1987-93	New architectural faculty building of the University of Porto
1988-93	Galician Museum for Modern Art, Santiago de Compostela, Spain
1992	Pritzker Architecture Prize
1995-98	Portuguese Pavilion for the 1998 World Exposition in Lisbon, Portugal

6

James Stirling with Michael Wilford

Neue Staatsgalerie | STUTTGART 1977–1984

1

James Stirling has said of his Neue Staatsgalerie, or New State Gallery, that although some critics deem it "too monumental," he considers the structure to be "an essential element in a city." The Neue Staatsgalerie was conceived as a history of monuments as well as a contribution to the city of Stuttgart, and has since been considered one of the central works of postmodern architecture.

The design of the museum is intricate, both spatially and stylistically. Temporary exhibitions are organized in the open areas of the interior, while the permanent collection is housed in rooms that recall the layout of nineteenth-century museums. Stirling gestures to earlier art museums with an enfilade of galleries connected by openings that are framed with classically-inspired pediment surrounds. The most overt historical reference made by the plan is to Karl Friedrich Schinkel's Altes Museum in Berlin (1824–28), which Stirling invokes with the rotunda that is located at the center of the complex. This space is not actually part of the museum interior at all; the rotunda is open to the weather and serves as a gathering place for pedestrians that is connected to a pathway that runs across the site. Like the rotunda at the heart of the Altes Museum, the central drum at the Neue Staatsgalerie is the focal

point of the plan, but it departs from the historic precedent by way of its actual physical connection to the city.

A series of ramps around the museum, which is built on a steep site, vaguely recalls the approach to the Acropolis in Athens, while also suggesting another twentieth-century building that likewise invoked this "promenade" experience: the Villa Savoye by Le Corbusier. Stirling painted some of the metal elements employed on the building's exterior in bright colors, perhaps to cite more recent modernist works, such as the Centre Georges Pompidou in Paris. These references to modernist buildings are thrown into violent contrast against the light-colored masonry blocks, the traditional material of monumental architecture. Furthermore, certain aspects of the Neue Staatsgalerie appear to have been derived from earlier Stirling projects. Thus the gallery embodies the history of monumental architecture, as well as the history of the architect's own career. Seen in a less complimentary light, Stirling's Neue Staatsgalerie represents a contradictory postmodernist pastiche of various historic references.

Despite this irony, Stirling insisted that serious urban intentions were the underpinning of his design. The architect argued that the museum constituted one means of repairing the damage that had been done to Stuttgart by "war and post-war rebuilding," and in particular by the highway that separates the site from the city. Stirling also managed to incorporate the ruins of the original 1838 museum building on the site, making the connection to history clear: the postmodern historicism of the Neue Staatsgalerie refers to earlier monumental architecture, as well as to the existing city that it seeks to complement.

K.D.M.

JAMES STIRLING

1926	Born on April 22 in Glasgow, Scotland
1945–50	Attends the University of Liverpool School of Architecture, England
1953–56	Senior assistant with Lyons, Israel, Ellis and Gray, Architects, London
1956	House on the Isle of Wight, England
1956–63	Partnership with James Gowan, London
1958	Teaches at the Cambridge University School of Architecture, England
1959–63	Engineering Department Building, University of Leicester, England
1964–70	Private practice in London; History Building, Cambridge University (completed in 1967); Andrew Melville Hall, St. Andrews University, Scotland (completed in 1968)
1966–71	Florey Building, Queen's College, Oxford University, England
1967–	Davenport Professor, Yale University, New Haven, Connecticut
1969–76	Olivetti Training School, Haslemere, Surrey, England (completed 1972); low-cost housing projects for Lima, Peru

1971	Partner with Michael Wilford; the firm is named James Stirling, Michael Wilford and Associates, London
1977–84	Neue Staatsgalerie, Stuttgart, Germany
1979	Named a fellow of the Royal Institute of Arts, London; work is shown in the exhibition "Museum Projects" at Dortmund University, Germany; additions to the Architecture School at Rice University, Houston, Texas (completed in 1981); new building for the Fogg Art Museum, Harvard University, Cambridge, Massachusetts (completed in 1984)
1981	Pritzker Architecture Prize
1985	Tate Gallery Extension (Turner Museum), Millbank, London
1985–92	B. Brown Melsungen Factory Complex, Melsungen, Germany
1986–96	School of Music, Stuttgart (completed by Michael Wilford and Partners)
1992	Dies on June 25 in London

2

3

5

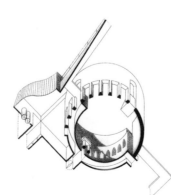

4

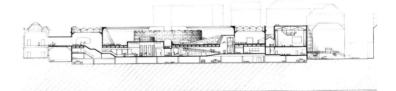

6

1 | Detail of raking, curved glazed
    wall to foyer
2 | External view of foyer at night
3 | View into rotunda
4 | Axonometric drawing of rotunda
5 | General view of exterior
6 | Longitudinal section

Andres Duany and Elizabeth Plater-Zyberk

Seaside | FLORIDA 1978-1983

If you could tour each corner of the world, take the best urban design had to offer, and create a new city, how would you do it? And why? Real estate developer Robert Davis and architects Andres Duany and Elizabeth Plater-Zyberk (DPZ) offer the Town of Seaside in Florida as a built answer to both questions. What post-World War II urban planning has failed to do — generate attractive, decent neighborhoods — Davis and DPZ show is not only preferable, but also imminently possible.

Using a master plan and an urban code called Traditional Neighborhood Development (TND), DPZ, Davis, and local residents found a way to make Seaside an appeal for and proof of effective community-building all in one. The basis of

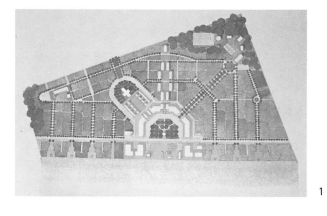

1

TND is simple: honor the human over all else, public spaces over private, and the town plan concept over its architectural parts. Originally, Seaside was envisioned as an inexpensive, low-rise, high-density vacation community of 2,000 residents, organized around civic institutions such as the town hall and public spaces such as parks, streets, walks, and beach. Privately owned houses and shops were to fill in around the core public realm using the five-minute-walk principle: no building would be more than a quarter mile from the civic center, an average of five minutes on foot. This would reduce dependency on cars and encourage residents to meet one another in public, thus creating a neighborhood out of a development.

What architects have built at Seaside in the 20 years since its inception is the result of DPZ's balance of tight urban controls and architectural flexibility. Although the sister to Sea-

side's urban guideline, the building code, is based on traditional local vernacular styles, it does allow for variation. Thus, well-known modernists such as Robert A.M. Stern and Steven Holl have built at Seaside, along with numerous up-and-coming New Urbanists. More importantly, local builders and craftspeople have produced excellent, characteristic buildings at Seaside, demonstrating that DPZ's guidelines are practicable tools for anyone to use, no matter their level of expertise. And perhaps most revealing of the town's significance, Leon Krier, the traditional architect and theoretician who in some 30 years of designing and drafting had refused to build in the modernist condition, completed his very first structure, a wood balloon-frame house, at Seaside in 1989. One year later, the American Academy in Rome gave Seaside its vote of confidence, awarding Davis the prestigious Rome Prize in Architecture.

For all of its success, Seaside is not without shortcomings: its popularity and rarity caused property values to soar shortly after it was founded, resulting in an exclusive resort community instead of the average American town for which the planners had hoped. And, as some critics are quick to note, some of its buildings are so cute as to be kitschy. But Seaside succeeds as a proof of New Urbanist principles not only in its built fabric, but also in its underlying hypothesis: nothing, not even design, is more important in a town or city than the people who live there.

C.W.H.

ANDRES DUANY AND ELIZABETH PLATER-ZYBERK

1949	Andres M. Duany is born on September 7 in New York City; grows up in Cuba until immigrating to the U.S. in 1960
1950	Elizabeth Plater-Zyberk is born on December 20 in Paoli (near Philadelphia), Pennsylvania
1971-74	Both Duany and Plater-Zyberk earn degrees in architecture from Princeton University, Princeton, New Jersey, and graduate degrees from Yale University School of Architecture, New Haven, Connecticut
1974-80	Duany and Plater-Zyberk are founding members of the firm Arquitectonica
1975	Duany and Plater-Zyberk begin teaching architecture and urban planning at the University of Miami, Florida
1978-83	Seaside, Walton County, Florida
1980	Duany and Plater-Zyberk leave Arquitectonica to found their own firm; numerous projects
1993	Along with other reform-minded architects, Duany and Plater-Zyberk are co-founders of the Congress for a New Urbanism
1998-	Duany and Plater-Zyberk develop 140 urban plans in 18 years, including municipal revitalization projects in Los Angeles, St. Louis, Missouri, and Miami; current projects include an urban extension of Toronto, Canada

1 | Master plan
2 | Aerial view of development
3 | Street view
4 | Leon Krier's house
5 | View of gardens

2

3

4

5

1 | Postmodern ornamental gable
2 | Mall
3 | Overall view at dusk
4 | Drawing: elevations and details

1

AT&T (today Sony) Building | NEW YORK CITY 1978-1984

New York's tall buildings or skyscrapers come in two types: the boring and the flamboyant. Philip Johnson helped contribute to both.

Few buildings in recent memory have created such excitement and commentary as the AT&T, from the moment it appeared in an unusual front page article in the *New York Times*, on March 30, 1978, through its ensuing construction, completion, and occupancy. The AT&T Building gave legitimacy to postmodernism, or POMO, which in the late '70s existed on the periphery of acceptable architectural thought. Here in New York City, the world's largest corporation, instead of choosing a safe, ordinary, and boring design, Johnson opted for the fast lane. The AT&T Building became the first POMO skyscraper in New York, and perhaps even killed the movement with parody.

In many respects a simple building, it rises as a vertical slab of 647 feet (197 meters) and 36 stories on Madison Avenue between 55th and 56th Streets. Its uniqueness comes from three features: its ground level, its skin, and its top, or crest. The building faces Madison Avenue with a central entrance arch 116 feet high, while on either side open 60-foot-high rectangular groin-vaulted bays, creating a loggia or arcade for passersby. Historical references abound for the base, with the most commonly cited being the Pazzi Chapel in Florence. At the rear, behind the arcade, sits a 100-foot-high glazed canopy that provides mid-block passage and whose inspiration came from Milan's Galleria Vittorio Emanuele. For the skin of the structure, the architect chose a tan Connecticut granite, which contrasted with the standard employment of glass, aluminum, or other metal panels, commonplace in skyscraper design for over 30 years. Finally, at the top of this tripartite composition sits the crown, or plume, a huge gable-like form with raised molding. Was the top Palladian? Or Baroque? Or, as "wise guy" critics claimed, Johnson had created a giant Chippendale highboy.

One salient feature of POMO was its irony, and the AT&T Building was no exception: during its construction, the company was broken up under court order, and soon after initial occupancy AT&T vacated the building. The Sony Corporation became the new tenant and filled in the arcades with shops. For Philip Johnson, the AT&T Building represented the latest turn in a career that began as an avowed modernist back in 1932 when he, in conjunction with Henry-Russell Hitchcock, unleashed radical European modernism, or the International Style, on America. His Glass House of 1949 was rigorously modern, but beginning in the 1960s he became increasing formalist; with the AT&T he converted to POMO, before moving on, once again, to his latest interest, deconstructivism. As Johnson has said many times, "I would rather be interesting than good."   R.G.W.

PHILIP JOHNSON

1906	Born on July 8 in Cleveland, Ohio
1923-30	Attends Harvard University, Cambridge, Massachusetts, studying classics and philosophy
1932	Mounts the exhibition "Modern Architecture: International Exhibition" at the Museum of Modern Art in New York City; co-authors a book with Henry Russell-Hitchcock, *The International Style: Architecture since 1922*; remains at the MOMA as the director of the Department of Architecture and Design until 1934
1937-43	Studies architecture under Walter Gropius and Marcel Breuer at Harvard University
1946-54	Director of the Department of Architecture and Design, Museum of Modern Art
1949	Glass House, New Canaan, Connecticut
1951	Hodgson House, New Canaan, Connecticut
1953	Sculpture court for the Museum of Modern Art
1954-58	Associate architect with Mies van der Rohe, Seagram Building, New York City
1967-88	Practices architecture in New York City, in partnership with John Burgee
1968	Designs the Kunsthalle in Bielefeld, Germany
1970-76	Pennzoil Place, Houston, Texas
1973	IDS Center, Minneapolis, Minnesota, first major high-rise
1978-84	AT&T Building, New York City, and the somewhat neogothic Pittsburgh Plate Glass Building
1979	Pritzker Architecture Prize
1988	"Deconstructivist Architecture" exhibit at the Museum of Modern Art

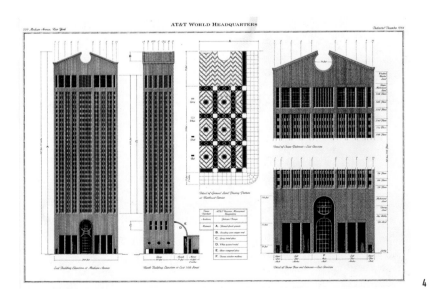

4

Helmut Jahn

James R. Thompson Center | CHICAGO 1978-1985

1

At the Thompson Center (formerly the State of Illinois Center) one finds a remarkable confluence of factors shaping our modernist cities.

James R. Thompson, governor of Illinois between 1977 and 1991, selected Helmut Jahn, the rising star of one of Chicago's oldest and most famous architectural firms, to design the building. The architect's "Romantic Modernism" seeks a revival of modernism's trajectory into a technologically-driven future.

Ironically, Jahn's emphasis on innovative uses of materials and construction technology sometimes pushes architecture dangerously beyond its limits. For instance, the roof of a major arena collapsed; the Thompson Center's original curtain wall was too expensive and unbuildable; and the building's complicated HVAC system required extensive retrofitting. Extending the forms of familiar modernist building types or designs beyond familiar bounds has also led to the ridicule of nicknames — "The Cash Register"; "The Pile of Luggage"; "The Building Coupling with the Board of Trade."

Jahn's work is located in the world at large and in the future, not in an identifiable locale or in a continuity with a premodernist past. His classification of buildings follows modernist types which he calls mats (low or wide buildings), tower buildings, urban block buildings, and transportation buildings. Some structures, especially the larger ones, are composites. Tradition is limited to formal motifs, as in evoking the Chrysler Building in several of his towers, or the central space of the traditional American state capitol with the Thompson Center's rotunda.

The Thompson Center is Jahn's most important completed public commission. It is enclosed almost completely by sleek 17-story curtain walls except at the southeast corner. Here, beyond a shallow apron, a slanted, three-step cylinder sheers back the vertical enclosure, gathering up the open space of the large civic plaza fronting the city and county government buildings diagonally opposite it. Beyond the entrance and visible from a distance is the vast interior rotunda, 160 feet (49 meters) in diameter. Projecting as a cylinder above the building's lower mass, its top, a drum without a dome, slants to inflect toward the plaza. The 1,150,000 square feet (106,800 square meters) of office space for 156 state agencies is arrayed between the rotunda's skin and the outer walls.

Within the rotunda escalators plunge into the commercial concourse linking several blocks and subway routes. Ringing its interior are ascending ranks of offices laced together with catwalks, stairways, and files of glass elevators. Brightly painted, exposed structural members high above and all around; polished colored stone floors; glistening panels of reflective, clear, and opaque glass in various shades of patriotic red, white, and blue; all this in a volume raked by direct sunlight flowing through the drum and extensive exterior glazing produces a vertiginous effect. Here clear focus and easy comprehension are impossible. Here, in what is clearly not the past, one must be in the future.   C.W.W.

HELMUT JAHN

1940	Born on January 4 in Nuremberg, Germany
1965	Graduates from the Technische Hochschule in Munich, Germany; works briefly for Munich architect P.C. von Seidlein
1966-67	In Chicago he pursues graduate studies at the Illinois Institute of Technology, working with the successors of renowned architect Mies van der Rohe
1967-73	Works under Mies' student Gene Summers, a principal at C.F. Murphy Associates
1973-74	Kemper Arena, Kansas City, Missouri
1975	Corporate member, American Institute of Architects
1978-82	Xerox Center, Chicago (completed 1980); Chicago Board of Trade extension
1978-85	The State of Illinois Center, subsequently renamed the James R. Thompson Center, Chicago
1981	First of various teaching positions, at the University of Illinois in Chicago; principal, then president (1982), and finally president and CEO, Murphy/Jahn (1983)
1983-87	United Airlines Terminal, O'Hare International Airport, Chicago
1984-87	Northwestern Atrium Center, Chicago, on the site of a historic railway station
1984-88	Wilshire/Westwood Tower, Los Angeles; One Liberty Plaza, Philadelphia, Pennsylvania
1985-91	Messe Tower/Messe Hall, Frankfurt-am-Main, Germany
1988-94	Hitachi Tower/Caltex House, Singapore (completed in 1993); Ku-Damm 70, Berlin
1989-94	Munich Order Center, Munich (completed in 1993); Pallas Office Building, Stuttgart, Germany; Hotel Kempinski, with Munich Airport Center (1990-96)
1993-99	21st Century Tower, Shanghai, China (completed in 1997); Sony Center, Berlin
1994-	Bangkok International Airport

1 | The building in its
    urban context
2 | Inside the rotunda
3 | Plan of center
4 | Section

2

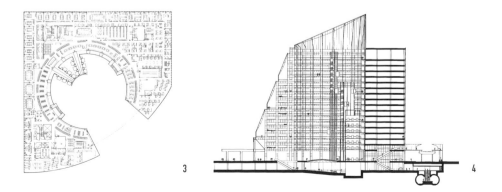

3

4

Richard Rogers

Lloyd's of London | LONDON 1979-1984

Richard Rogers won the commission to design Lloyd's of London as the result of a limited competition. The brief was for a building that would cater to the needs of the market into the 21st century. The flexibility of the high-tech design has been proven as it has successfully coped with an organization which, when the building opened, still used handwriting for the majority of transactions, but which, within five years, was fully computerized.

The origins of Lloyd's date back to the seventeenth century, when the business of insuring risks was carried out in the coffeehouses of the city. It is now the center of world insurance, but the methods of business still follow the traditional practices of the market place. The syndicates of underwriters work from "boxes" or stalls in the large open space of the double height "Room" which is the heart of the structure. From its center, the atrium rises to the full height of 305 feet (93 meters), bringing light down into the Room; it also allows the expansion of the market area upwards into the building. At the base of the atrium is the Lutine bell, which is rung at times of disaster when the insurers are likely to have to pay out.

The most remarkable aspect of the Lloyd's building is the externalization of the services, which allowed the architect to provide a clear and unobstructed space within the main office areas. The separation of the services from the main building structure is geared to the life cycles of the various elements. Whereas the main building has a long life expectancy, the towers are fitted with service equipment which is changed at regular intervals. The lifts, toilets, kitchen, and fire stairs, crowned by the three-story plant rooms, sit on a precast concrete framework, and are easily accessible for

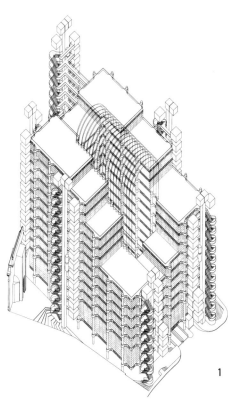

1

maintenance and replacement. Each element, clad in stainless steel, is designed to express its function clearly and to differentiate the parts of the building.

The variety and complexity of the facades respond to the rich architecture of the surrounding city. The fragmented silhouette fits more appropriately with the historic skyline than the pure geometric form of many modern structures.

The main building facade uses triple glazing with a cavity through which surplus warm air is drawn. This creates a near constant temperature on the inner glass surface, providing a comfortable perimeter zone and ideal conditions for operating the heating and air conditioning. Exhaust air is extracted through the large circular light fittings located in each ceiling coffer.

All the structural, cladding, and internal components of the six service towers were prefabricated off-site and assembled as a kit of parts. The 33 toilet modules were delivered to the site fully clad and fitted out, including the marble washbasins. In contrast, the eighteenth-century Committee Room at the top of the building was designed by Robert Adam for Bowood House in Wiltshire, and its neoclassical plasterwork was restored and rebuilt within the new building.   P. M.

RICHARD ROGERS

1933	Born on July 23 in Florence, Italy
1954–59	Studies architecture at the Architectural Association School, London
1961–62	Studies at the Yale University School of Architecture, New Haven, Connecticut
1963–68	Team 4, partnership with Sue Rogers and Norman Foster and his wife
1967	Reliance Controls Factory, Swindon, Wiltshire, England
1971–77	Partnership with Renzo Piano, London/Genoa; Centre Georges Pompidou in Paris with Piano
1977	Founds Richard Rogers Partnership, London
1979–84	Lloyd's of London Headquarters, London
1982	Microprocessor Factory, Newport, Wales
1986	Chevalier de l'Ordre Nationale de la Légion d'Honneur
1988	Renovation of Billingsgate Market, London
1991	Rogers is knighted
1992	Commercial building Kabuchi-cho, Tokyo
1994	Channel 4 Building, London
1995	European Court for Human Rights, Strasbourg, France
1996	Member of the House of Lords, Labour peer
1997–	Millennium Dome, Greenwich, England
1998–	New Area Terminal (NAT), Barajas International Airport, Madrid, Spain

1 | Axonometric drawing
2 | Atrium: "The Room"
3 | Overall view
4 | Section

2

3

4

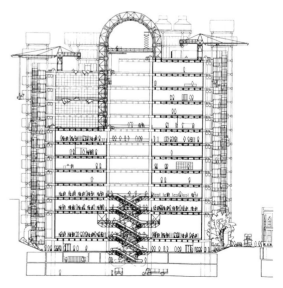

1 | Detail of atrium
2 | Overall view
3 | East–west section
4 | Atrium

1

2

Norman Foster

Hong Kong & Shanghai Bank | HONG KONG 1979-1986

In 1979, Michael Sandberg, president of the Hong Kong & Shanghai Banking Corporation, invited seven architects to design "the most beautiful bank in the world." Norman Foster, the winner of the competition by unanimous vote, gave Sandberg what was at that time the most expensive building in the world. The 47-story, 590-foot (180-meter) high administrative headquarters of the bank, built on the site of the former first branch office amidst the steepling skyscrapers of Hong Kong Island, cost some 5 billion Hong Kong dollars.

Foster was 44 years old at the time, and the Hong Kong & Shanghai Bank was the first skyscraper in his list of works. Without any great experience in the field of high-rise building, he made a close study of the site and the urban environment at the beginning of the competition. For an enthusiastic advocate of technology such as Foster, the dense, dramatic urban context represented a fascinating challenge. With great élan and in collaboration with the structural engineers Ove Arup & Partners in London, the architects set about defining and investigating all previous high-rise architecture.

In addition to optimizing the economic performance of the building — for example, through built-in flexibility and energy-saving measures — an improved working environment was also to be achieved. Maximum exploitation of daylight, open working areas, and extensive open spaces became the leitmotifs of the planning. The formal design and the fitting out were to be entirely new; no standard elements were used. In developing the details of the building, many models were created, some of which were constructed to full size, also contributing to the high cost of the scheme.

Foster finally decided in favor of a rectangular plan form with service towers at the east and west ends. The building has a steel load-bearing structure, consisting of eight masts — each comprising four linked cylindrical members — tied together at three levels by huge girders. The individual stories are suspended from this structure, facilitating the creation of open facades and allowing views out of the building to the north and south. The processes of prefabrication and assembly also formed part of the planning. The restricted area of the site and the resulting lack of storage space led to the prefabrication of all elements, from the steel frame structure to complete mechanical service modules. Only the final assembly and installation took place on site.

Without doubt, the architectural sensation of the scheme is that one does not simply walk into the building, but "experiences" the act of entry. Customers and other visitors ascend into the main banking hall via two escalators that lead through a curved glass membrane, a transparent "belly." Extending above this is a 10-story-high atrium space. Flooded with natural light refracted from a "sunscoop" on the outer face of the building, this space bears a certain resemblance to the interior of a cathedral. Two bronze lions keep guard outside the bank. They are the only surviving elements of the former building. According to popular belief, to touch them before entering the bank brings good luck. C.B.

NORMAN FOSTER

1935	Born on June 1 in Manchester, England
1956-62	Studies architecture in Manchester and at the Yale University School of Architecture, New Haven, Connecticut
1963	Team 4 architectural practice founded with Richard and Sue Rogers and Wendy Cheeseman, who later becomes Foster's first wife
1967	Founding of Foster Associates together with Wendy Foster
1968-83	Collaboration with Richard Buckminster Fuller and others on the Climatroffice project
1969	Administration and leisure center for Fred Olsen Ltd., London
1975	Administrative headquarters for Willis, Faber and Dumas, Ipswich, England
1978	Sainsbury Centre for the Visual Arts, University of East Anglia, Norwich, England
1979-86	Hong Kong & Shanghai Bank, Hong Kong
1983	Sales center for Renault UK Ltd. in Swindon, England
1985-87	Furniture system for Tecno, Milan, Italy
1989	Office building for Stanhope Securities, Stockley Park, near London
1990	Broadcasting building for the British TV channel ITN in London
1991	Stansted Airport, London's third airport, and the Century Tower, Tokyo
1993-98	Reichstag redesign, Berlin
1994	Gold Medal, American Institute of Architects
1997	Commerzbank, Frankfurt am Main, Germany

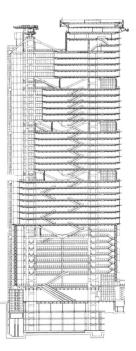

3

4

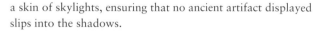

1

Rafael Moneo

Museum of Roman Art | MÉRIDA (SPAIN) 1980-1985

The steep brick walls of the Museum of Roman Art in Mérida, Spain, may appear to pay homage to neighboring ancient structures, but this more than 43,000-square-foot (4,000-square-meter) building shares little of the classical character of the adjacent Roman theater and aqueduct, and is minimally contextual, relying fully on modern functionalist principles for appearance and program. Its Corbusian clarity made Rafael Moneo famous, and introduced the world to the architect's mature work and dedication to modernist principles of design.

The structure's exterior offers a variety of profiles and perspectives: the eastern elevation, belonging to the administrative wing, is a surprisingly domestic, two-story building with shuttered dormer windows. This block also includes the principal, south-facing entrance, marked by a massive marble plinth spanning a broad brick arch, announcing, MVSEO. The south, west, and north faces of the far larger exhibition hall reveal a completely different character, an unscaleable Gothic box rhythmically articulated by buttressing and punctuated with high-set industrial windows.

Moneo organized the interior of the three-level museum around a central atrium according to administration, exhibition, and restoration spaces. A ramp leads down from the entry portal into the gallery space, a cavernous interior draped in webs of semi-circular arches. Critics have likened the effect of light streaming in from warehouse-like windows set high in the gallery walls to John Soane's Bank of England and Piranesi's prisons. However, the interior is kept bright by a skin of skylights, ensuring that no ancient artifact displayed slips into the shadows.

Contrary to its Romantic atmosphere, the exhibition space is rationally composed of a series of parallel walls bridged by semi-circular brick arches, creating one central nave and a series of corridors running perpendicular to it. To give this masonry grid a modern mien, Moneo applied an updated version of an ancient construction method known to the Romans as *opus caementitium*: the result is an almost uncomfortably tight built fabric and an intentionally abstract look that is eased somewhat by the pale yellow-pink tone of the Seville bricks themselves. The contrast between ancient technique and Moneo's updated approach can be seen in the museum's basement level, where arches open over an ancient cemetery, basilica, and house preserved in situ, with a tunnel connecting the museum to the adjacent archaeological site.

The third functional element, restoration workshops, is connected to the gallery and administration wings by a series of steel-railed ramps and stairways around the atrium space, a centralizing force in the overall composition. Dependent as the building is upon these elements to perform as a museum, and eschewing, as it does, the classical approach that employs building types, the structure could hardly be called a bridge to antiquity. Instead, it is a bridge over antiquity, a leap out of the current of tradition and the lessons of ancient architecture into a self-referential style of building, custom-made to fit the site, and tailored to contemporary modernist expectations.

C.W.H.

RAFAEL MONEO

1937	Born on May 9 in Tudela, Navarra, Spain
1956–61	Diploma in architecture, Technical School of Architecture in Madrid, Spain; works in the offices of architect Francisco Javier Sáenz de Oíza
1961–62	Works with Jørn Utzon, architect of the Sydney Opera House, in Hellebaek, Denmark
1963	Two-year fellowship to the Spanish Academy in Rome; subsequent professorships at the Universities of Madrid and Barcelona, Spain
1968–71	Urumea Apartment House in San Sebastián, Spain, with Marquet, Unzurrunzaga, and Zulaica
1973–76	Bankinter Headquarters in Madrid and the Longroño Town Hall, Spain, with Ramón Bescós
1976–77	Visiting professor at the Institute for Architecture and Urban Studies in New York City, and various other universities
1980–85	Museum of Roman Art in Mérida, Spain
1982–88	Bank of Spain Headquarters in Jaén, Spain, and the Provisión Española Insurance Co. Headquarters in Seville, Spain
1985–90	Chairman of the Architecture Department, Harvard University Graduate School of Design, Cambridge, Massachusetts
1987–92	San Pablo Airport in Seville and the Pilar & Joan Miró Foundation, Palma de Mallorca, Spain
1988–93	Diagonal Building, Barcelona, with Manuel de Solá-Morales
1994–98	Museums of Modern Art and Architecture, Stockholm, Sweden
1996	Pritzker Architecture Prize; Gold Medal of the French Academy of Architecture; Gold Medal of the International Union of Architects
1998–	Projects being completed: the Potsdamer Platz Hotel and Office Building, Berlin (begun in 1993), and the Audrey Jones Beck Building for the Museum of Fine Arts, Houston, Texas

2

3

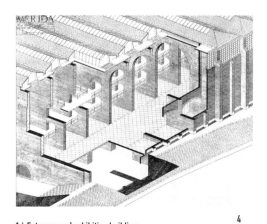

4

5

6

1 | Entrance and exhibition building
2 | Aerial view during construction
3 | Exhibition hall
4 | Isometric drawing
5 | Roof lights between walls with
   round-arched openings
6 | Access to the three levels via stairs
   and bridges

Jean Nouvel

Institut du Monde Arabe | PARIS 1981-1987

1

"The most important material in this building, as in Arab architecture, is light." Jean Nouvel

Relations between the Arabs and the French have been, historically, somewhat ambivalent. It is all the more remarkable, then, that a center dedicated to the culture of the Arab world should be planned and built in the heart of Paris during the Mitterrand era. The competition, held jointly in 1981 by France and 19 Arab states, was won by the French architect Jean Nouvel. With the Institut du Monde Arabe, which has been highly acclaimed by architectural critics, he achieved an international breakthrough.

The design brief required a museum, together with a library, conference rooms, and space for the administration, that would promote understanding of the Arab world in France. Two of the aims of this scheme were fraught with problems: the concept of linking Arab and European traditions, and the urban context on the left bank of the Seine, where the buildings of the Jussieu University dating from the 1960s impinge upon the old urban fabric of Paris. Nouvel exploited these oppositions in an attempt to create a synthesis of European, rational, highly technological architecture and Arab culture on the one hand, and a synthesis of the traditional urban tissue of Paris and modern university life on the other hand.

As a first step, Nouvel placed two large, strictly geometric volumes on the site to respond to the varying urban contexts. The northern tract, which houses the exhibition spaces, takes up the curving line of the Seine, while the southern tract, containing the library, is oriented to the neighboring university. The two volumes are divided by a narrow slit that begins in a square courtyard modeled on similar spaces in Arab palaces, and which is aligned at its opposite end with the cathedral of Notre Dame. It is a symbol, therefore, of the dialogue between European and Arab cultures, and thus one of the central metaphors of the complex. Another major design element is the multi-layered quality of the facades. The north face is turned toward the historical city of Paris and adopts the horizontal articulation of its facades. The silhouette of the city with its main monuments was printed on the Institut's glass front using a silk-screen process, so that when one looks across to the Ile Saint-Louis, serigraph and reality are overlaid.

The highlight of the complex, however, is the south facade, the sunscreening of which takes the form of thousands of diaphragms that open and close, depending on the angle of incidence of the sun. The ornamental effect was inspired by latticework window screens in Arab architecture. Inside the building, a rich interplay of light and shade is created. The theme of Nouvel's architecture — to move away from a purely sculptural quality, as still postulated by modern architecture, toward an ever greater degree of dematerialization — is particularly evident in this work. Light, which dissolves matter, becomes the main design element. A game of transparency and light deflection, an interplay of substantial and insubstantial elements, is set in motion, and lends the building its sense of poetry.   K.W.

JEAN NOUVEL

1945	Born on August 12 in Fumel, southwest France
1966-71	Studies at the Ecole des Beaux-Arts in Paris
1970	Sets up his first office, together with François Seigneur, while still a student
1981-87	Institut du Monde Arabe, Paris; awarded the Equerre d'Argent prize for the best architectural work in France in the year of its completion
1985-87	Experimental housing, Nemausus 1, Nîmes, France
1986-93	Opera House, Lyons, France; also awarded the Equerre d'Argent in 1993
1988	Architectural practice Jean Nouvel, Emmanuel Cattani et Associés (until 1994)
1991	Mediapark, Cologne, Germany
1991-94	Foundation Cartier, Paris
1991-95	Euralille Center, Lille, France
1991-96	Galeries Lafayette, Berlin

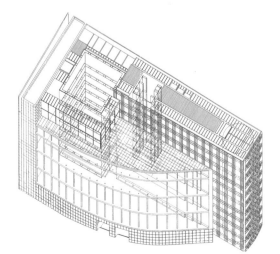

2

1 | View from courtyard to sky
2 | Axonometric drawing
3 | View from northwest
4 | Conference room
5 | Detail of library facade
6 | South face with latticework
    ornamentation to windows

3

4

5

6

Arata Isozaki

Tsukuba Center Building | TSUKUBA (JAPAN) 1983

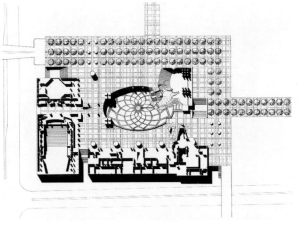

1

"It seems to me," the architect Arata Isozaki said in an interview in 1986, "that Japan is strangely disunited. It has no clear form anymore and no character of its own. . . . That was a real problem for me; for how is one to represent something that no longer has a clear-cut definition?"

By the 1970s, incredible industrial growth and the urban expansion to which this led had destroyed all traces of an independent Japanese culture. No generally accepted rules existed anymore, and in such an environment, there was scarcely anything that could surprise anyone. With his Tsukuba urban center, Isozaki sought a way out of this dilemma for himself by designing an artificial counter-world. What at first glance seems simply to be playful architecture run wild was in fact the first development to criticize the typically heterogeneous and chaotic Japanese cityscape, and at the same time to recognize it as a source of inspiration.

ARATA ISOZAKI

1931	Born on July 23 in Oita, Japan
1954	Completes studies in the Faculty of Architecture, University of Tokyo; works in Kenzo Tange's office
1959–60	Oita Medical Hall, Oita
1963	Arata Isozaki & Associates founded in Tokyo
1966–67	Fukuoka City Bank, Oita Branch
1966–70	Expo '70 — Festival Plaza, Osaka, Japan
1968–71	Fukuoka City Bank, Head Office, Fukuoka, Japan
1971–74	Museum of Modern Art, Gunma, Japan
1972–74	Kitakyushu City Museum of Art, Fukuoka
1973–74	Fujimi Country Club, Oita
1976–78	Kamioka Town Hall, Gifu, Japan
1981–86	Museum of Contemporary Art, Los Angeles
1983	Tsukuba Center Building, Tsukuba, Japan
1983–85	Palladium Club, New York City
1984–90	Sant Jordi Olympic Hall, Barcelona, Spain
1986–90	Art Tower Mito, Ibaraki, Japan
1987–90	Team Disney Building, Orlando, Florida
1991–92	Guggenheim Museum, Soho, New York City
1991–95	Kyoto Concert Hall, Kyoto, Japan
1992–96	Nara Convention Hall, Nara, Japan; Nagi Museum of Contemporary Art, Nagi, Japan
1992–97	Office building, Potsdamer Platz, Berlin

Tsukuba, a city of science 50 miles (80 kilometers) from Tokyo, has been under construction for 30 years. The brief with which Isozaki was confronted for the Tsukuba Center was characteristic of the situation at the time when it was drawn up. It required an 11-story hotel with the usual banqueting and festival halls, an auditorium, and an underground shopping center. The nondescript mixture of modern functions foreseen for the new urban development had been repeated throughout Japan in the 1970s with the regularity of a metronome. Isozaki's achievement lay in making the arbitrariness of this program and of the environment the actual inspiration for his architecture. He thereby liberated himself from the constraints of modernism and rationalism, which had determined the appearance of architecture in Japan since World War II.

Isozaki created a complex laid out about a courtyard, the center of which is a direct quotation — in the form, dimensions, and design of the pavings — of the Campidoglio (Capitoline Hill) in Rome. The striking oval layout of the sixteenth-century public space was created by Michelangelo, and is one of the most important architectural works of the Italian Renaissance. In Tsukuba, the square also contains fountains, amphitheaters, and artificial trees, which ultimately differentiate it from the Roman model. In the middle of Japan, a bizarre, decorative, and rather uncanny world of three-dimensional quotations has been created whose references are to be found everywhere and nowhere. The buildings laid out about this mannerist ensemble are also alienated by means of architectural collage. The uniform facades are broken down into an unexpected variety of contradictory materials and geometric forms. Polished, gleaming metal elements are juxtaposed with primitive, roughly hewn stone, or, as in the hotel, large colored windows are contrasted with an industrially prefabricated facade system. Isozaki created a world of baroque profusion in which various ages and cultures collide with each other. The architect developed a range of instruments by which architectural forms could be generated in a new and hitherto unknown manner — a superimposition of new and old, familiar and unfamiliar elements that still provoke strong critical reactions today.

W. K.

2

3

4

1 | Site plan
2 | View from east
3 | Hotel tower
4 | Courtyard design with architectural
quotations and references
5 | Architectural collage

5

Coop Himmelb(l)au

Attic Conversion | VIENNA 1983; 1987-1988

They wanted to change the world, but whether that would ever be possible through architecture was uncertain. The firm's original name, "Coop Himmelblau," meaning literally, Coop "The Blue of the Heavens," was more a description of a vital consciousness, the *joie de vivre* of the '60s, than of an architectural practice. In contrast to the tough, politically committed designers of that generation, the cooperative, as part of the international situationist movement, initially sought to gain possession of urban space with various happenings. Slogans such as "Architecture is now!" that could just as well have come from an advertising agency were tossed to journalists who lay in wait, watching for built results.

The attic conversion for a lawyers' practice in Vienna's historic city center proceeded slowly against this background. The initial sketches were produced in 1983, but when translated into proper plans, the scheme seemed too risky and had trouble gaining planning permission. Since the design did not provide a continuous roof surface, oriels, and turrets, and did

not respect the materials, proportions, and colors found in the existing urban context, the authorities failed to recognize it as a building at all. The mayor at that time found a way out of the dilemma: he declared the roof to be a work of art, and gave the project his blessing.

The "skin" of this sculptural space was supported by a raking steel-trussed girder with welded tie members. Supported at the sides and spanning the corner of the building, like the vertebrae of an exposed spine, it points like an energy vector down toward the street. Fixed to this cold bolt of lightning, which forms the principal element of the load-bearing structure, are folded plates, planar structures, and trussed struts. The roof membrane of the roof comprises curved sheets of glass, sheet-metal latticework, panels, and shingles. The whole resembles a snapshot of a disastrous collision, yet nothing actually moves. According to the structural engineer, the complexity of the calculations required for the load-bearing structure lay between those for a "bridge and an aircraft." The scheme's impenetrable deconstructivism — a movement for which the architects actually showed no great enthusiasm — obviously made the engineers uncomfortable.

The various coverings on the exterior determine the views out and the ingress of daylight for the large conference room, which has a maximum height of almost 26 feet (8 meters), and also contains a gallery level. The roof swerves over the lawyers' vast conference table like a constructional thunderstorm, inevitably with a number of unorthodox abutments between the various elements.

Since this project's completion, Coop Himmelb(l)au has addressed the issue of true construction. The parentheses around the letter "l," which the firm added to its name in 1990, is one indication of this, changing "the blue of the heavens" into "real building." "The harder the times, the harder the architecture," they once remarked — and they have remained true to their motto.   W.B.

COOP HIMMELB(L)AU

1942	Wolf D. Prix is born on December 13 in Vienna
1944	Helmut Swiczinsky is born on January 13 in Posen, Poland; grows up in Vienna
1962-69	Prix studies at the University of Technology in Vienna, the Southern California Institute of Architecture in Los Angeles, and the Architectural Association in London
1963-69	Swiczinsky studies at the University of Technology in Vienna and at the Architectural Association in London
1968	Prix, Swiczinsky, and Rainer Michael Holzer found Coop Himmelblau in Vienna; Holzer leaves the group in 1971
1977	Reiss Bar, Vienna
1981	Roter Engel Song Bar, Vienna
1983-89	Open House, Santa Monica, California (unrealized project); attic conversion, Falkestrasse, Vienna
1985	E. Baumann Studio, Vienna
1986	Wahliss Arcade, Vienna; directors' story, ISO Holding, Vienna
1987	Ronacher Theater, Vienna (unrealized project)
1988	Architectural Prize of the City of Vienna; the firm opens an office in Los Angeles
1988-89	Funderwerk, St. Veit/Glan, Austria
1991	Frank Stepper becomes a partner in the firm
1991-95	Seibersdorf Office and Research Center, Seibersdorf, Austria
1993-94	East pavilion of the Groningen Museum, Groningen, the Netherlands
1993-98	UFA cinema center, Dresden, Germany
1994-98	SEG housing tower, Vienna
1996	Austrian representatives at the Venice Biennale

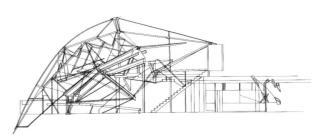

2

3

5

4

1 | Section
2 | Conference room
3 | View to Baroque urban surroundings
from conference room
4 | Plan of layout
5 | Roof (de)construction

Johan Otto von Spreckelsen with Paul Andreu

La Grande Arche | PARIS 1983-1989

Together with the Louvre Pyramide, the Parc de la Villette, and the new Bibliothèque Nationale, La Grande Arche was one of the first of the Paris "Grands Projets" to be realized. Completed in 1989, it forms part of a spectacular program of urban redevelopment in the city undertaken in the 1980s and pursued with great vigor by the late president, François Mitterrand.

Situated to the west of the city at the center of a gigantic concrete platform, on which the tower blocks of La Défense rise to form a late-modernist urban crown, the tall, cubic, gate-like structure of La Grande Arche extends the historical east-west axis from the Louvre, via the Champs-Elysées and the Avenue Charles de Gaulle, and sets a new urban landmark at its terminus. The gateway also establishes a modern counterpart to the neoclassical Arc de Triomphe built by Jean-François-Thérèse Chalgrin between 1806 and 1835.

La Grande Arche was the outcome of an international competition held in 1983 and won by the Danish architect Johan Otto von Spreckelsen. His idea was not only to set a new architectural landmark at the end of the historical axis, but to create a powerful urban center in the office and residential district of La Défense, which had been built at the beginning of the 1960s and had since then suffered from increasing desolation.

JOHAN OTTO VON SPRECKELSEN

1929	Born on May 4 in Copenhagen, Denmark		"Grands Projets": his project initially ties for
1958	Builds his own house near Copenhagen		first prize with that of Jean Nouvel, and is sub-
1967	Wins first prize for town design from the		sequently chosen as the winning entry out of
	Danish State Art Foundation		a total of 424 submissions
1968–80	Builds housing and churches in Copenhagen	1984	Begins his formal association with Frenchman
1971	Wins another first prize in town design		Paul Andreu, an engineer and architect who
	for a new development in Kristiansstad,		had won the Grand Prix d'architecture in 1977,
	Sweden		and whose specialty is airport design
1978–87	Director of the architecture department at the	1984–89	Von Spreckelsen and Andreu build La Grande
	Royal Academy of Fine Arts, Copenhagen		Arche, which is completed after von Spreckel-
1983	Enters the competition for La Grande Arche in		sen's death
	Paris, one of President François Mitterrand's	1987	Dies on March 18 in Copenhagen

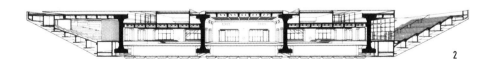

2

Von Spreckelsen's project originally comprised an open cube 361 feet (110 meters) high and 348 feet (106 meters) wide, the roughly 62-foot (19-meter) wide side tracts of which were to contain 35 stories of office and conference space. The platform at the base was to form an architectural environment, where, under the cover of broad glass sails, the urban life that was decaying between the dreary high-rise housing blocks would be reinvigorated by a wide range of activities. Of these ambitious plans, perhaps one of the most striking features to be realized was the system of open, panoramic lifts that takes inquisitive tourists day by day up between the glazed office slabs to the viewing platform on the roof. Structural constraints in the placing of the foundations were largely responsible for the open cube being turned at a six-and-half-degree angle to the historical axis. This and the funnel-like form of the arch heighten its monumental effect when seen from close up, and account for its striking appearance when viewed from a distance. The smooth, planar inner faces are splayed at a 45-degree angle and are clad in white Carrara marble. At the base, a broad, shallow, open flight of stairs draws one into the gargantuan gateway, the vertiginous height of which is alleviated by a white tent structure. Spanned between the inner faces of the hollow cube, which are divided into square glazed grids, the tent is meant to counteract the awe-inspiring dimensions of the monumental arch with an element of lightness and movement, and with proportions that are related to the human scale.

La Grande Arche represents an effective modern reinterpretation of the evocative Parisian motif of the triumphal arch. It also attempts to derive a modern meaning from its urban function. Perhaps it is of some significance that what has triumphed in its current use is something that already dominates the urban space in La Défense today: large-scale office complexes for the service industry.   A.G.

1

3

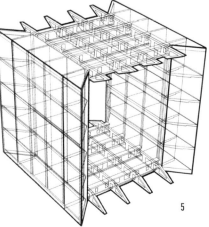

4

1 | View up to tent canopy
2 | East–west section of the roof
3 | Overall view
4 | Aerial photo, showing axis to Arc de Triomphe
5 | Isometric drawing of structural system

5

I.M. Pei

Pyramide, Le Grand Louvre | PARIS 1983-1993

4

Originally a thirteenth-century castle, and transformed over the centuries by a series of regal palaces, Paris' Le Grand Louvre has long been a destination for art enthusiasts. As the number of museum visitors skyrocketed in the 1970s and 1980s, the pitfalls of the Louvre's labyrinth-like structure became more pronounced: the L-shape building was not easily accessible to pedestrian or bus traffic, the museum lacked sufficient bathrooms, cafes, and other conveniences, and the staff operated with only a fraction of the 40 percent support space required for most major museums. In 1981, French President François Mitterrand proposed that the Louvre be expanded and better integrated with the surrounding city while preserving the historic grandeur of its buildings. For this delicate task he chose the Chinese-born American modernist I.M. Pei.

In the political storms that beset the modernization of the Louvre, the group of pyramids became a lightening rod for critics who feared that such severe forms would overwhelm the surrounding buildings. Not since the erection of the Eiffel Tower in the nineteenth century had an architectural project cut so close to the cultural heart of Paris. Pei understood the weighty responsibility entrusted to him, and his design reflects a great sensitivity to the preexisting buildings.

Although the Louvre pyramids follow the basic proportions of their Egyptian predecessors, their fabrication relied heavily on contemporary building technology. The 675 diamond-shape and 118 triangular panes are held in place by a web of steel girders and thin cables. For the strong, ultra-light joinings or "nodes" which hold the tension structure in place, Pei turned to a Massachusetts-based company that made rigging for the America's Cup yachts. A specially manufactured colorless glass preserves the view of the historic palace both inside and outside the entrance, and a series of reflecting pools gives the impression that the structure floats upon water. The 79-foot (24-meter) tall pyramid is flanked by three smaller pyramids which illuminate the subterranean concourses that lead to the three wings of the museum.

The glass pyramid entrance in the central courtyard is only the tip of the iceberg in Pei's expansion of the Louvre. A two-level complex of reception areas, shops, and exhibition spaces sprawls below ground. By moving the Ministry of Finance from the Richelieu Wing, the museum expanded to fill the entire Louvre and thereby assumed a U-shape with the pyramids occupying the center. These changes make the Louvre the largest museum in the world, with nearly 1.4 million square feet (130,000 square meters) of space.

The latest in a series of additions spanning eight centuries, Pei's design has transformed the Louvre into an efficient, modern museum with only a minimal amount of intrusion upon its historic exterior. His pyramids are a rigorous, modern presence, but the transparency and lightness of these ancient geometric forms help to maintain the historic continuity of Le Grand Louvre.   J.G.

I.M. PEI
Architect's biography on p. 118

1

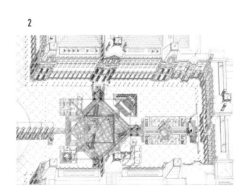

2

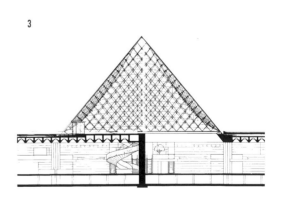

3

1 | View to historic palace
2 | Axonometric drawing of site
3 | Section through main pyramid
4 | Main pyramid in the Louvre
courtyard
5 | Plan: roof of main pyramid
6 | Entrance area

5

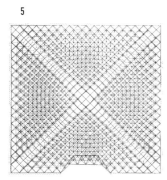

6

1 | Foyer to concert hall
2 | Overall view of Cité de la Musique from east
3 | Loggia in western part of complex
4, 5 | Pavilions in western part of complex
6 | Drawing of overall site layout
7 | Concert hall

Ten years in the making, the Cité de la Musique is the most complex, and perhaps the least well-known in the series of major new public and civic buildings commissioned by the French government for Paris during the last 20 years. Christian de Portzamparc won the competition for the commission in 1984 while still relatively young, but the building represents the most comprehensive exploration to date of the ideas which had brought him to the fore in the architectural and planning debate in Paris during the 1970s.

Fundamental to de Portzamparc's work was the belief that a new understanding of urban form had to supersede the outdated modernist vision of Le Corbusier's Plan Voisin. In the two phases, west and east, of the Cité de la Musique, he set out his manifesto for the formal diversity of objects, integrated with significant space, as the basis of a new vision of the city. The complex was designed not as a freestanding monument, like many of the other Grands Projets, but as a setting for people and events: a new urban territory forming a threshold between the nineteenth-century city along Avenue Jean Jaures, and the "twenty-first-century" Parc de la Villette in the northeast of Paris.

The initial west phase of the complex comprises accommodation for the National School of Music and Dance, while the east phase, completed some years later, centers around a public auditorium and a museum of music, with additional office space and student housing. The two elements face each other across a central open area in front of the Grande Halle, a converted nineteenth-century market building on the edge of the Parc de la Villette. De Portzamparc designed the composition to be asymmetrical to avoid any suggestion of beaux-arts formalism.

In terms of architectural conception, the west phase was planned essentially to be as open and permeable as possible, presenting a new formulation of the cultural institution and its relationship to the city. The east phase is more introverted, creating an insulated realm for musical performance where audiences would be able to detach themselves from the everyday life of the world beyond its walls. The formal idea behind the east phase is a spiral with the auditorium at its heart, while the west phase comprises a series of linked but detached pavilions, creating a rhythmic sequence of solid and void, transparent and opaque.

This concept was important for the School of Music, where de Portzamparc wanted to create a gradually unfolding series of spaces, and areas of openness, conviviality, and relaxation as a contrast to the intensely concentrated nature of the activities taking place in the enclosed, acoustically-sealed clusters of classrooms and practice rooms. The collection of spaces and volumes is gathered around an open garden at the heart of the school, and is given formal coherence along the main road by a prominent, oversailing roof. Using this language of forms, de Portzamparc brings a solid intellectual agenda to his work which provides a basis for discussion about the future of the city. C.M.

CHRISTIAN DE PORTZAMPARC

1944	Born on May 9 in in Casablanca, Morocco
1968	While studying architecture at the Ecole des Beaux-Arts in Paris, he plays an important role in the student uprising of 1968
1971	First project: water tower in Marne-la-Vallée, France
1978	Low-cost housing, rue des Hautes-Formes, Paris
1980	Participates in the Venice Biennale organized by Paolo Portoghesi entitled, "The Presence of the Past," a showcase for postmodernist work
1981-88	Housing in Marne-la-Vallée; the Music Conservatory and Home for the Elderly, rue de Nicot, Paris; Home for the Elderly, rue de Chateau des Rentiers, Paris; the project for the Ecole de Danse de l'Opera de Paris at Nanterre shows de Portzamparc moving away from the language of postmodernism, and back to his earlier structuralist interests
1984-95	Cité de la Musique, Paris
1994	Pritzker Architecture Prize
1995	Achieves international prominence with the completion of the Cité de la Musique

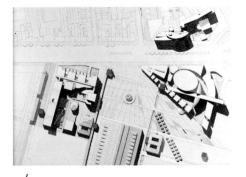

6

7

Peter Eisenman

Wexner Center for the Visual Arts | COLUMBUS, OHIO 1985-1989

At the time of the completion of the Wexner Center for the Visual Arts in Columbus, Ohio, Peter Eisenman's production of literary and theoretical projects had been so great and his output of built work so small, that one magazine announced the building with the headline, "Eisenman Builds." Could such an intellectually-charged ideologue successfully complete a large-scale building on a complicated site for a major university in America's heartland?

The site was an important location between the main entrance to the Ohio State University campus and its primary green space, the oval, but it was crowded with existing buildings. Most of the designs submitted took fairly conventional approaches to creating discrete new buildings in interstitial spaces. However, Eisenman, with Trott & Bean Architects of Columbus, seized the opportunity to produce a built reconsideration of some of architecture's most fundamental principles.

Eisenman's theoretical investigations had been focusing on post-structuralist theory and literary deconstruction. From these studies he derived a skepticism about the desire for humanism and unity in Western traditions of thought, suggesting that these impulses were really constructs which suppressed realities full of conflict, ambiguity, and disjunction.

1

PETER EISENMAN

1932	Born on August 11 in Newark, New Jersey
1951-55	Bachelor of architecture at Cornell University, Ithaca, New York
1957-58	Works for Percival Goodman in New York City
1959	Works for The Architects' Collaborative, Cambridge, Massachusetts
1959-60	Master's degree in architecture, Columbia University, New York City
1960-63	Doctorate in the theory of design, Cambridge University, Cambridge, England
1963	Publishes "Towards an Understanding of Form in Architecture" in *Architectural Design*
1964	Co-founds CASE (Conference of Architects for the Study of the Environment)
1967-68	Series of ten numbered houses of a very abstract, theoretical nature
1967-82	Founds and directs the Institute for Architecture and Urban Studies (IAUS); acts as a clearing-house for avant-garde architectural theory

1972	The book *Five Architects* is published, featuring Eisenman and four other designers; sparks international debate on the merits of modernism and postmodernism in architecture
1973-82	Editor of the IAUS magazine *Oppositions*
1981-87	Designs and constructs apartments on the Kochstrasse, Berlin
1982	After years of small independent commissions and extensive academic work, Eisenman opens an architectural office; the scope and number of his commissions increase dramatically
1985-89	Wexner Center for the Visual Arts, Ohio State University, Columbus, Ohio
1989-92	Columbus Convention Center, Columbus; after completing this building, Eisenman bragged that its irregularly intersecting volumes made one visitor physically ill

Accordingly, the Wexner Center seems less like a building than an accumulation of value-laden fragments between and around the pre-existing neighboring buildings, Weigel Hall and Mershon Auditorium. A three-dimensional grid, or "scaffolding," runs for several hundred feet through the entirety of the complex. It marks entrances to the building, but defies any specific function in favor of making obscure reference to the greater planning grid which governed the original surveys by the state. Its 12-degree shift from the main hall — which is further articulated by glass and metal grids — only heightens the sense of disunity in the building. A seemingly haphazard accumulation of crenelated brick slivers cites an armory which occupied the site until 1958. The intention is to question the ability of architectural form to convey time and history adequately. Such rhetorical games continue throughout the building. Columns and beams end in mid-air to question notions of structure and its representation. Windows in the floor question notions of vision. Meanwhile, visitors to the building raise basic functional queries, such as how to find the art library.

The Wexner Center has generated a certain amount of praise amid a barrage of criticism. It won the competition for the commission, according to the jury report, because it "best captured the spirit, dynamism, and open-endedness of the center's programmatic needs." Indeed, the formal chicanery belies a complex program of exhibition, curatorial, performance, library, studio, and administrative spaces. Reactions to the building have ranged from complaints that its design is too obscure to objections that it is too accessible. In this sense, Eisenman has responded to questions about his capabilities as an architect not with an answer, but with a very provocative built question.
C.L.R.

2

1 | Interior view
2 | Entrance area with brick towers
3 | Three-dimensional grid structure
4 | Aerial view of entire development

3

4

Oswald Mathias Ungers

Contemporary Art Wing | HAMBURG 1986-1996

The gallery does not live from art alone. Architecture is part of its presence: a public building assignment that has its own symbols and history. The museum also exists in its own environment, which is usually an urban one, with which it has to communicate about its own function, about the interests of others, about the location and its history, and last but not least, about the process of building itself. To reconcile all these aspects is no simple task, especially when one is concerned with the extension of an important museum and art gallery such as the Kunsthalle in Hamburg, Germany, which occupies a prominent location — the Glockengiesserwall between the main station and the Binnenalster.

Oswald Mathias Ungers took the task of building the extension, the Contemporary Art Wing, very seriously. He drew the new structure forward into the front row, into the line of buildings that encloses the waters of the Binnenalster like a square in the city center. The way the building forms a part of this panorama yet retains a respectable distance from it is as precisely gauged as the relationship of the extension to the central Kunsthalle building, which dates to the nineteenth century. With the splayed granite plinth, Ungers recalls that the Glockengiesserwall, part of the old city ramparts, once stood here. On top of the plinth, he placed a cubic volume clad in light-colored limestone and identical on all faces. Window veins rise vertically up the facades, marking the central axes. The cube, the three-dimensional form developed from a square, is a shape that has proven its adaptability in the architect's work over a period of many decades — from functional trade fair buildings to prestigious, unique works such as the residence of the German ambassador in Washington, D.C. The Contemporary Art Wing is also based on a square modular unit from which all elements of the main building are derived, from the recessed light fittings to the layout itself.

Internally, the central hall draws the eye upwards through all stories to the very top, where the view leads out through a glazed roof. Two flights of stairs wind around the hall, and here, too, the proportions are lofty, almost sublime.

The secluded exhibition spaces form a second, outer circulation route. On the second floor, Ungers does not hesitate to expose the art displayed to the city outside, which in turn enters the exhibition spaces through the large windows. Art is seen as part of the gallery and as part of the urban culture in which it has its origins.

The concepts and designs of Oswald Mathias Ungers have had an enlivening influence on architectural developments for decades now. His aesthetic single-mindedness has contributed to the fact that architecture is again referred to, with increasing frequency, as the "art of building," having for years threatened to waste away in functionalism. On the other hand, it is the same quality of seriousness that distinguishes his work from the self-indulgent trifles of postmodernism and its offshoots, to which the new building for the Hamburg Kunsthalle — an etude on the theme of architecture — responds with the richness and diversity of elemental design.   U.M.S.

OSWALD MATHIAS UNGERS

1926	Born on July 12 in Kaisersesch-in-der-Eifel, Germany
1947-50	Studies architecture at the University of Technology, Karlsruhe, Germany, with Egon Eiermann as tutor
1958-59	Builds his own house in Müngersdorf, Cologne, Germany, a manifesto of rational and sculptural architecture (1989-90 extended by a library)
1963	Begins teaching at the University of Technology, Berlin
1964-65	Creates ensembles in the student hostel in Enschede, the Netherlands, the Museum of Prussian Cultural Collection, Berlin, and the German embassy in the Vatican
1969-86	Lectureship at Cornell University in Ithaca, New York
1973	His competition design for the Tiergarten district of Berlin introduces the notion of complex order to urban planning theory through large-scale architectural forms
1977	Publication of "Die Stadt in der Stadt: Berlin — das grüne Stadtarchipel"
1979-84	Conversion of a villa on the River Main, Frankfurt, into the German Architecture Museum
1980-	Hall 9 and the "Galleria" on the Frankfurt Trade Fair site (1980-83): the Alfred Wegener Institute for Polar and Marine Research, Bremerhaven (1980-84): the State Library of Baden, Karlsruhe (1980-92): the Federal Prosecutor's Office in Karlsruhe (1985-97), all in Germany
1982	Publication of "Morphologie — City Metaphors"
1983	Publication of *Die Thematisierung der Architektur*
1983-84	Gatehouse, Frankfurt-am-Main
1986-	Begins the Contemporary Art Wing in Hamburg, completed ten years later: professor of architecture at the Academy of Art in Düsseldorf, Germany, until 1990
1988-94	Residence of the German ambassador in Washington, D.C.
1992-96	Block 205, Friedrichstadt arcades, Berlin

1 | Overall view with granite plinth
    and forecourt
2 | Exhibition space
3 | Window to central top-lit hall
4 | Longitudinal section

1

2

3

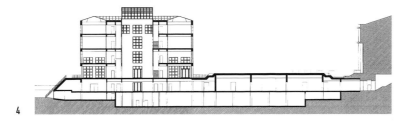

4

Tadao Ando

Church of the Light | OSAKA (JAPAN) 1987-1989

1

TADAO ANDO

Before turning to architecture, Tadao Ando was a boxer, and even as an architect, he has assumed an extreme stance. Despite the minimalist reduction that characterizes his buildings, disturbance and conflict are always themes of his work. The Church of the Light in Osaka, Japan, is one striking example: it consists of a clearly defined cubic form that is abruptly intersected at an angle by a lower wall slab. At the points where the wall penetrates the body of the church, it is surrounded and thereby isolated by glazed openings. The main structure is axially oriented to the rising sun, whereas the wall takes its alignment from another church nearby.

The hermetically closed building reveals its function only in the show front to the southeast, where a glazed cross is sharply incised in the facade. The cruciform opening does not allow a view into the church, however; the glass reflects the outdoor surroundings.

The entrance to the church is situated at the point where the raking concrete wall, which flanks the ambulatory on one side, intersects the nave wall; but the entrance is on the far side of this. The first path one takes, therefore, is a dead end that terminates in a window affording a glimpse into the church's interior. If one wishes to enter the church, one has to return to the starting point of the ambulatory and follow the wall along its outer face. This route leads the visitor, via a brightly lit, triangular vestibule, into the prayer hall. One enters the Church of the Light from the side, and at first glance, the internal space would seem to lack what the name promises: it is dark. But as soon as one enters and turns to face the altar, one is confronted with an overwhelming and dramatic scene. During the morning service, visitors can witness the rising sun burning a cross of light in the southeast altar wall. Only at this point do its rays directly penetrate the hermetically sealed concrete volume. Only here does light possess the power to cleave walls. The Divine manifests itself in the brightness that floods into this space, and that, through the agency of the architecture, forms the sign of the cross.

Although the labyrinthine route and the false entrance may be alien to Europeans, paths of this kind are linked to the traditions of Japanese tea houses and temples. The destination can be reached only via a roundabout path that leads the visitor out of the everyday world and prepares the way for the rites ahead.

Ando is a mediator between East and West. He chooses to build almost exclusively in concrete, and although this material is inseparably linked with the Modern Movement in Europe, in Ando's work it evokes an Oriental aesthetic. One might say, there is concrete, and there is Tadao Ando concrete: in his hands, the material seems as supple as tissue paper and freed of all weight. The carefully shuttered wall surfaces refract the light that enters the building, and seem almost immaterial as a result of the different patterns of shade cast on them. "Light wakens architecture to life" is the artistic credo of this autodidact. For Ando, architectural means of expression do not exhaust themselves in the haptic forms of concrete or wood. They include light, wind, and water as phenomena that can be experienced through the senses.   M.H.

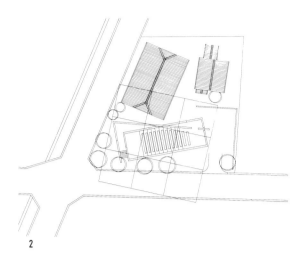

2

3

5

4

1 | View from southeast
2 | Site plan
3 | Section through church
4 | Church space
5 | Cross of light on floor

Rem Koolhaas

Gallery of Contemporary Art | ROTTERDAM 1987-1992

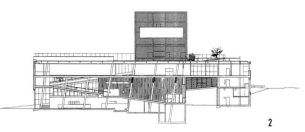

2

1

Few people would doubt that Rem Koolhaas is one of the most important architects of the last years of the twentieth century. He is also one of the most controversial figures of the profession. While some observers extol the wit and originality of his designs, his "neo-modernist" architecture for the common man, without elitist pretensions and formal excesses, others reject the ugliness and cheapness, the "do-it-yourself aesthetic" of his work. Koolhaas is acclaimed as a thinker, realist, and urbanist who takes a sober view of the city. At the same time, he is criticized for his rejection of a European urban identity. These contradictions are clearly evident in his Gallery of Contemporary Art in Rotterdam, the Netherlands.

The building is docked at the edge of an urban expressway that runs along the crest of a dyke, a place where there is really no question of "urban identity." To the north, toward the museum park, the ground falls away steeply. Based on a square plan, three large exhibition halls and two galleries are stacked at the bottom of the slope, with a hall and a cafe between them. The north-south access route cuts the complex into two unequal parts. The external and internal ramps along this axis cross an east-west road that passes under the building. This system of routes divides and at the same time

links the various areas in such a way that the development becomes a complex, ingeniously constructed whole.

In contrast to this sophisticated spatial layout, the halls seem at first sight to be a collage made up of odds and ends from a builder's yard. Every facade, for example, has a different appearance; and tinted glass of various colors heightens this effect. The mechanical services on the roof are enclosed with gratings in a seemingly makeshift manner. Inside the hall, every conceivable type of translucent plastic is employed as cladding which reveals more than it hides. The fluorescent tubes seem to be installed at random rather than in accordance with a lighting plan, and the flooring consists of simple metal gratings. In the hall facing the park, the steel columns are "camouflaged" as tree trunks, and help to create a flowing transition between the internal space of the building and the garden; between art and artificial nature. Walking around this art center, one becomes aware that it does not want to be a museum. The exhibits are not raised on pedestals; the art is on display at a tangible distance.

For Koolhaas, architecture no longer has anything heroic about it. He is interested in neutral things, things unfettered by taste, or form. His 1,376-page book *S,M,L,XL* reveals his main preoccupations. The texts are concerned with concepts that are relevant to architectural theory today: concepts of "bigness" and the "generic city," that have to do with the question of size and the notion of a metropolis without individual features. In his work, Koolhaas calls upon architects and urban planners to abandon notions such as context and identity and to accept the chaos, speed, and disjunctions that characterize present-day urban development, instead of (tearfully) lamenting a lost past. The profession of the architect, in his opinion, has to be reinvented.

Architects still listen to these arguments in perplexity; in the meantime, Koolhaas' ideas have gained renown at universities and other seats of learning. S.S.

REM KOOLHAAS

1944	Born on November 17 in Rotterdam, the Netherlands
1952–56	Lives in Indonesia; works as a journalist for the *Haagse Post* in Amsterdam, the Netherlands, and as a screenwriter
1968–72	Studies at the Architectural Association in London
1972–73	Studies at Cornell University, Ithaca, New York
1975	Teaches at the Institute for Architecture and Urban Studies and Columbia University, both in New York City, and at the University of California Los Angeles; co-founds the Office for Metropolitan Architecture in London
1976	Teaches at the Architectural Association in London
1978	Publishes the book *Delirious New York*
1987–92	Gallery of Contemporary Art, Rotterdam
1988–89	Teaches at the University of Technology in Delft, the Netherlands
1990–	Professor at Harvard University, Cambridge, Massachusetts
1991–92	Teaches at Rice University, Houston, Texas
1996	Publishes the book *S,M,L,XL*
1997	"Design for an Asian City of the 21st Century," Ottoneum, documenta X, Kassel, Germany

1 | Entrance
2 | Section
3 | Overall view: street face
4 | Rear face
5 | Auditorium
6 | Diagram of circulation system
    and link to street
7 | Ramp

3

4

5

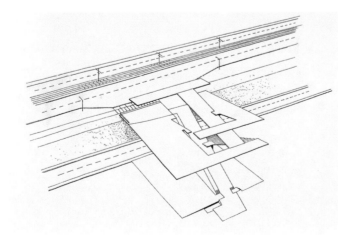

6

7

1 | Aerial view of airport
2 | Interior of terminal
3 | Cross-section
4 | Overall view
5 | Design sketch

1

2

3

4

Kansai International Airport | OSAKA (JAPAN) 1988-1994

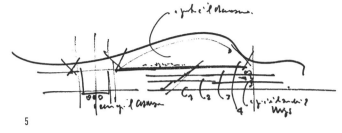

5

The Japanese city of Osaka, with its 3 million inhabitants, suffers from an acute shortage of space. For that reason, a decision was made to build the new Kansai International Airport offshore in Osaka Bay. Since there was no island that could be developed for this purpose, an artifical platform had to be built up on the sea bed. The new airport is linked to the mainland by a bridge more than two miles long. Some 6.4 billion cubic feet (180 million cubic meters) of earth and sand and over 1,000 piles were required for this outstanding engineering achievement. The piles extend down through 66 feet (20 meters) of water and a 66-foot layer of mud before being rammed just as far again into the bedrock. The airport president justly drew attention to the fact that, with the construction of Kansai Airport, Japan had increased in size by nearly six square miles.

In 1988, when he first saw the "site" in the open sea, Renzo Piano, the winner of the international competition, said he felt like a shipwrecked soul: "We were lost in infinity and intoxicated by the space around us. We therefore began

to look for points of reference beyond the physical context — in the collective unconscious, in the memory and in the culture."

The only points of reference from which the competitors could derive their bearings were the movement of the waves, the tides, fluid forms — and the wind. Piano based his concept on transient structures, on the notion of air; in other words, he designed elongated, lightweight forms, not least to withstand the earthquakes that can occur in this region. The shape of the airport terminal roof is based on the dynamic flow of air currents.

The almost 1 million square feet (90,000 square meters) of roof skin, which is in the form of a series of curves of different radii, consists of 82,000 identical stainless-steel panels laid over exposed girders. The reversed aerodynamic form of this structure ensures that air currents within the passenger hall can be controlled without the use of closed air-conditioning ducts, and can be expelled at the runway end.

Viewed from above, the airport resembles a glider resting on the ground. The main building can be seen as the fuselage; the access roads formally resemble the ailerons of the tail section; and the 5,570-foot (1,700-meter) long passenger-handling tract with its 42 gates forms the outstretched wings.

As a result of financial problems, the Japanese clients decided, when the project was at an advanced stage of development, to implement strict savings and impose a new cost limit. Piano reacted in a headstrong and provocative manner. He knew that it was impossible to omit a single section of the complex without destroying the balance of the whole. He therefore suggested shortening the wings, of all things. This tactical bluff resulted in more funds being raised, and the wings were executed to the length originally foreseen.

Between 1990 and 1994, some 6,000 construction workers worked on the site at any one time — 10,000 at peak times — in realizing one of the largest structures ever built. Kansai International Airport in Osaka, which can handle a volume of 100,000 passengers a day, thus represents one of the outstanding feats of engineering art and architecture of the late twentieth century.   C. W. J.

RENZO PIANO

1937	Born on September 14 in Genoa, Italy
1964	Completes architectural studies in Milan, Italy, and works in his father's office
1965-70	Collaboration with Louis I. Kahn in Philadelphia, Pennsylvania, and Z.S. Makovsky in London
1971-77	Joint practice with Richard Rogers, London/ Genoa; Centre Georges Pompidou in Paris
1981-86	Museum for the Menil Collection, Houston, Texas
1985-93	Conversion of the Fiat Lingotto Factory, Milan, Italy
1987-89	San Nicola Football Stadium, Bari, Italy
1988-94	Kansai International Airport, Osaka, Japan
1992-97	Master plan for Potsdamer Platz, Berlin
1994-97	Fondation Beyeler, art museum, Basel

Dominique Perrault

Bibliothèque Nationale de France | PARIS 1989-1995

1

The Bibliothèque Nationale in Paris is a building of many paradoxes. Dominique Perrault did not design it as a solid volume, but as a void inserted into the urban tissue in threefold form: firstly, by means of a plinth, which accentuates the special quality of this place within the city; secondly, as an implied space between four corner towers, an area whose geometric clarity assumes final form only in the mind of the observer — in other words, a mental space par excellence; and finally, as a sunken garden, enclosed and inaccessible, nature as the mythical core of a culture full of meaning.

The design concept is also paradoxical, especially in the way landscaping elements, such as the open, embankment-like flight of steps along the road, are used to create an urbane location. Another riddle lies in the alternative ways in which one can interpret the forms. On the one hand, the towers are wholly geometric abstractions, crystalline and possessing a Platonic clarity; on the other hand, they can be read figuratively, as open books. Wholly contradictory, it would seem, is the garden. Situated at the center of a public development, it is nevertheless inaccessible. As a living, growing jungle, it evokes the untouchable quality of nature; on the other hand, it has been brought to this place with highly sophisticated technology and with an enormous investment of time and money.

By means of these paradoxes, Perrault transforms what at first glance seems a minimalist, rationalist building into a complex entity, rich in mental associations and allusions as a result of its evident conceptual oppositions. It stirs the emotions through its sheer size, yet ultimately lacks any comprehensible scale; and it appeals to the senses through the contrast of its materials, which range from warm-toned tropical timbers to cool steel mesh and dissolving glass cladding.

Although Perrault presses the reception areas and the reading rooms into the plinth with the primal force of nature, so to speak, and heaves the offices and book stores aloft with a titanic display of strength, it is not so much the actual dimensions that lend the library its magnitude. With a height of 262 feet (80 meters) each, the towers are easily outstripped by many office blocks. The space between these structures has the dimensions of the well-proportioned Palais Royal; and the garden is sunk below the surface of the plinth to a depth of 69 feet (21 meters), precisely the eaves height of the average Parisian street block. Far more, it is the formal stringency that lends the project its greatness and gives expression to the inner context. There are, after all, 12 million books to be accommodated here, for which more than 260 miles (420 kilometers) of shelving has been installed at present — a most impressive quantity.

This final, most important, and largest of François Mitterrand's "Grands Projets" is, therefore, not just a hybrid epitaph to the late president. It is also an ambivalent swan song to an era, or, perhaps more accurately, to a certain direction that, as an expression of modernism, seeks independent new ground. The modernity of this complex, however, no longer points to the future, which will follow a different path — an ecological one. The Bibliothèque Nationale celebrates its own apotheosis, which, with a series of supreme paradoxes, brings this very modernism to a deceptively archaic end.   W. S.

DOMINIQUE PERRAULT

1953	Born on April 9 in Clermont-Ferrand, France
1978	Completes architectural studies at the Ecole Nationale Supérieure des Beaux-Arts in Paris
1979	Certificate of urban planning at the Ecole Nationale des Ponts-et-Chaussées in Paris
1980	Diploma from the Ecole des Hautes Etudes en Sciences Sociales in Paris
1981–	Own practice in Paris
1984-87	Ecole Supérieure d'Ingénieurs en Electronique et Electrotechnique (E.S.I.E.E.) in Marne-la-Vallée, France
1986-90	Hôtel Industriel Berlier in Paris
1989-95	Bibliothèque Nationale de France, Paris
1992	Opens an office in Berlin
1992-98	Cycling and swimming hall in Berlin
1993	Grand prix national d'architecture
1996	Wins the competition for the European Court of Justice in Luxembourg

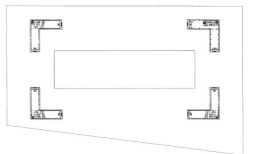

2

3

1 | View of complex from the Seine
2 | Site plan
3 | View between two library towers
4 | Central garden
5 | Reading room
6 | Corridor along glass facade

4

5

6

Daniel Libeskind

Berlin Museum Extension | BERLIN 1989-1998

Author and composer E.T.A. Hoffmann once administered Prussian law in the Superior Court of Justice, a symmetrical, rectilinear Baroque building in which the Berlin Museum has been housed since 1969. After his official duties, Hoffmann would reflect in a less formal manner in his droll and sometimes anarchic tales about the society in which he lived.

Society and the dialectic of its psychological and historical development also inspired Daniel Libeskind in his design for the extension to the Berlin Museum to house the Jewish Department when he took part in the international competition held by the Berlin Senate in 1989, before the Wall came down. Libeskind's programmatic title, "Between the Lines," embodies his interpretation of two conflicting historical currents, which he represents with a rational, straight-line volume intersected at various points by a serpentine, zig-zagging form. At the points of conflict — i.e., where the lines intersect — are so-called "voids," which are to be found throughout the building and are excluded from the exhibition activities of the museum. For the most part, they can be seen only through narrow viewing slits. In these multistory gray concrete shafts, light, sound, and time stand still. Nothing penetrates these empty spaces but the distant echo of a past age. According to Libeskind, they represent an "impenetrable void" that is meant to symbolize the absence of the Jewish community of Berlin.

Access to the museum is via the main entrance of the former Superior Court building. Here, the history of Berlin is depicted down to the founding of the German Reich in 1870. A "voided void" that penetrates the existing building vertically provides access to the basement. A subterranean corridor leads into the extension, which has a floor area of approximately 130,000 square feet (12,000 square meters) and houses the collection covering the period after 1870. Almost immediately three possible routes present themselves. The first leads to the Jewish Department, situated in a dead-end passage that is terminated by the Holocaust void. The second route leads directly to the labyrinthine open-air E.T.A. Hoffmann Garden, which represents the state of exile. The third route, an extension of the entrance corridor, leads via straight flights of stairs to the three exhibition levels. The top floor of the building accommodates the administration, workshops, and library, and is not open to the general public.

The power of Libeskind's building was evident at an early stage, and indeed manifested itself throughout the arduous process of realization, from the competition in 1989 and the laying of the foundation stone in 1992 to the completion of the project in 1998. The building's plan — like a bolt of lightning — has exercised a magical attraction ever since. It was derived from a distorted form of the Star of David, and other cultural references, which range from Walter Benjamin to Arnold Schönberg, are also to be found here. In spite of the complex, contentious, and often confusing architectural language of the building, Libeskind attempts to shape something compellingly simple, which, as he says, represents the greatest challenge of all, "namely, to erect the museum about an empty space that extends through the entire building."   C.B.

DANIEL LIBESKIND

1946	Born on May 12 in Lodz, Poland
1957	Parents emigrate to Israel; begins studying music
1960	Moves to the U.S.; studies painting and mathematics
1965	U.S. citizenship; begins studying architecture at Cooper Union, New York City
1971	Master's degree in architectural theory at the University of Essex, England
1978-85	Dean of the Faculty of Architecture at the Cranbrook Academy of Art, Michigan
1986-89	Founder and director of the Architectural Intermundium, Milan, Italy
1987	First prize for City Edge, Berlin
1989-	Own architectural offices, Berlin; first prize for the extension of the Berlin Museum, completed in 1998
1993	Special prize for the Sachsenhausen Memorial, Oranienburg, Germany
1995	First prize for the Felix Nussbaum Museum, Osnabrück, Germany
1996	First prize for the extension of the Victoria & Albert Museum, London
1997	First prize for the Imperial War Museum of the North, Manchester, England

1

2

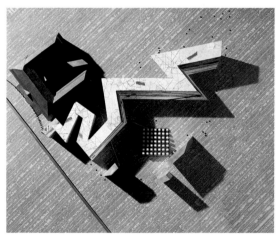

3

1 | Detail of facade
2 | Overall view
3 | Model
4 | Staircase

4

Santiago Calatrava

Satolas TGV Station | LYON (FRANCE) 1990–1994

Eighty offices took part in the international architectural competition held in 1987 for the Satolas TGV Station in the north of Lyon, France. In the final round, the scheme by Santiago Calatrava narrowly beat that from Richard Rogers. The development contains an approximately 1,475-foot (450-meter) long hall with connecting routes to the airport. The construction period for the entire works, external and internal, lasted from January 1990 to July 1994, in the process of which the cost estimate was exceeded by 50 percent — a fact that this self-assured architect scarcely contends.

Calatrava adopted the nineteenth-century tradition of the station as an urban super-sign, but transposed it into the present-day context which clings with fetishistic faith to the principle of "time is speed is money." In his allusions to organic forms, he succeeds in finding, in the image of a huge bird with elegant wings, a poetic-architectural symbol for the romantic ideas associated with travel — optimism, ease, weightlessness, velocity, and even vivacity — establishing a link between the notion of a train speeding like an arrow to its destination and the metaphor of flying. Visual impressions of alpine scenery and of the safe, protective function of a pair of spread wings are also implied; and from certain angles, Calatrava's bird of passage may even remind one of the menacing, death-bringing beauty of an American Stealth bomber.

The danger of organic architecture parlante lies in its overtly pictorial character. Calatrava escapes this by adopting, with a highly sensuous, physical immediacy, some of the abstract principles of the engineering tradition that are a recognized part of the art of building. He fuses these with symbolic visual images, organic processes, and mathematical-musical rhythms.

Aesthetics and function, motion and dynamics thus enter into a synthesis. The architect describes his scheme as an exercise in light and transparency, but it is much more than that. It is a model piece of work by an experimental engineer and artist. Since writing his dissertation on foldable framed structures, Calatrava has proved himself to be an outstanding designer in the field of folded sheet-steel construction. Here, he reveals himself to be a brilliant sculptor in concrete and glass, as well.

C.W.T.

SANTIAGO CALATRAVA

1951	Born on July 28 in Benimamet, Valencia, Spain
1968–69	Studies at the University of Art in Valencia
1969–74	Studies architecture at the Escuela Técnica Superior de Arquitectura de Valencia
1975–79	Engineering studies at the ETH in Zurich, Switzerland
1979–81	Doctorate at the ETH in Zurich; dissertation on the "Foldability of Load-Bearing Frame Structures"; assistant at the Institute for Structural Engineering and Building Construction of the ETH, Zurich
1981	Opens his own architectural and engineering practice in Zurich
1987	Member of the Federation of Swiss Architects (BSA); Auguste Perret Prize of the Union Internationale des Architectes (UIA)
1988	City of Barcelona Prize for Art for the Bach-de-Roda Bridge; several other awards for bridges, including the Fritz Schumacher Prize; honorary member of the Federation of German Architects (BDA); monographic exhibition at Columbia University, New York City
1990	Médaille d'Argent de la Recherche et de la Technique, Paris
1990–94	Satolas TGV Station, Lyon, France
1992	Member of the Real Academia de Bellas Artes de San Carlos, Valencia; Brunel Award for Stadelhofen Station, Zurich; Gold medal of the Institute of Structural Engineers, London
1993	Exhibition of bridge structures in the Deutsches Museum, Munich, Germany; exhibition in the Museum of Modern Art, New York City
1998	Completion of the Lisbon east station, Portugal

1

2

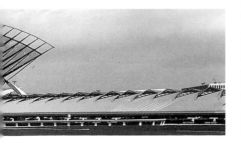

3

1 | Overall view
2 | External view of station hall
3 | Interior of station hall
4 | Section

4

Peter Zumthor

Thermal Baths | VALS (SWITZERLAND) 1990-1996

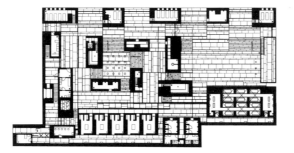

1

Imagine a typical modern amusement park pool with turquoise tiles, curving cascades and pools, a water chute, palm trees, the smell of chlorine, florid decorations, and the noise of people enjoying themselves: shrieking, screaming, loud music, and gushing water. Then imagine the opposite of all this: "the quiet intrinsic experience of bathing, of purification, of relaxing in water; the physical sensation of water of different temperatures in different spaces; the contact with stone. . . ." This is Peter Zumthor's idea of recreation, and at the same time the concept underlying his "rock spa" thermal baths in Vals.

The only warm spring in the Grisons Canton in Switzerland rises in Vals, a remote village in the upper Rhine Valley. This was reason enough for the local council to invest 24 million Swiss francs in the construction of a new thermal baths. As early as 1986, Zumthor was commissioned to draw up a design concept. At that time, he was making a name for himself with timber protective structures over Roman excavations in Chur, the regional capital of the Grisons.

The rock springs were completed in 1996. The smooth-faced volume clad in Vals stone is hidden behind an ensemble of hotel buildings and housing blocks dating from the 1960s, and is half sunk into the slope of the site. The spa facilities are reached via the hotel corridors, and the guest enters a contemplative semi-dark zone that has a distinctly calming influence. Like the external facades, the bathing space is clad entirely in indigenous rock — not just the walls, but the surfaces of the pools and the stairs, as well. One has the impression of being in an artificial grotto, a hollowed-out block of stone with massive, rectangular piers left standing in the space. Concealed between these irregularly placed piers are small pools, which one discovers one after another — the red fire bath (107.6 °F/42 °C), the blue ice bath (57 °F/14 °C), and the aromatic marigold bath. They, too, lie in a state of semi-darkness. The water is illuminated only from below, and in the main space, a strange iridescent light shines through a row of square, blue-glazed top lights. This opens out toward the valley with a series of large windows and an external pool with terraces.

In its minimalism, the rock pool is reminiscent of the thermal baths in antiquity: just water and stone, here combined with a limited number of brass fittings and balustrades. Martin Steinmann, a Swiss professor of architecture, remarks that the simple volumetric forms of Zumthor's buildings result in attention being focused on the surfaces and, above all, on how they are composed. Zumthor himself says his ideal is to create "an architectural object that is in a state of equilibrium."

Since setting up his own practice, Zumthor has exerted a strong influence on the work of young architects, both in the Grisons and much further afield — in particular through buildings such as the Sogn Benedetg Chapel in Sumvitg (1985–88), Switzerland, and the Kunsthaus, or art gallery, in Bregenz (1990–97), Austria. As an architect, he has done more to preserve local culture and create an appropriate form of construction in the mountains than in the 11 years when he worked as a conservator of ancient monuments.   S.S.

PETER ZUMTHOR

1 | Site plan: entrance and bathing level
2 | Main pool
3 | Cubic volume of building in Vals stone
4 | Terrace
5 | Front face

Cesar Pelli

Petronas Towers | KUALA LUMPUR (MALAYSIA) 1992–1997

2

On April 12, 1996, the U.S.-based Council on Tall Buildings and Urban Habitat named Petronas Towers the World's Tallest Building. On July 10, 1997, it muddied the distinction by subdividing the designation into three categories. Regardless of these changes, Petronas Towers represents the Malaysian government's bid to express economic prosperity in the Western-style architectural form of a gargantuan office and retail complex. As part of an 18 million-square-foot (1.67 million-square-meter) development on a 100-acre site, this building encloses 7.5 million square feet (697,000 square meters) of space in a twin tower structure whose 1,483-foot (452-meter) height has spent at least some tenure as the world's tallest. Intended as a new gateway to the city of Kuala Lumpur, the 88-story behemoth occupies the site of a former race track. The new facility includes a petroleum museum, symphony hall, and multi-media conference center, as well as parking for 4,500 cars and shops for the people who drive them.

Several structural innovations made the soaring towers possible. Concrete columns at the building perimeter slope at the setbacks to eliminate the need for bulky transfer elements. Concrete ring beams connect the columns to complete the outer frame. Steel finds limited application: in supports for the

CESAR PELLI

1926	Born on October 12 in Tucuman, Argentina
1950	National University in Tucuman, diploma in architecture
1952	Moves to the U.S. to study architecture at the University of Illinois at Champaign–Urbana
1954	Completes a master's degree in architecture; works for Eero Saarinen in Bloomfield Hills, Michigan; project designer, TWA Terminal at John F. Kennedy Airport, New York City; buildings at Yale University in New Haven, Connecticut
1961	Begins teaching at the Yale School of Architecture
1964–68	Director of design for Daniel, Mann, Johnson & Mendenhall in Los Angeles
1968–76	Partner for design at Gruen Associates in Los Angeles; Pacific Design Center in Los Angeles; U.S. Embassy in Tokyo
1977	Opens Cesar Pelli & Associates; Museum of Modern Art Expansion and Residential Tower in New York City
1981–88	World Financial Center, New York City
1992–97	Petronas Towers, Kuala Lumpur, Malaysia
1995	Gold Medal, American Institute of Architects

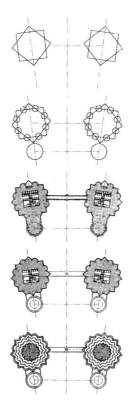

1

1 | Development of plan forms
2 | Twin towers with skybridge
3 | Towers during construction

concrete-filled metal decks on each floor, and as framing for the dramatic 190-foot (58 meter) long skybridge connecting the towers. In the foundations, 208 so-called "barrette piles" are anchored, amazingly, in the dense sandy soil.

These technical achievements play a supporting role figuratively as well as literally. Even in a project of outlandish size, architectural expression here emphasizes elegance and restraint over technical exuberance. These qualities have characterized Pelli's work consistently throughout his career.

Pelli's architectural considerations have always gone far beyond the isolated object. His World Financial Center in New York City, 1981–88, is as frank an expression of building technology as any of his earlier designs. Yet it also refers and defers to the surrounding Manhattan skyline with a genteel urbanism that never even remotely suggests kitsch in the way so many of its contemporaries do. At the ground level, its plaza and winter garden show that architectural design can be an instrument for bringing private lives into public spaces. Even though he has worked successfully with many other building types, Pelli earned a reputation as a skyscraper designer for a series of urban office and retail high-rises that began with the World Financial Center and culminated in the Petronas project.

Petronas Towers may be more than simply an upward reach. The floorplate derives its shape from Islamic geometric principles, and the tower spires echo minarets. It is doubtful that these formal cues provide sufficient contextualizing in a place which lacks a century of skyscraper urbanism as precedent: Malaysia's industrialization has been rapid and recent. The question remains whether a Western, essentially American building type is appropriate to this culture — not how high the building rises, but how well it is grounded.   C.L.R.

1 | Control tower
2, 3 | Interior of terminal
4 | Model
5 | Site layout
6 | View from approach road

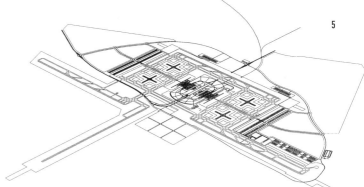

At the end of the twentieth century, airports represent the most complex building assignments confronting architects and their clients. The sheer dimensions, functional requirements, and security technology — coupled with the magic that is still attached to the whole idea of flying — make the design and construction of an airport a major challenge. What is more, airports today are often the first picture one has of a foreign country; they have a representative function to fulfill that would not have been conceivable a few years ago. In this context, creating an unmistakable physiognomy for an internationally identical function is proving to be more and more of a problem — one that cannot be overcome simply by relying on outstanding technological achievements.

The growth of air transport has led the up-and-coming industrial nations of Asia to build airports of unprecedented dimensions. One can recognize in them the structural, functional, and constructional clarity of a modern form of architecture that is appropriate to the purpose it has to fulfill.

In 1992, the Japanese architect Kisho Kurokawa was entrusted with the development of the new airport in Kuala Lumpur, Malaysia. When completed, it will be used by up to 25 million passengers a year, who will pass through a main terminal with a satellite building set in front. The activities of the airport will be handled in optimal fashion in a building five stories high, and with an area of more than 4.3 million square feet (400,000 square meters). During peak periods of construction, up to 20,000 workers were employed on the site. Coordinating their activities successfully was a logistical miracle in itself. An extension of the complex is already planned for the next century, which should increase the capacity to 90 million passengers. Kurokawa is also drawing up plans for new cities around this international transport node.

What is immediately striking in developments on such a large scale is the flexibility of the functional processes, which is an essential factor to their success. This is a quality passengers take for granted, however. This new airport has its own unique features as well. In the design and planning, Kurokawa was inspired by the image of a forest, which was to become a symbol of the whole complex. The forest, which once covered

large areas of Malaysia, was to be reflected in the structure of the new airport. It was probably the power of this symbol that helped gain Kisho Kurokawa the commission to plan and build the project within a period of only six years. The new airport superimposes on Malaysia's heritage an unobtrusive yet modern high-technology plan in which great importance is attached to the climatic characteristics of the country. Passengers entering the main terminal are prepared for the adventure of flying by elegant shell and tent roof structures with top lights, while the same structures extend to welcome visitors to Malaysia in the semi-shade of a protective forest.

The concept of an airport forest pursued by Kurokawa in this project is not specific to Malaysia. It is echoed, for example, by the profound conviction of the Japanese that a harmony of nature and technology is both desirable and possible. The airport in Kuala Lumpur, therefore, really is a new Asian building, and as such, deserves special attention. W.K.

KISHO KUROKAWA

1934	Born on April 8 in Nagoya, Japan
1957	Completes studies in the faculty of architecture at the University of Kyoto, Japan
1959	Completes studies in the faculty of architecture at the University of Tokyo under Kenzo Tange
1960	Active participation in the architectural Metabolist movement; utopian designs for new cities
1962	Establishes his own architectural office; numerous prizes and honors, teaching activities, publications on architecture, exhibitions
1972	Nakagin Capsule Tower, Tokyo
1976	Sony Tower, Osaka, Japan
1986	Médaille d'Or, Académie Française d'Architecture
1988	Museum for Contemporary Art, Hiroshima, Japan; Japanese–German Center, Berlin
1991	Melbourne Center, Australia
1992	Museum for Photography, Nara, Japan; Pacific Tower, Paris
1992–98	International Airport, Kuala Lumpur, Malaysia

6

Frank O. Gehry

Guggenheim Museum | BILBAO 1993-1997

1

FRANK O. GEHRY

1929	Born on February 28 in Toronto, Canada
1954-	Bachelor of Architecture degree from the University of Southern California, Los Angeles; goes on to study city planning at Harvard University's Graduate School of Design, Cambridge, Massachusetts
1957-61	Apprentices with various architectural firms
1962	Founds his own firm, Frank O. Gehry and Associates, in Santa Monica, California
1978	Designs his own house in Santa Monica
1979-80	Spiller Residence, Venice, California; Temporary Contemporary Museum, Santa Monica Place
1981-84	Loyola Law School and California Aerospace Museum, Los Angeles
1987	Fish Dance Restaurant, Kobe, Japan
1989	Pritzker Architecture Prize
1991	Chiat/Day/Mojo Advertising Agency, Venice, California
1992	University of Toledo Center for the Visual Arts, Ohio; University of Iowa Laboratories Building, Iowa City
1993-97	Guggenheim Museum, Bilbao, Spain
1994	Vitra Headquarters in Basel, Switzerland; American Center in Paris
1998	Current work includes a contemporary music museum in Seattle, Washington, and the Walt Disney Concert Hall, Los Angeles

Adjectives like "organic" or "sculptural" are inadequate to describe this branch of the Guggenheim Museum completed in Bilbao, Spain, in late 1997. "A force of nature" seems better, since the titanium-clad elements of this 258,000-square-foot (24,000-square-meter) assemblage so strongly resemble unfurling tree leaves, budding branches, or spreading roots.

Gehry's working method is much closer to that of a sculptor than to that of an architect. In dozens of drawings and in models, some of which were assembled from the crudest cardboard and crumpled paper, he and colleagues studied the design, tore it apart, and refined it in an iterative process that relied almost entirely on the architect's intuition.

To realize Gehry's complex shapes, his architectural practice — based in Santa Monica, California — pioneered the use of a highly sophisticated computer-modeling application called CATIA, more commonly used in industry. The contours of Bilbao's physical model were traced with a special wand so that the computer could digitize the design. Once the design was completed, the computer defined the form for the computer-aided fabrication of the titanium skin and analyzed the supporting steel structure, conveying to the fabricator the loads and geometries of the connections, greatly reducing the time needed to calculate their proper strength.

To the casual observer, the completed building appears to slouch aimlessly along the bank of the Nervion River, but the itinerary the visitor follows is in fact carefully considered. One enters from either the street, down a grand flight of stairs, or a from a ramped riverside promenade. These routes meet in a lofty central atrium that can be compared to the hollowed-out interior of a tree trunk. A stair twists crazily upward, clad in metal that is skinned with scales of glass. Curved wedges, finished in plaster or stone, appear to sway in the dappled light cast by skylights tilted at various angles. Gallery suites open out from this central space like tree branches. Gehry has seemingly pushed, pulled, or twisted every surface and space. Each move is echoed in the exterior, where the titanium shingles pick up the light as if this were a giant hammered-silver serving dish.

Some critics have taken Gehry's work to task for overpowering the art with dramatic forms. Bilbao may not be suitable for small works of great delicacy, but it seems to please artists willing to enter into a dialogue with the architect's sensuous spacemaking. On the other hand, the nearly unanimous praise the project has received has vindicated the faith of Guggenheim Director Thomas Krens, who saw a chance to transform a fading industrial city through the marriage of Basque cultural aspiration and a great collection — one that could never fully be displayed in its original Frank Lloyd Wright-designed building in New York City.   J.S.R.

2

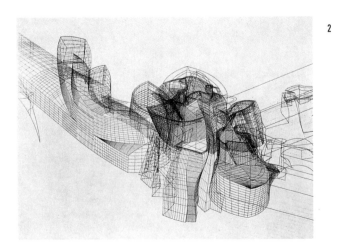

3

4

5

1 | Entrance
2 | Computer drawing
3 | Overall view
4 | Detail of facade with
   titanium cladding
5 | Atrium

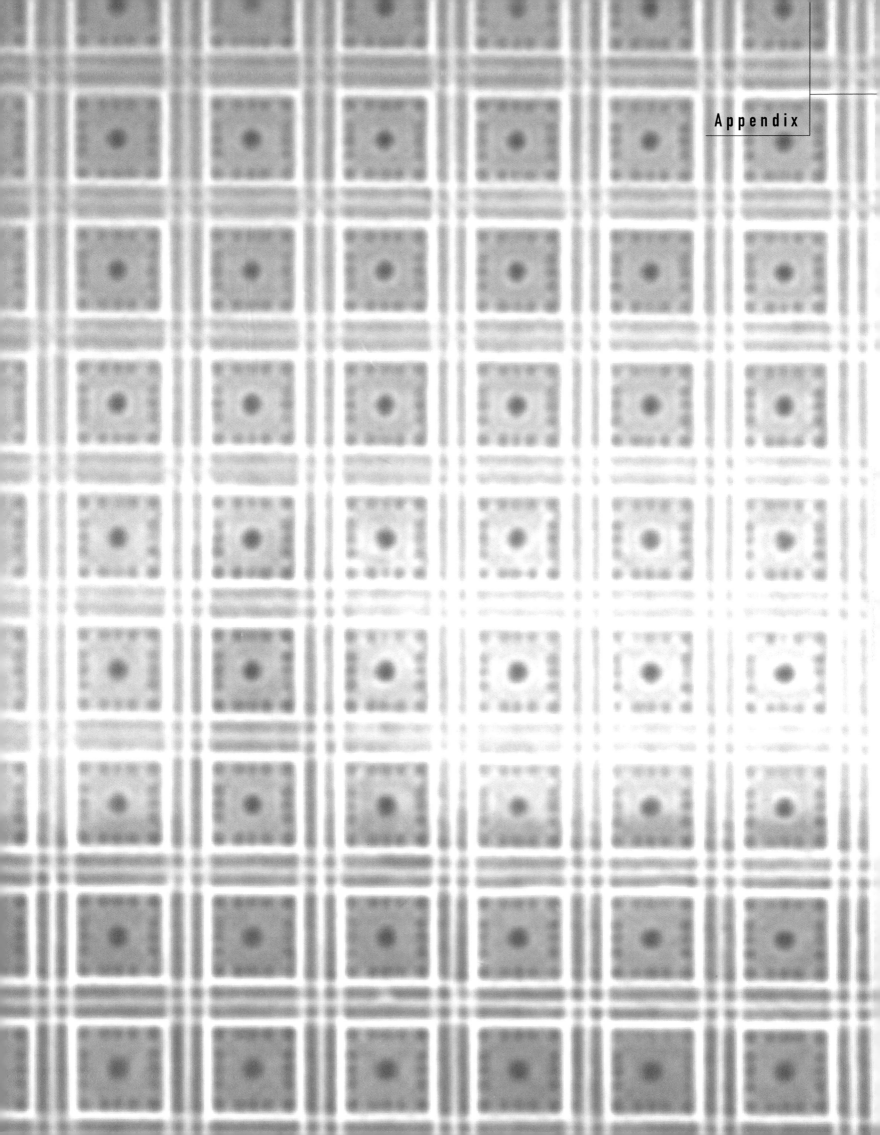

Selected Bibliography

Suggestions for further reading, listed in the order of the projects featured:

Antoni Gaudí, Sagrada Familia   p. 10
Güell, Xavier (ed.): *Antoni Gaudí,* Bologna 1986 (reprint, Barcelona 1992); Zerbst, Rainer: *Gaudí 1852–1926: Ein Leben für die Architektur,* Cologne 1988

Hendrik Petrus Berlage, Stock Exchange   p. 12
Bock, Manfred: *Anfänge einer neuen Architektur: Berlages Beitrag zur architektonischen Kultur der Niederlande im ausgehenden 19. Jahrhundert,* The Hague 1983; Polano, Sergio: *Hendrik Petrus Berlage: Complete Works,* New York 1988

Charles Rennie Mackintosh, Glasgow School of Art   p. 14
Macaulay, James: *Glasgow School of Art: Charles Rennie Mackintosh, Architecture in Detail,* London 1993; Steele, James: *Charles Rennie Mackintosh: Synthesis in Form,* London/New York 1994; Kaplan, Wendy (ed.): *Charles Rennie Mackintosh,* New York/London/Paris 1996; Fiell, Charlotte and Peter: *Charles Rennie Mackintosh (1868–1928),* Cologne/London 1997

Daniel H. Burnham, Fuller Building (Flatiron)   p. 16
Moore, Charles: *Daniel H. Burnham: Architect, Planner of Cities,* 2 vols., Boston/New York 1921; Hines, Thomas S.: *Burnham of Chicago: Architect and Planner,* New York 1974; *Flatiron: A Photographic History of the World's First Steel Frame Skyscraper,* Washington, D.C. 1990

Auguste Perret, Apartment Building, rue Franklin   p. 18
Collins, Peter: *Concrete: The Vision of a New Architecture — A Study of Auguste Perret and His Precursors,* London 1959; Zahar, Marcel: *D'une doctrine d'architecture — Auguste Perret,* Paris 1959

Otto Wagner, Postal Savings Bank   p. 20
Graf, Otto Antonia: *Otto Wagner: Das Werk des Architekten,* Vienna/Cologne/Graz 1985; Österreichische Postsparkasse (ed.): *Otto Wagner: Die österreichische Postsparkasse,* Vienna 1996

Josef Hoffmann, Sanatorium   p. 22
Sekler, Eduard: *Josef Hoffmann: Das architektonische Werk,* Salzburg/Vienna 1982

Eliel Saarinen, Main Station   p. 24
Hausen, Marika: *The Helsinki Railway Station in Eliel Saarinen's First Versions 1904,* Studies in Art History, 3, Helsinki 1977; Hausen, Marika/Mikkola, Kirmo/Amberg, Anna-Lisa/Valto, Tytti: *Eliel Saarinen: Projects 1896–1923,* Helsinki 1990

Joseph Maria Olbrich, Hochzeitsturm and Exhibition Building   p. 26
Olbrich, Joseph Maria: *Architektur,* 3 vols., Berlin 1901–14 (reprint, Tübingen 1988); Latham, Ian: *Joseph Maria Olbrich,* Stuttgart 1981; *Joseph M. Olbrich 1867–1908,* exh. cat., Darmstadt 1983

Peter Behrens, AEG Turbine Factory   p. 28
Buddensieg, Tilmann/Rogge, Henning (eds.): *Peter Behrens und die AEG 1907–14,* Berlin 1980; Heuser, Mechthild: "Die Fenster zum Hof: Die Turbinenhalle, Behrens und Mies van der Rohe," in Pfeifer, Hans-Georg (ed.): *Peter Behrens: "Wer aber will sagen, was Schönheit sei?",* exh. cat., Düsseldorf 1990

Adolf Loos, Goldman & Salatsch Building   p. 30
Czech, Hermann/Mistelbauer, Wolfgang: *Das Looshaus,* Vienna 1976; Rukschcio, Burkhard/Schachel, Roland: *Adolf Loos: Leben und Werk,* Salzburg/Vienna 1982

Walter Gropius with Adolf Meyer, Fagus Factory   p. 32
Nerdinger, Winfried: *Der Architekt Walter Gropius: Zeichnungen, Pläne, Fotos, Werkverzeichnis,* Berlin 1985; Futagawa, Yukio (ed.): *Walter Gropius: Bauhaus, Dessau, Germany, 1925–26, Fagus Factory,* Tokyo 1994

Albert Kahn, River Rouge Plant   p. 34
Hildebrand, Grant: *Designing for Industry: The Architecture of Albert Kahn,* Cambridge (Mass.)/London 1974; Bucci, Federico: *Albert Kahn: Architect of Ford,* New York 1994

Erich Mendelsohn, Einstein Tower   p. 36
Zevi, Bruno: *Erich Mendelsohn,* Zurich 1983; Achenbach, Sigrid (ed.): *Erich Mendelsohn: Ideen Bauten Skizzen,* exh. cat., Berlin 1987; Klotz, Heinrich (ed.): *Erich Mendelsohn: Das Gesamtschaffen des Architekten,* Brunswick 1989; *Erich Mendelsohns Einsteinturm in Potsdam,* Brandenburgisches Landesamt für Denkmalpflege, vol. 5, Potsdam 1994

Gunnar Asplund, Municipal Library   p. 38
Caldenby, Claes/Hultin, Olof (eds.): *Asplund,* Stockholm 1985; Caldenby, Claes/Lindvall, Jöran/Wang, Wilfried (eds.): *20th-Century Architecture: Sweden,* Munich/New York 1998

Fritz Höger, Chilehaus   p. 40
Binding, Rudolf G.: *Das Chilehaus,* Berlin 1939; Busch, Harald/Sloman, Ricardo Federico: *Das Chilehaus in Hamburg, sein Bauherr und sein Architekt,* Hamburg 1974; Nicolaisen, Dörte: *Das Chilehaus als Schiff,* Nimwegen 1986; Bucciarelli, Piergiacomo: *Fritz Höger. Hanseatischer Baumeister 1877–1949,* Berlin 1992

Rudolph Michael Schindler, Lovell Beach House   p. 42
Sarnitz, August: *R.M. Schindler: Architekt 1887–1953. Ein Wagner-Schüler zwischen internationalem Stil und Raum-Architektur,* Vienna/Munich 1986; Noever, Peter (ed.): *MAK Center for Art and Architecture: R.M. Schindler,* Munich/NewYork 1995

Gerrit Thomas Rietveld, Rietveld-Schröder House   p. 44
Overy, Paul/Büler, Lenneke/den Oudsten, Frank/Mulder, Bertus: *Das Rietveld-Schröder-Haus,* Brunswick/Wiesbaden 1988; Küper, Marijke/van Zijl, Ida: *Gerrit Th. Rietveld 1888–1964: Het volledige Werk,* exh. cat., Utrecht 1992

Walter Gropius with Adolf Meyer, Bauhaus   p. 46
Gropius, Walter: *Bauhausbauten in Dessau,* Munich 1930 (facsimile, Mainz 1974); Isaacs, Reginald: *Gropius: An Illustrated Biography of the Bauhaus,* Boston 1991

J.A. Brinkman and L.C. van der Vlugt, Van Nelle Factory   p. 48
Adriaansz, Elly: *Leen van der Vlugt, Wiederhall Architectural Series,* 14, Amsterdam 1993

Ludwig Mies van der Rohe and others, Weissenhof Estate   p. 50
Kirsch, Karin: *Die Weißenhofsiedlung: Werkbundausstellung "Die Wohnung,"* Stuttgart 1927/1987; Cramer, Johannes/Gutschow, Niels: *Bauausstellungen: Eine Architekturgeschichte des 20. Jahrhunderts,* Stuttgart/Berlin 1984

Konstantin Melnikov, Rusakov Workers' Club   p. 52
Chan-Magomedow, Selim O.: *Pioniere der sowjetischen Architektur,* Vienna/Berlin 1983; Schlögel, Karl: *Moskau lesen,* Berlin 1984; *Avantgarde II: Sowjetische Architektur 1924–1937,* exh. cat., Stuttgart 1993

William Van Alen, Chrysler Building   p. 54
Chrysler Tower Corporation: *The Chrysler Building,* New York 1930; Breeze, Carla: *New York Deco,* New York 1993

Ludwig Mies van der Rohe, Tugendhat House   p. 56
Tegethoff, Wolf: *Mies van der Rohe: the Villas and Country Houses,* Cambridge (Mass.) 1985; Schulze, Franz: *Ludwig Mies van der Rohe: Eine kritische Biographie,* Berlin 1986, pp. 168–178; Sapák, Jan: "Das Alltagsleben in der Villa Tugendhat," in: *Werk, Bauen und Wohnen,* 42, vol. 12, 1988, pp. 15–23

Le Corbusier with Pierre Jeanneret, Villa Savoye   p. 58
Boesiger, Willy, and others (eds.): *Le Corbusier et Pierre Jeanneret: Oeuvre complète,* vol. I: 1910–1929 and vol. II: 1929–1934, Zurich 1935; Benton, Tim: "Villa Savoye and the Architect's Practice," in: *Architectural Design,* vol. 55, no. 7–8, 1985, pp. 9–30

Pierre Chareau with Bernard Bijvoët, Maison de Verre   p. 60
Frampton, Kenneth/Vellay, Marc: *Pierre Chareau: Architect and Craftsman 1883–1950,* New York 1985; Brace Taylor, Brian: *Pierre Chareau: Designer and Architect,* Cologne 1992

Giuseppe Terragni, Casa del Fascio   p. 62
Zevi, Bruno: *Giuseppe Terragni,* Bologna 1980; Ciucci, Giorgio: *Giuseppe Terragni: Opera completa,* Milan 1996

Alvar Aalto, Sanatorium   p. 64
Schildt, Göran: *Alvar Aalto: The Decisive Years,* Helsinki 1986; Schildt, Göran: *Alvar Aalto: The Complete Catalogue of Architecture, Design and Art,* Helsinki 1995; Schildt, Göran: *Alvar Aalto: The Master Works,* New York 1998

Shreve, Lamb, and Harmon, Empire State Building   p. 66

Goldman, Jonathan: *The Empire State Building Book,* New York 1980; Tournae, John: *The Empire State Building: The Making of a Landmark,* New York 1995

George Howe and William Lescaze, PSFS Building   p. 68

Jordy, William H.: "PSFS: Its Development and Its Significance in Modern Architecture," in: *Journal of the Society of Architectural Historians,* no. 21, May 1962, pp. 47–102; Jordy, William H./ Wright, Henry: "PSFS Revisited," in: *Architectural Forum,* no. 120, May 1964, pp. 124–129

Frank Lloyd Wright, Fallingwater   p. 70

Alofsin, Anthony: *Frank Lloyd Wright — The Lost Years, 1910–22,* Chicago 1993; Levine, Neil: *The Architecture of Frank Lloyd Wright,* Princeton 1996

Adalberto Libera, Casa Malaparte   p. 72

Talamona, Marida: *Casa Malaparte,* Milan 1990; *Adalberto Libera: Opera completa,* Milan 1989

Arne Jacobsen with Fleming Lassen, Town Hall   p. 74

Faber, Tobias: *Arne Jacobsen,* New York 1964; Dyssegard, Søren: *Arne Jacobsen — A Danish Architect,* Copenhagen 1972

Frank Lloyd Wright, Solomon R. Guggenheim Museum   p. 76

Jordy, William H.: *American Buildings and Their Architects: The Impact of European Modernism in the Mid-Twentieth Century,* vol. 5, chap. V, New York/Oxford 1972; Levine, Neil: *The Architecture of Frank Lloyd Wright,* Princeton 1996

Lev Rudnyev, Lomonosov University   p. 78

Ikonnikov, Andrei: *Russian Architecture of the Soviet Period,* Moscow 1988; Noever, Peter (ed.): *Tyrannei des Schönen: Architektur der Stalin-Zeit,* Munich/ New York 1994

Kenzo Tange, Peace Center   p. 80

"Kenzo Tange: Il centro della Pace ad Hiroshima," in: *Casabella,* no. 212, Sept.– Oct. 1956, pp. 13–18; "Kenzo Tange. Friedenszentrum in Hiroshima," in: *Bauen + Wohnen,* no. 1, Jan. 1960, pp. 2–7; *Kenzo Tange and Associates: 40 Ans d'urbanisme et d'architecture,* Tokyo 1987; Bettinotti, M. (ed.): *Kenzo Tange 1946–1996: Architecture and Urban Design,* Milan 1996

Le Corbusier, Notre-Dame-du-Haut Chapel   p. 82

Boesiger, Willy, and others (ed.): *Le Corbusier et son atelier rue de Sèrres 35: Oeuvre complète,* vol. VI: 1952–57, Zurich 1957; Le Corbusier: *Ronchamp, les carnets de la recherche patiente,* Zurich 1957; Petit, Jean: *Le livre de Ronchamp,* Paris 1961; Pauly, Danièle: *La Chapelle de Ronchamp — the Chapel at Ronchamp,* Paris/Boston 1997

Ludwig Mies van der Rohe, Seagram Building   p. 84

Blaser, Werner: *Mies van der Rohe: Less is More,* New York 1986; Spaeth, David: *Mies van der Rohe: Der Architekt der technischen Perfektion,* Stuttgart 1986, pp. 140–149

BBPR, Torre Velasca   p. 86

Kallman, G.M.: "Modern Tower in Old Milan," in: *Architectural Forum,* no. 2, Feb. 1958; "BBPR: Tre problemi di ambientamento — Chiarimento," in: *Casabella,* no. 232, Oct. 1959; Samonà, Giuseppe: "La Torre Velasca a Milano," in: *L'Architettura,* no. 40, Feb. 1959

Pier Luigi Nervi, Palazzetto dello Sport   p. 88

Desideri, P./Nervi, Pier Luigi Jr./Positano, G.: *Pier Luigi Nervi,* Bologna 1979 (Zurich 1982); *Gestalten in Beton: Zum Werk von Pier Liugi Nervi,* Cologne 1989

Eero Saarinen, TWA Terminal   p. 90

Temko, Allan: *Eero Saarinen,* New York/London 1962; Fisher, Thomas: "Landmarks: TWA Terminal," in: *Progressive Architecture,* no. 73, May 1992, pp. 96–107; Hart Leubkeman, Christopher: "Form Swallows Function," in: *Progressive Architecture,* no. 73, May 1992, p. 108

Hans B. Scharoun, New Philharmonic   p. 92

Bürkle, J.C.: *Hans Scharoun,* Zurich 1993; Wisniewski, Edgar: *Die Berliner Philharmonie und ihr Kammermusiksaal,* Berlin 1993; Geist, Johann Friedrich/Kürvers, Klaus/Rausch, Dieter: *Hans Scharoun: Chronik zu Leben und Werk,* exh. cat., Berlin 1994; Blundell-Jones, Peter: *Hans Scharoun,* London 1995

Carlo Scarpa, Museo di Castelvecchio   p. 94

Dal Co, Francesco/Mazzariol, Giuseppe: *Carlo Scarpa 1906–1978,* Milan 1984; *Carlo Scarpa: Architektur,* Niederteufen 1986; Los, Sergio: *Carlo Scarpa,* Stuttgart 1995.

Jørn Utzon, Opera House   p. 96

Utzon, Jørn: "The Sydney Opera House. What Happened and Why," in: *Architectural Record,* May 1967, pp. 189–192; Wilson, Forrest: "The Sydney Opera House: A Survivor," in: *Architecture,* Sept. 1989, pp. 103–110

Oscar Niemeyer, Congress Buildings   p. 98

Staubli, Willi: *Brasilia,* London 1966; Underwood, David: *Niemeyer and the Architecture of Brazil,* New York 1994

Alison and Peter Smithson, Economist Building   p. 100

Dunster, David (ed.): *Alison and Peter Smithson, Architectural Monograph 7,* London 1982; Webster, Helena (ed.): *Modernism without Rhetoric: Essays on the work of Alison and Peter Smithson,* London 1997

Robert Venturi, Vanna Venturi House   p. 102

Dunster, David: *Key Buildings of the 20th Century: Houses 1945–1989,* London 1990; Schwarz, Frederic (ed.): *Mother's House: the Evolution of Vanna Venturi's House in Chestnut Hill,* New York 1992

Kenzo Tange, Olympic Stadia   p. 104

Banham, Reyner: *Megastructures: Urban Futures of the Recent Past,* New York 1970; Kultermann, Udo: *Kenzo Tange,* Zurich 1978; *Kenzo Tange and Urtec 1946–1979,* SD (Space Design), Tokyo 1979; *Kenzo Tange and Urtec 1983,* SD, Tokyo 1983; *Kenzo Tange Associates 1987,* SD, Tokyo 1987; *Kenzo Tange Associates 1991,* SD, Tokyo 1991

Louis I. Kahn, Parliament Buildings   p. 106

Ronner, Heinz/Jhaveri, Sharad: *Louis I. Kahn: Complete Works 1935–1974,* second expanded edition, Basel/Boston 1987; Brownlee, David/De Long, David G. (eds.): *Louis I. Kahn: In the Realm of Architecture,* exh. cat., Los Angeles/New York 1991; Futagawa, Yukio (ed.): *Louis I. Kahn: National Capital of Bangladesh, Dhaka, Bangladesh, 1962–83,* Tokyo 1994; *GA — Global Architecture,* no. 72, Tokyo 1994

Richard Meier, Smith House   p. 108

"Le Corbusier à la Mode," in: *Architectural Design,* Jan. 1971, p. 24; Eisenman, Peter: "Letter to the Editor," in: *Architectural Design,* Aug. 1971, p. 520; *Richard Meier Houses,* New York 1997

Skidmore, Owings & Merrill, John Hancock Center   p. 110

Architecture of Skidmore, Owings & Merrill 1963–1973, New York 1974; *Bruce Graham of SOM,* New York 1989

Richard Buckminster Fuller, Pavilion for the World Exposition   p. 112

Krausse, Joachim (ed.): *Bedienungsanleitung für das Raumschiff Erde und andere Schriften,* Hamburg 1973; Ward, James (ed.): *The Artifacts of R. Buckminster Fuller,* 4 vols., New York/London 1985

Günter Behnisch with Frei Otto, Olympic Games Complex   p. 114

Gauzin-Müller, Dominique: *Behnisch & Partner: 50 Jahre Architektur,* Berlin 1997

Herman Hertzberger, Centraal Beheer Office Building   p. 116

Hertzberger, Herman: *Vom Bauen: Vorlesungen über Architektur,* Munich 1995; van Bergeijk, Herman: *Herman Hertzberger,* Basel 1997

I.M. Pei, East Building of the National Gallery of Art   p. 118

Huxtable, Ada Louise: "Geometry with Drama," in: *New York Times,* May 7, 1978; Amery, Colin: "Inside the NGA," in: *Architectural Review,* Jan. 1979; Wiseman, Carter: *I.M. Pei: A Profile in American Architecture,* New York 1990

Sverre Fehn, Archaeological Museum   p. 120

Museum of Finnish Architecture: The Poetry of the Straight Line, Helsinki 1992; Norberg-Schulz, Christian: *Skandinavische Architektur,* Stuttgart 1993

Minoru Yamasaki, World Trade Center   p. 122

"The Architect Was Told 'World Trade,' So He Planned Big," in: *Smithsonian,* Jan. 1978; Yamasaki, Minoru: *A Life in Architecture,* New York/Tokyo 1979

Selected Bibliography

Aldo Rossi, San Cataldo Cemetery   p. 124

Arnell, Peter/Bickford, Ted: *Aldo Rossi: Buildings and Projects*, New York 1985; Ferlenga, Alberto (ed.): *Aldo Rossi: Architetture Opera completa*, 3 vols., Milan 1987–96; Rossi, Aldo: *Wissenschaftliche Selbstbiographie*, Bern 1988

Skidmore, Owings & Merrill, Sears Tower   p. 126

Architecture of Skidmore, Owings & Merrill 1963–1973, New York 1974; *Bruce Graham of SOM*, New York 1989

Renzo Piano and Richard Rogers, Centre Georges Pompidou   p. 128

Nakamura, Toshio (ed.): *Richard Rogers 1978–1988*, Tokyo 1988; Silver, Nathan: *The Making of Beaubourg*, Cambridge (Mass.) 1994; Burdett, Richard (ed.): *Richard Rogers Partnership. Bauten & Projekte*, Stuttgart 1996

Hans Hollein, Museum Abteiberg   p. 130

Pehnt, Wolfgang: *Hans Hollein Museum in Mönchengladbach: Architektur als Collage*, Frankfurt am Main 1986; Nash, Douglas: "Simulated Space: Hans Hollein and the Contemporary Museum," in: *The Politics of Space: Architecture, Painting and Theater in Postmodern Germany*, New York 1996

Álvaro Siza Vieira and others, São Victor District Housing   p. 132

Álvaro Siza: Professione poetica, Milan 1986; *Álvaro Siza 1954–1988*, *a+u* extra edition, 6, 1989; Trigueiros, Luiz: *Álvaro Siza, 1986–1995*, Lisbon 1996; Testa, Peter: *Álvaro Siza*, Basel/Boston/Berlin 1996

James Stirling with Michael Wilford, Neue Staatsgalerie   p. 134

Jencks, Charles: "The Casual, the Shocking and the Well-Ordered Acropolis," in: *Architectural Design*, no. 54, 3/4, 1984, pp. 48–55; "Stirling in Stuttgart," in: *Progressive Architecture*, no. 65, Oct. 1984, pp. 67–85; Rodiek, Thorsten: *James Stirling: Die Neue Staatsgalerie Stuttgart*, Stuttgart 1984

Andres Duany and Elizabeth Plater-Zyberk, Seaside   p. 136

Katz, Peter: *The New Urbanism: Toward an Architecture of Community*, New York 1991; Sexton, Richard: *Parallel Utopias*, San Francisco 1995

Philip Johnson, AT&T (today Sony) Building   p. 138

Johnson, Philip: *Writings*, New York 1979; Schulze, Franz: *Philip Johnson: Life and Work*, New York 1994

Helmut Jahn, James R. Thompson Center   p. 140

Miller, Nory: *Helmut Jahn*, New York 1986; Dobney, Stephen (ed.): *Murphy/Jahn: Selected and Current Works*, Victoria (Australia) 1995; Blaser, Werner: *Helmut Jahn: Transparency/Transparenz*, Basel/Boston/Berlin 1996

Richard Rogers, Lloyd's of London   p. 142

Appleyard, Bryan: *Richard Rogers: A Biography*, London 1986; Sudjic, Deyan: *The Architecture of Richard Rogers*, London 1994; Powell, Kenneth: *Lloyd's Building: Richard Rogers Partnership*, London 1994

Norman Foster, Hong Kong & Shanghai Bank   p. 144

Chaslin, François (ed.): *Norman Foster*, Stuttgart 1987; Lambot, Ian (ed.): *Norman Foster: Team 4 and Foster Associates: Buildings and Projects*, London 1989; Treiber, Daniel: *Norman Foster*, Basel 1992

Rafael Moneo, Museum of Roman Art   p. 146

"Support, Surface: Rafael Moneo's Design for the Archaeological Museum of Mérida," in: *Lotus International*, no. 35, 1985, pp. 86–92; "Rafael Moneo: Museum Mérida, Spain," in: *Progressive Architecture*, no. 67/1, 1986, pp. 73–83

Jean Nouvel, Institut du Monde Arabe   p. 148

Patrice, Goulet: *Jean Nouvel*, Paris 1987; Blazwick, Iwona/Jacques, Michel/Withers, Jane (eds.): *Jean Nouvel Emmanuel Cattani et Associés*, Zurich/Munich/London 1992; Boissière, Olivier: *Jean Nouvel*, Basel/Boston/Berlin 1996

Arata Isozaki, Tsukuba Center Building   p. 150

"Isozaki, Arata. Rhetoric of the Cylinder," in: *The Japan Architect*, April 1976, pp. 61–63; Futagawa, Yukio (ed.): *Arata Isozaki*, vol. 1, 1959–1978, Tokyo 1991, p.160

Coop Himmelb(l)au, Attic Conversion   p. 152

Coop Himmelblau: *Sie leben in Wien*, Vienna 1975; Coop Himmelblau: *Architektur ist jetzt*, Stuttgart 1983; Coop Himmelblau: *Die Faszination der Stadt/The Power of the City*, Darmstadt 1988

Johan Otto von Spreckelsen with Paul Andreu, La Grande Arche   p. 154

Peters, Paulhans: *Paris: Die großen Projekte*, Berlin 1992; Gleiniger, Andrea/Matzig, Gerhard/Redecke, Sebastian: *Paris: Contemporary Architecture*, Munich/New York 1997

I.M. Pei, Pyramide, Le Grand Louvre   p. 156

Loriers, M.C.: "The Pyramid Prevails," in: *Progressive Architecture*, no. 70, 6, 1989; Wiseman, Carter: *I.M. Pei: A Profile in American Architecture*, New York 1990

Christian de Portzamparc, Cité de la Musique   p. 158

Jacques, Michel (ed.): *Christian de Portzamparc/arc en rêve centre d'architecture*, Basel/Boston 1996; Melhuish, Clare: *Cité de la Musique*, typescript to be published in: *Architecture in Detail*, London

Peter Eisenman, Wexner Center for the Visual Arts   p. 160

Johnson, Philip/Wigley, Mark: *Deconstructivist Architecture*, New York 1988; *Peter Eisenman*, Progressive Architecture special edition, Oct. 1989

Oswald Mathias Ungers, Contemporary Art Wing   p. 162

Ungers, Oswald Mathias: *Architektur 1951–1990*, Stuttgart 1991; Kieren, Martin: *Oswald Mathias Ungers*, Zurich 1994

Tadao Ando, Church of the Light   p. 164

Ando, Tadao: *The Colours of Light*, London 1996; Drew, Philip: *Church on the Water, Church of the Light: Tadao Ando*, London 1996

Rem Koolhaas, Gallery of Contemporary Art   p. 166

Rem Koolhaas, arch +, no. 132, June 1996; *OMA/Rem Koolhaas 1992–96*, el croquis, no. 79, 1996; OMA/Koolhaas, Rem/Mau, Bruce: *S,M,L,XL*, New York 1995 (Cologne 1997)

Renzo Piano, Kansai International Airport   p. 168

Buchanan, Peter: *Renzo Piano Building Workshop*, London 1993; Piano, Renzo: *Mein Architektur-Logbuch*, Ostfildern-Ruit 1997, pp. 150–163

Dominique Perrault, Bibliothèque Nationale de France   p. 170

Jacques, Michel (ed.): *Bibliothèque Nationale de France 1989–1995: Dominique Perrault Architecte*, Paris 1995; *Dominique Perrault: Des Natures — Jenseits der Architektur*, Basel/Boston/Berlin 1996

Daniel Libeskind, Berlin Museum Extension   p. 172

Feireiss, Kristin (ed.): *Daniel Libeskind: Erweiterung des Berlin Museums mit Abteilung Jüdisches Museum*, Berlin 1992; Müller, Alois Martin (ed.): *Daniel Libeskind: Radix-Matrix*, Munich/New York 1997

Santiago Calatrava, Satolas TGV Station   p. 174

Santiago Calatrava 1983–1993, el croquis, no. 38+57, 1994; Edelmann, Frédéric/Rheinert, Patrick: "Zwei Annäherungen an den TGV-Bahnhof Satolas, Lyon," in: *Bauwelt*, no. 31, 1994, pp. 1696–1703; "Santiago Calatrava Lyon Airport, Railway Station," in: *Architecture and Urbanism*, no. 298, July 1995, pp. 10–25

Peter Zumthor, Thermal Baths   p. 176

Thermalbad Vals: Exemplary Projects, Architectural Association, London 1997; *Peter Zumthor: Kunsthaus Bregenz*, Archiv Kunst Architektur, Stuttgart 1997; *Peter Zumthor Häuser 1979–1997*, Baden (Switzerland) 1998; *Peter Zumthor: Architektur denken*, Baden (Switzerland) 1998

Cesar Pelli, Petronas Towers   p. 178

Crosbie, Michael J.: *Cesar Pelli: Selected and Current Works*, Mulgrave (Australia) 1993; Sullivan, Ann C.: "Petronas Towers," in: *Architecture*, Sept. 1996, pp. 160ff.

Kisho Kurokawa, International Airport   p. 180

Kurokawa, Kisho: *Metabolism in Architecture*, London 1977; Kurokawa, Kisho: *From Metabolism to Symbiosis*, London 1992

Frank O. Gehry, Guggenheim Museum   p. 182

"Project Diary: Guggenheim Museum Bilbao," in: *Architectural Record*, Oct. 1997; van Bruggen, Coosje: *Frank O. Gehry: Guggenheim Museum Bilbao*, New York/Ostfildern 1997; Forster, Kurt W./Hadley Soutter, Arnold/Dal Co, Francesco: *Frank O. Gehry: The Complete Works*, New York 1998

W.B. Wolfgang Bachmann holds a Ph.D. in engineering and is the editor-in-chief of *Baumeister* magazine in Munich, Germany.

C.B. Christian Brensing works for Arup, Inc., in Berlin, the German subsidary of Ove Arup & Partners, London.

J.G. John Garton is a Ph.D. candidate in art history at the Institute of Fine Arts, New York University, New York City.

A.G. Andrea Gleiniger, Ph.D., former curator of the Deutsches Architektur-Museum in Frankfurt am Main, Germany, is a lecturer at the Staatliche Hochschule für Gestaltung in Karlsruhe, Germany.

D.A.G. Dale Allen Gyure is a Ph.D. candidate in architectural history at the University of Virginia, Charlottesville, Virginia.

R.H. Ruth Hanisch is an assistant lecturer at the Department of Urban History at the Eidgenössische Technische Hochschule (ETH), Zurich, Switzerland.

M.H. Mechthild Heuser, Ph.D., is an art and architectural historian in Berlin who writes for various magazines, including *Casabella*, *Archithese*, and *Bauwelt*.

H.I. Hans Ibelings is a curator at the NAi (Nederlands Architectuurinstituut) in Rotterdam, the Netherlands.

M.J. Markus Jager is an art historian living in Berlin who works as a freelance collaborator for the Deutsches Architektur-Museum in Frankfurt am Main, Germany, and writes for the *Neue Zürcher Zeitung*.

T.J. Teppo Jokinen, Ph.D., is a research assistant at the Institut für Geschichte und Theorie der Architektur at the Eidgenössische Technische Hochschule (ETH), Zurich, Switzerland.

W.K. Wilhelm Klauser is an engineer, architect, and publicist who has lived and worked in Tokyo since 1992.

S.K. Steffen Krämer, Ph.D., is an assistant researcher at the Kunsthistorisches Institut, Ludwig-Maximilians-Universität, Munich.

R.K. Reyer Kras is the head conservator of the Department of Design at the Stedelijk Museum in Amsterdam, and a freelance designer.

V.M.L. Vittorio Magnago Lampugnani, Ph.D., is a professor at the Department of Urban History at the Eidgenössische Technische Hochschule (ETH), Zurich, Switzerland.

B.M. Bruno Maurer is a research coordinator at the Institut für Geschichte und Theorie der Architektur at the Eidgenössische Technische Hochschule (ETH), Zurich, Switzerland.

C.M. Clare Melhuish, former reviews editor at the architectural weekly *Building Design*, is an author and lecturer on architecture based in London.

K.D.M. Kevin D. Murphy is an associate professor at the Department of Architectural History, School of Architecture, University of Virginia, Charlottesville, Virginia.

P.M. Peter Murray is the director of Wordsearch Communications in London, and a member of the Royal Academy Architecture Committee.

E.P. Elizabeth Prelinger is the Chair of the Department of Art, Music and Theatre at Georgetown University, Washington, D.C.

C.L.R. Charles L. Rosenblum is a Ph.D. candidate in architectural history at the University of Virginia who lives in Pittsburgh, Pennsylvania, and contributes to various publications, including *Architectural Record* and *New Art Examiner*.

J.S.R. James S. Russell, A.I.A., is an editor-at-large at *Architectural Record* in New York City, and writes for the *Philadelphia Inquirer* and the *New York Times*.

A.S. Angeli Sachs is an art historian at the Institut für Geschichte und Theorie der Architektur at the Eidgenössische Technische Hochschule (ETH), Zurich, Switzerland.

M.S. Manfred Sack, Ph.D., was the architectural critic for the weekly newspaper *Die Zeit* from 1959 to 1997, and is currently a freelance writer living in Hamburg, Germany.

S.S. Sabine Schneider is an editor at *Baumeister* magazine in Munich, Germany.

U.M.S. Ulrich Maximilian Schumann is an assistant lecturer at the Department of Urban History at the Eidgenössische Technische Hochschule (ETH), Zurich, Switzerland.

P.S. Pia Simmendinger is a research assistant at the Department of Urban History at the Eidgenössische Technische Hochschule (ETH), Zurich, Switzerland.

W.S. Wolfgang Sonne is an assistant lecturer at the Department of Urban History at the Eidgenössische Technische Hochschule (ETH), Zurich, Switzerland.

M.-T.S. Marie-Theres Stauffer is a research assistant at the Department of Urban History at the Eidgenössische Technische Hochschule (ETH), Zurich, Switzerland.

W.J.S. Wolfgang Jean Stock is the executive editor at *Baumeister* magazine in Munich, Germany, and a freelance architectural critic for the *Süddeutsche Zeitung* daily newspaper.

C.W.T. Christian W. Thomsen, Ph.D., is a founding member and professor at the Department of English and Media Studies at the Universität Gesamthochschule, Siegen, Germany.

W.V. Wolfgang Voigt, Ph.D., is the executive director of the Deutsches Architektur-Museum in Frankfurt am Main, Germany.

C.W.J. Christine Waiblinger-Jens is an engineer, architect, and art historian in Cologne, Germany.

K.W. Katharina Walterspiel is an engineer, architect, and freelance editor in Berlin.

C.W.H. Claudine Weber-Hof is an editor in Munich and a correspondent for *Architectural Record*.

C.W.W. Carroll William Westfall is the Chair of the School of Architecture at the University of Notre Dame, South Bend, Indiana.

R.G.W. Richard Guy Wilson is the Chair of the Department of Architectural History, School of Architecture, University of Virginia, Charlottesville, Virginia.

V.M.Y. Victoria M. Young is a Ph.D. candidate in architectural history at the University of Virginia, Charlottesville, Virginia.

Index

Photo Credits

Our special thanks to the architects who made illustrative material available for this volume.

The numbers listed below refer to pages and figures, respectively.

Alvar Aalto Foundation 65 (4)
Aldo Acquadro/LOOK 113 (2–3)
Graphische Sammlung Albertina, Vienna/Adolf Loos Archiv 30 (1), 31 (2–3)
J. Apicella/Cesar Pelli & Associates 178/79 (2)
Architectural Drawing Collection, University of California, Santa Barbara 42 (1), 43 (3, 5–6)
Archiv für Kunst und Geschichte 33 (portrait), 57 (4)
Archives nationales/Institut français d'architecture, Fonds Perret 18 (1–3), 19 (portrait)
Yann Arthus-Bertrand/Bildagentur Schuster/Altitude 129 (5), 155 (4)
Kazi Khaleed Ashraf 107 (3)
Bässler/Interfoto 41 (4)
Jeremy Baker 101 (portrait)
Sina Baniahmad/Atelier Hollein 130 (portrait)
Arnaud Baumann 148 (portrait)
Josef Beck/allOver 11 (5)
Jordi Bernadó 75 (2–4)
Dida Biggi 147 (6)
Bildarchiv Foto Marburg 32 (3), 57 (6–7)
Bildarchiv Preussischer Kulturbesitz 40 (2)
Bitter + Bredt 173 (2, 4)
Michel Boesveld 48 (1, 4)
Nicolas Borel 158 (2), 159 (6–7)
Marcus Brooke/allOver 14 (1), 15 (2), 97 (2)
David B. Brownlee 107 (5)
Orlando R. Cabanban 126 (1)
Michael Carapetian 100 (4), 101 (5)
Lluís Casals 146 (2–3), 147 (3)
Centro Studi Giuseppe Terragni 62 (portrait), 63 (2, 4)
Helge Classen 50 (1), 51 (4–8)
Stephan Couturier/Arcaid 149 (3)
Jan Derwig 12 (1–2), 48 (2–3)
Deutsches Architektur-Museum, Frankfurt am Main 112 (portrait), 113 (4)
Todd Ebele 182 (portrait)
Ellert/Postsparkasse 21 (3)

Georges Fessy 148 (1), 149 (4, 6), 170 (portrait, 1), 171 (3–6)
Klaus Frahm/Contur 38 (1), 39 (2, 5), 41 (3), 46 (3–4), 63 (1, 3), 146 (1), 147 (5), 163 (2), 172 (4)
Michael Freeman 43 (2, 4), 76/77 (1), 77 (3)
Michael Gackstatter/allOver 97 (5)
Gaston 149 (5)
Dennis Gilbert/VIEW Pictures 92 (1, 3)
Glasgow School of Art 15 (5)
Jeff Goldberg/Esto 160 (1), 161 (2–4)
Jan Greune/LOOK 144 (1)
Rainer Grosskopf/allOver 77 (2), 123 (5)
Ingbet Grüttner 118 (portrait)
Thomas Güller 94 (1), 95 (2–5)
Udo Haafke/allOver 25 (4)
Roland Halbe/Contur 28 (1–2)
Daniela Hartmann 162 (portrait)
Hedrich-Blessing 127 (4)
Christian Heeb/LOOK 54 (1), 55 (4), 111 (4), 119 (5), 122 (1–2), 123 (3), 138 (1–3), 143 (2–3)
Silke Helmerdig 29 (5)
Helmsley-Spear, Inc./Empire State Building 67 (3–5)
Doris Herlinger/Postsparkasse Wien 21 (4)
Hilbich/Archiv für Kunst und Geschichte 32 (1)
K. Hiwatashi 168 (1)
Tom Hoenig/allOver 129 (4), 156 (1)
Dieter E. Hoppe/Archiv für Kunst und Geschichte 28 (3)
Koji Horiuchi/Pei Cobb Freed & Partners 156/57 (4, 6)
Angelo Hornak 84 (1), 85 (5)
Timothy Hursley 110 (1)
Xavier Iglesias/Duany Plater-Zyberk 137 (3, 5)
Interfoto 12 (portrait), 40 (portrait), 70 (portrait)
Shunji Ishida 168 (2)
Yasuhiro Ishimoto 151 (2–5)
Wolfram Janzer/Contur 124 (1)
Ferdinand Jendrejewski/allOver 128 (1–2)
Karl Johaengtes/LOOK 15 (4)
Martin Jones/Arcaid 100 (1)
Albert Kahn Associates 34 (portrait), 35 (1–4)
Werner Kaminsky/allOver 154 (1)
Christian Kandzia/Behnisch & Partner 114 (1), 115 (4–5)

M. Kapanen/Alvar Aalto Museum 65 (1)
Atelier Klaus Kinold 25 (2–3), 46 (1–2, 5), 52 (1), 53 (1), 58 (1, 3–4), 65 (3), 116 (portrait), 117 (2, 4–5), 124 (2), 125 (5)
Kirchner/Postsparkasse Wien 21 (2)
Roland Koch/Kulturinstitute der Stadt Darmstadt 27 (2)
Foto-Design Waltraud Krase 134/35 (1–3, 5)
Kulturinstitute der Stadt Darmstadt 26 (portrait, 1), 27 (3, 4)
Günter Lachmuth/Architektur-Bilderservice Kandula 16 (1), 17 (4), 127 (2)
Ian Lambot 144 (2), 145 (4)
Robert/Andrea Lautmann Photography 118 (2)
Fondation Le Corbusier 58 (2), 59 (portrait), 82 (1), 83 (5)
Edmund Lill/Bauhaus-Archiv 32 (4)
Alex S. MacLean 137 (2)
Rainer Martini/LOOK 10 (1), 11 (2)
Mitsuo Matsuoka 164 (1), 165 (4–5)
Fotostudio Meyska 131 (3)
J.T. Miller 102 (portrait)
Bernhard Moosbrugger 83 (2–3)
Hank Morgan 178 (portrait)
Stefan Müller 163 (1, 3)
Osamu Murai 80 (1), 81 (2, 4), 104 (1, 3)
Gerhard Murza 37 (3)
Nederlands Architectuurinstituut, Rotterdam (NAi)/Berlage Archiv 12 (portrait), 13 (4–5)
NAi/Brinkman en Van der Vlugt Archiv 49 (1)
NAi/Library 49 (portrait on right)
NAi/Private collection 49 (portrait on left)
NAi/Stichting Wonen Archiv 13 (1, 3)
Cathleen Naundorf/LOOK 99 (2–3)
Universität von Parma/P.L. Nervi Archiv 88 (1–2), 89 (3)
John Nicolais 119 (4)
Axel Nordmeier/allOver 67 (2)
Tomio Ohashi 180 (4)
Frank den Oudsten 45 (1, 4–5)
Sanne Peper 166 (portrait)
Postsparkasse Wien/Library 20 (portrait, 1)
Gunay Reha 107 (2)

Albert Renger-Patzsch/Bauhaus-Archiv 32 (2)
Ralph Richter/Architekturphoto 166 (1), 167 (3), 174/75 (2–3)
Christian Richters Fotograf 167 (4–5, 7), 177 (2–5), 182 (1), 183 (3–5)
Tomas Riehle/Contur 53 (2), 176 (portrait)
Karsten de Riese 114 (2), 115 (3), 179 (3)
Georg Riha 131 (2, 4)
Paul Rocheleau 71 (2–5)
Rollin La France 103 (2–4, 6)
Paolo Roselli 174/75 (portrait, 1)
Lukas Roth 158 (1, 5)
Manfred Sack 57 (2–3, 5)
Jordi Sarrá 60 (1–2), 61 (3–5)
Ulli Seer/LOOK 111 (2)
Schwarz/Postsparkasse Wien 21 (5)
Shinkenchiku-Sha 168/69 (4)
Snoek 100 (3)
Terje Solvang 120 (2), 121 (3–5)
Margherita Spiluttini 22 (3), 23 (5)
Stadtplanungsamt Stuttgart 50 (2)
Dan Stevens 142 (portrait)
Ezra Stoller/Esto 90/91 (2–4), 108/09 (1–2, 4), 111 (3), 119 (2)
Studio Arch. Alberico Barbiano di Belgiojoso 86 (portrait), 87 (1–3)
Sabine Thiel-Siling 66 (1), 77 (4)
Jussi Tiainen 65 (2)
Luca Vignelli 172 (portrait)
Ton van Vliet/allOver 155 (3)
Sybolt Voeten 116 (1)
Wolfgang Voigt 72 (2), 73 (3–4)
Andrew Ward 145 (portrait)
James Ward (ed.): The Artifacts of R. Buckminster Fuller, Vol. 4/2, New York/London 1985, p. 99 top right 112 (1)
Tom Weber/allOver 97 (3)
The Frank Lloyd Wright Foundation 70 (1)
Reiner Wulf/Archiv für Kunst und Geschichte 40 (1)
Loo Keng Yip 180 (1–3), 181 (6)
Gerald Zugmann 152 (portrait), 153 (2–3, 5)
Gerald Zugmann/Raiffeisenlandesbank NÖ-Wien 31 (4)

Front cover: Chrysler Building, New York City (also on spine; photo: Rainer Grosskopf/allOver), Sagrada Familia, Barcelona (photo: Ferdinand Hollweck/allOver), Solomon R. Guggenheim Museum, New York City (photo: Rainer Grosskopf/allOver), Olympic Games Complex, Munich (photo: Karsten de Riese), Opera House, Sydney (photo: Marcus Brooke/allOver), Centre Georges Pompidou, Paris (photo: Ferdinand Jendrejewsky/allOver), Pyramide, Le Grande Louvre, Paris (photo: D. v. Schaewen)

Back cover: Guggenheim Museum, Bilbao (photo: Christian Richters), Einsteinturm, Potsdam (photo: Gerhard Murza), Bauhaus, Dessau (photo: Klaus Frahm/Contur), Empire State Building, New York City (photo: Axel Nordmeier/allOver), Lloyd's of London, London (photo: Christian Heeb/LOOK), Satolas TGV Station, Lyon (photo: Ralph Richter/Architekturphoto)

Library of Congress Cataloging-in-Publication Data
Icons of architecture : the 20th century / edited by Sabine Thiel-Siling : with contributions by Wolfgang Bachman . . . [et al.].
p.   cm.
Includes bibliographical references and index
ISBN 3-7913-1949-3 (acid-free paper)
1. Architecture. Modern--20th century.   2. Architects--Biography.
I. Thiel-Siling, Sabine.   II. Bachman, Wolfgang.
NA680.I26   1998
724'.6--dc21   98-34623   CIP

Die Deutsche Bibliothek – CIP-Einheitsaufnahme
Icons of architecture : the 20th century / ed. by Sabine Thiel-Siling. With contributions by: Wolfgang Bachmann ... [Contributions transl. from the German by Peter Green. Contributions transl. from the Dutch by Robyn de Jong-Dalziel and Graham Broadribb]. – Munich; London; New York: Prestel, 1998
Dt. Ausg. u.d.T.: Prestel, 1998
ISBN 3-7913-1949-3

Edited by Claudine Weber-Hof

Prestel-Verlag
Mandlstrasse 26 · 80802 Munich · Germany
Tel. +49 (89) 38 17 09-0; Fax +49 (89) 38 17 09-35
and 16 West 22nd Street, New York, NY 10010, USA
Tel. (212) 627-8199; Fax (212) 627-9866

Prestel books are available worldwide.
Please contact your nearest bookseller or write to either of the above addresses for information concerning your local distributor.

Contributions translated from the German by Peter Green, Munich
Contributions translated from the Dutch by Robyn de Jong-Dalziel, Heemstede, the Netherlands, and Graham Broadribb, Düsseldorf
Photo research: Petra Böttcher and Alexandra Loidl
Coordination and research, U.S.: Victoria M. Young

Design: Angela Dobrick, Hamburg
Layout and production: Matthias Hauer, Munich
Lithography: Repro Brüll, Saalfelden
Typesetting: ABC Team, Munich
Production editing: John Stuart, Danko Szabó, Munich
Paper: profiStar from 2H-Papier, Garching
Printing: Passavia Druckservice, Passau
Binding: Oldenbourg, Feldkirchen

Printed in Germany on acid-free paper

ISBN 3-7913-1949-3